ACHIEVE

PMP ®

EXAM SUCCESS ■ 4th EDITION

A Concise Study Guide for the Busy Project Manager

MARGARET CHU, PMP
DIANE ALTWIES, PMP
JANICE PRESTON, PMP

Copyright ©2009 by Core Performance Concepts, Inc.

ISBN 978-1-60427-018-1

Printed and bound in the United States. Printed on acid-free paper.
10 9 8 7 6 5 4 3 2 1

Library of Congress Cataloging-in-Publication Data

Chu, Margaret Y.
    Achieve PMP exam success; a concise study guide for the busy project
manager / by Margaret Chu, Diane Altwies and Janice Preston.-4th ed.
        p. cm.
Includes index.
        ISBN 978-1-60427-018-1 (pbk. : alk. paper)
        1. Project management--Examinations, questions, etc. I. Altwies,
Diane, 1962- II. Preston, Janice, 1947- III. Title.
        HD69.P75C476 2009
        658.4'04'076--dc22
                    2009008404

Direct all inquiries to J. Ross Publishing, 5765 N Andrews Way,
Ft. Lauderdale, FL 33309. Phone 954-727-9333; Fax 561-892-0700;
Web www.jrosspub.com.

Core Performance Concepts, Inc., is a Registered Education Provider of PMI.
PMI, PMP, PMBOK and CAPM are registered certification marks of Project
Management Institute, Inc. PMI does not endorse or otherwise sponsor this
publication.

Attention: Corporations, Professional Organizations, Universities and Colleges.
Quanity discounts are available on bulk purchases of this book. For information
contact: salesandmarketing @jrosspub.com

TABLE OF CONTENTS

FOREWORD

What a clever idea: to create a PMP examination study guide to be used alongside the *PMBOK® Guide*! As a PMP who has helped hundreds of Project Management Institute (PMI) members prepare to take the exam and as a leader within the PMI community for more than 15 years, I have frequently wished for such a source of valuable information to help PMP candidates achieve success.

Let's face it, we all know the *PMBOK® Guide* is useful but no one ever said it was a quick read! The variety of material and the length and breadth of the PMP exam questions have stumped and intimidated many would-be candidates. As one who in a previous career was a university Reading and Study Skills Specialist, I know how helpful a study guide can be. It helps keep one awake while reading slow-going material and ensures that the reader gets the critical information from his or her reading in the most effective manner possible.

This particular study guide is excellent. Chapter 1 provides the information that the project manager needs and wants to know right away — what will the exam be like? And how does one go about studying and preparing for it? Adults who have been out of college for a few years usually do not really know how to study or have forgotten how to take multiple choice exams. The study techniques in this guide are well-researched and proven. (I should know; I prepared the original recommendations for the PMI-LA chapter PMP preparation workshop many years ago!) Chapter 1 also includes a preassessment test of 40 sample questions, giving you, the reader, a taste of the nature and content of examination questions. The next 11 chapters follow the structure of the *PMBOK® Guide*, with project management framework, the project management processes and the nine knowledge areas. The 13th chapter covers the performance domain of professional responsibility, an important additional topic on the exam. Each of these chapters contains sample exam questions for practice and confirmation that learning has taken place. In addition, real-life case study exercises provide opportunities to learn the key aspects of the topic. The book concludes with a post-assessment exam of 60 questions. But that's not all; a CD-ROM features over 1200 additional sample exam questions. Wow!

Although this study guide is designed to help PMP candidates pass the exam, it provides background and knowledge to any busy project participant who wants to improve his or her skills. This study guide ensures that the reader gets the essential information in an efficient manner. Bravo Margaret, Diane and Janice! You've created a tool that we've all needed for years now. I wish this guide had been available when I was a PMP exam candidate; my study time could have been cut in half, by far.

Ida Harding, PMP

PMI Professional Awards Member Advisory Group (2008 – 2009)
PMI Component Services Member Advisory Committee (2005 – 2007)
PMI Chapter LDEC Chair and Co-chair (2003 – 2004)
PMI Association of Chapter Presidents (ACP) VP (Coordinator for
   Regional Mentor Program) (2002 – 2003)
PMI Educational Foundation BOD (2002 – 2003)
PMI-LA Chapter Trustee (2001 – 2009)
PMI REP Advisory Committee (2001 – 2002)
PMI District Regional Advocate (Region 7, 2000 – 2001)
PMI Chapter President of the Year (PMI-LA Chapter, both 1999
   and 2000)
PMI Information Systems SIG, Co-chair Seminar Symposium Track
   (1997 and 1998)
PMI-LA Chapter, miscellaneous other positions (1993 – 1998)

As most project managers know, PMI updates the *PMBOK® Guide* every four years. The most recent update, released in December, 2008, is officially called the *PMBOK® Guide*, Fourth Edition, but is popularly known as the *PMBOK® Guide* 2008. Within one year the changes in the *PMBOK® Guide* will be reflected in the PMP exam. For the 2008 Guide, the exam changes go into effect in July of 2009. The PMP Exam consists of 200 questions. 25 of those questions are field testing questions to see if they are appropriate. The 25 trial questions will NOT count towards the pass/fail determination. So only 175 of the 200 questions count towards your score.

For those who have been using the *PMBOK® Guide* 2004, the following paragraphs describe the major changes for *PMBOK® Guide* 2008. If you have not used the 2004 Guide, skip the remainder of this Preface.

The *PMBOK® Guide* Fourth Edition has been significantly improved from its prior editions. For those who are familiar with the *PMBOK® Guide* Third Edition, you will find that the new *PMBOK® Guide* addresses and speaks to the business community in general with major improvements in consistency as well. We will highlight a few of the key changes as they relate to helping students prepare for the PMP Exam. To see a full list of changes from the *PMBOK® Guide* Third Edition, reference Appendix A of the *PMBOK® Guide* Fourth Edition.

One of the major consistency changes made throughout the *PMBOK® Guide* is the adjusting of all processes to be written in verb/noun format. The table below lists the process name changes by each knowledge area.

Knowledge Area	*PMBOK® Guide* Third Edition Processes	*PMBOK® Guide* Fourth Edition Processes
Integration	• Develop Project Charter • Develop Preliminary Project Scope Statement (Deleted) • Develop Project Management Plan • Direct and Manage Project Execution • Monitor and Control Project Work • Integrated Change Control • Close Project	• Develop Project Charter • Develop Project Management Plan • Direct and Manage Project Execution • Monitor and Control Project Work • Perform Integrated Change Control • Close Project or Phase
Scope	• Scope Planning • Scope Definition • Create WBS • Scope Verification • Scope Control	• Collect Requirements • Define Scope • Create WBS • Verify Scope • Control Scope

Knowledge Area	PMBOK® Guide Third Edition Processes	PMBOK® Guide Fourth Edition Processes
Time	• Activity Definition • Activity Sequencing • Activity Resource Estimating • Activity Duration Estimating • Schedule Development • Schedule Control	• Define Activities • Sequence Activities • Estimate Activity Resources • Estimate Activity Durations • Develop Schedule • Control Schedule
Cost	• Cost Estimating • Cost Budgeting • Cost Control	• Estimate Costs • Determine Budget • Control Costs
Quality	• Quality Planning • Perform Quality Assurance • Perform Quality Control	• Plan Quality • Perform Quality Assurance • Perform Quality Control
Human Resources	• Human Resources Planning • Acquire Project Team • Develop Project Team • Manage Project Team	• Develop Human Resource Plan • Acquire Project Team • Develop Project Team • Manage Project Team
Communications	• Communications Planning • Information Distribution • Performance Reporting • Manage Stakeholders	• **Identify Stakeholders (Added)** • Plan Communications • Distribute Information • Manage Stakeholder Expectations • Report Performance
Risk	• Risk Management Plan • Risk Identification • Qualitative Risk Analysis • Quantitative Risk Analysis • Risk Reponse Planning • Risk Monitoring and Control	• Plan Risk Management • Identify Risks • Perform Qualitative Risk Analysis • Perform Quantitative Risk Analysis • Plan Risk Responses • Monitor and Control Risks
Procurement	• **Plan Purchases and Acquisitions (Combined)** • **Plan Contracting (Combined)** • **Request Seller Responses (Combined)** • **Select Sellers (Combined)** • Contract Administration • Contract Closure	• Plan Procurements • Conduct Procurements • Administer Procurements • Close Procurements

In comparing the *PMBOK® Guide* Third Edition to the *PMBOK® Guide* Fourth Edition, you will also note that a few processes have been removed, added or combined, but for the most part the major structure of the *PMBOK® Guide* processes has stayed in-tact. A total of 42 processes exist in the *PMBOK® Guide* Fourth Edition, reduced from the previous 44 processes in the prior edition. The nine knowledge areas and five process groups have not changed.

Since projects are initiated in an organization to enable the organization to grow and succeed, PMI has added clarification regarding the project charter and the scope statement. In addition, the *PMBOK® Guide* now addresses the importance of developing business cases and collecting requirements, both of which are critical inputs in determining the objectives of the project and ensuring project success.

Clarification has also been provided in comparisons of the project management plan and other commonly used project documents.

Some chapters have more extensive changes than others. Highlights of these chapters and their changes are:

Chapter 4: Project Integration Management

Clarification of the project charter and its relationship to the scope statement has been incorporated into this chapter. The project charter can be considered a more preliminary and higher-level document in which a summary of the project is included. The project charter serves as an input into the elaboration and more detailed specifications included in the project scope statement. The Define Preliminary Project Scope Statement process has been removed.

Chapter 5: Project Scope Management

The Scope Planning process was replaced with the Collect Requirements process. This change clarifies and recognizes the importance of defining the detailed requirements for the project.

Chapter 6: Project Time Management

The Arrow and Arrow-on-Arrow diagramming methods had limited and infrequent use, and so have been removed.

Chapter 9: Project Human Resource Management

The Manage Project Team process has been moved out of the monitoring and controlling process group and into the executing process group. This new edition of the *PMBOK® Guide* recognizes that the project manager's role in this knowledge area is not about the performance of the project itself, but is rather to provide general management skills, needed throughout the execution of the project.

Chapter 10: Project Communications Management

A new process was added to the communications management knowledge area, the Identify Stakeholders process. This process stresses the importance of knowing the stakeholders and understanding and defining their needs. The previous Manage Stakeholders process has been renamed Manage Stakeholder Expectations process.

Chapter 12: Project Procurement Management

This knowledge area has been simplified from six procurement processes into four. The four processes focus on the planning, conducting, administering and closing of procurements.

Margaret, Diane and Janice would like to recognize the hard work and contributions of the many individuals who helped us make this book a success:

Steve Buda and his team at J. Ross Publishing for their guidance and patience; Ed Walker, PMP, for his vision in helping Margaret and Diane achieve their goals; Cornelius Fitchner, PMP, for his assistance in helping us modify our course materials; Frank Reynolds, PMP, for support and guidance throughout the project and his many contributions to our collective project management knowledge; Jessica Haile for her diligent work as our editor; and Scott McQuigg for his technical expertise in bringing our CD-ROM to life.

Special thanks also to Ida Harding of the PMI-Los Angeles Chapter, various PMI chapters and our students at the University of South Florida for using our materials and providing invaluable feedback.

There are certainly others, whose names are not here but who contributed as participants in our workshops, challenging us to defend our statements and the answers to the PMP questions we wrote. Each course offering enhanced the material that has become this book. To each and every one of you, a million thanks from the bottom of our hearts. We could not have done this without you.

INTRODUCTION

Congratulations! Your curiosity about the project management profession and what is involved in attaining the elite status of a certified Project Management Professional (PMP) will lead you to many achievements. As you may know, the guide to the Project Management Body of Knowledge (*PMBOK® Guide*), which is published by PMI, is revised every four years. The revision of the *PMBOK® Guide* is followed by corresponding changes to the PMP certification exam questions. The current edition of the *PMBOK® Guide* is the 2008 edition (Fourth Edition) and it is often referenced as the *PMBOK® Guide* 2008. This study guide is closely related to the *PMBOK® Guide* and has been revised to match the *PMBOK® Guide* 2008. Before you begin, make sure you know what version of the *PMBOK® Guide* you need to study and determine your target time for taking the PMP exam. However, if your purpose is simply to find out more about the project management disciplines and the exam process, then any version will provide you with valuable information.

Our purpose in creating this study guide is to provide you with a consolidated source of material that, used together with the material contained in the *PMBOK® Guide* and your experiences as a project manager, should be all you need to pass the PMP exam. To help you succeed and to make effective use of your study time, the chapter topics match the chapters in the *PMBOK® Guide* and include material on PMI's professional responsibility performance domain. Each chapter contains a series of sample exam questions and, where appropriate, a hands-on exercise or two.

We have structured each of the chapters to present a list of the things you need to know to pass the exam. This list is based on 1) our personal experiences in preparing for and taking the exam, 2) our experiences in helping others prepare for the exam and 3) what our students and workshop participants have told us has been useful in helping them prepare for and pass the exam.

We have NOT included in the study guide all the inputs, outputs, tools and techniques described in the *PMBOK® Guide*. PMI has already done that and you MUST go through the *PMBOK® Guide* in detail to become familiar with the deliverables, tools and techniques of the many processes.

Our objective in providing to you this study guide is to add additional value to what is described in the *PMBOK® Guide* by offering forth explanations and examples, as well as going beyond the *PMBOK® Guide* to topics that reinforce these concepts and improve project manager competency.

The *PMBOK® Guide*, by design, is not meant to provide detailed step-by-step instructions to the project manager in a project setting. We hope you will find that this study guide provides the information needed to understand the concepts of the *PMBOK® Guide* and enable you to use its tools, techniques and methods in a real-world environment.

Remember also that the exam tests your knowledge of generally accepted project management processes. Your particular industry and/or area of specialization will have different ways of doing the same thing, but PMI is administering the test, so you need to know "the PMI way."

We have included an assessment test in Chapter 1 that you should take before you continue on to further chapters. It will help you focus on those areas of your knowledge and experience that are the weakest and save you time by allowing you to skim over the areas where you are already knowledgeable. These assessment questions may also help you decide if you need to take a course on project management principles or a PMP exam preparation course before attempting the exam. Chapter 14 is a final exam to help you confirm your understanding of the material.

PMI also administers a Certified Associate in Project Management (CAPM) exam. This is a shorter exam with less experience requirements for application approval. Use our *Achieve CAPM Exam Success: A concise study guide and desk reference* book to improve your project management skills and to help you pass the CAPM Exam.

Our CD-ROM allows the student to perform practice exams for both the PMP and CAPM exams. A key to success in passing the PMP Exam is taking several practice exams, in particular, automated exams such as we provide.

Finally, we would like to emphasize that you should by no means assume that studying this book replaces reading the *PMBOK® Guide*. Instead, both books should be used together. We suggest the following method of study:

- Start by doing an overview of a chapter in the *PMBOK® Guide* (paging through the chapter to get a big picture of what the chapter is about and how it is organized). This should take about two or three minutes.
- Do the same with the equivalent chapter in this study guide. Chapters 1 and 2 of the *PMBOK® Guide* are combined into Chapter 2 of this study guide.
- Now, read the *PMBOK® Guide* chapter carefully, asking yourself "What do I need to learn from what I am reading?"
- Next, read the study guide chapter carefully to find the tips and important points to learn.
- Then reread the *PMBOK® Guide* chapter in chunks, referring back to the study guide. Note concepts in the study guide that go beyond the *PMBOK® Guide*.
- Make notes or flash cards to help you remember essential information. Use these notes later to test yourself so you can narrow your focus on the information you may need to revisit.
- Next, do the sample exam questions in the study guide. If there are any concepts that you are weak in, you may want to read up on them by accessing the related reference material and practicing with additional exam questions.
- Use the CD-ROM of exam questions to practice taking online tests.
- Finally, reread the *PMBOK® Guide* chapter, this time very quickly, so you end with the overall picture rather than being buried in details.

Good studying and good luck with building your project management skills and knowledge. We look forward to hearing from you and celebrating your achievement. News of your success as well as any suggestions or comments on our study guide can be sent to us by email to info@cpconcepts.net.

Margaret Chu, Diane Altwies and Janice Preston

Core Performance Concepts, Inc.

In 2001 Diane Altwies, Margaret Chu and Ed Walker founded OuterCore Professional Development in Newport Beach, California. The partners realized that there was a need for low-cost assistance to improve the success rate of individuals taking the PMP certification exam. In addition, from their own experiences, Diane, Margaret and Ed saw an increased demand for well-trained project management professionals in every organization.

In 2009, OuterCore merged with another successful project management training organization, Vista Performance Group, led by Janice Preston, to form Core Performance Concepts, Inc. Core Performance Concepts, Inc., specializes in offering quality project management, program management and business analysis training across the globe.

Margaret Chu, PMP, has performed many roles within IT software development teams, over the last 20 years. She has successfully implemented process improvement at a large manufacturing firm utilizing the Software Engineering Institute-Capability Maturity Model Integration (SEI-CMMI). Her previously published book, *Blissful Data: Wisdom and Strategies for Providing Accurate, Meaningful, Useful, and Accessible Data for All Employees,* discusses the importance of overcoming people's resistance to change to ensure project success. Margaret is an active member of the Los Angeles chapter of PMI and serves on the board of directors of the Anaheim Breakfast Club of Toastmasters International, where she has achieved the levels of Competent Leader (CL) and Advanced Communicator Silver (ACS).

Diane Altwies, MBA, PMP, has been managing software development projects for over 20 years as a program manager or project manager in the insurance, financial services and healthcare industries. She is the CEO of Core Performance Concepts. She continues to teach and consult for organizations on various program management, project management and business analysis topics and develops advanced courseware topics for project managers. She is a frequent speaker at professional meetings and symposia across the country. In addition to this book, she has co-authored *Program Management Professional: A Certification Study Guide with Best Practices for Maximizing Business Results.*

Janice Preston, MBA, CPA, PMP, has been managing projects for more than 25 years in industries as diverse as real estate, finance, healthcare and technology. For more than 15 years, she has developed course curricula in project management and has been responsible for creating several project management certificate programs at leading universities. She writes and speaks on many project management topics, including team leadership, communication skills, earned value, cost control and procurement; she is considered an expert in the field of risk management and has consulted on updates to the *PMBOK® Guide*'s risk management knowledge area. She is a Fellow of PMI Orange County. She has an MBA in Finance and Accounting from the University of Missouri and a BA in Education from the University of Central Florida.

 Web
Added
Value™

Free value-added material is available from the
Download Resource Center at www.jrosspub.com.

At J. Ross Publishing we are committed to providing today's professional with practical, hands-on tools that enhance the learning experience and give readers an opportunity to apply what they have learned. That is why we offer free ancillary materials for download on this book and all participating Web Added Value™ publications. These online resources may include interactive versions of material that appears in the book or supplemental templates, worksheets, models, plans, case studies, proposals, spreadsheets and assessment tools, among other things. Whenever you see the WAV™ symbol in any of our publications, it means bonus materials accompany the book and are available from the Web Added Value Download Resource Center at www.jrosspub.com.

Downloads available for *Achieve PMP® Exam Success: A Concise Study Guide for the Busy Project Manager, 4th Edition* consist of a flashcard study aid of key terms and concepts, a self-study exercise on understanding the interdependencies of all 42 processes defined in the *PMBOK® Guide* and a training aid for better understanding process interdependencies.

CHAPTER 1 | EXAM OVERVIEW & ASSESSMENT EXAM

1

WHAT IS A PROJECT MANAGEMENT PROFESSIONAL (PMP)?

A PMP is a project management practitioner who:
- Has demonstrated a professional level of project management knowledge and experience by supporting projects using project management tools, techniques and methodologies
- Has at least 4,500 hours of experience as a project manager
- Has completed 35 hours of formal project management training
- Has passed a computer-based exam administered by the Project Management Institute (PMI)

PMP EXAM SPECIFICS

The exam has the following characteristics:
- It assesses the knowledge and application of globally accepted project management concepts, techniques and procedures
- It covers the six **Performance Domains** detailed in the *Project Management Professional (PMP) Examination Specification* (PMI 2005)
- It covers the nine **Knowledge Areas** and the five **Process Groups** as detailed in the Project Management Body of Knowledge Guide (*PMBOK® Guide*)
- It contains 200 multiple choice questions
- It includes 25 questions that are "preexam" questions being field-tested by PMI that do not affect your exam score
- It takes up to four hours

Table 1-1 on the following page summarizes the distribution of exam questions to each of the six performance domains based on the 2005 Project Management Professional (PMP) Exam Specifications. Note that the information in this chart may change from time to time. Consult the PMI website (www.pmi.org) for the most current information.

Table 1-1

Performance Domain	% of exam	# of questions
1. Initiating	11%	19
2. Planning	23%	40
3. Executing	27%	47
4. Monitoring & Controlling	21%	37
5. Closing	9%	16
6. Professional Responsibility	9%	16

STUDY TIPS

- Make a checklist of things you need to study
- Plan your study sessions with time limitations
- Vary tasks and topics during lengthy study periods
- Find one special place for studying and use it only for that
- Eliminate distractions
    - If daydreaming, walk away
    - Take brief breaks (5 to 10 minutes) after about 50 minutes of study
- Continue to test yourself
- Create your own exam
- Restate, repeat and put in your own words
- Understand the big concepts first
- Memorize key terms and important people
- Memorize formulas
- Use memorizing methods such as:
    - Flip-charts
    - Diagrams
    - Mnemonics
    - Memory searches (relate to past experiences)
- Prepare for the exam day
    - Get a good night's rest
    - Avoid last-minute cramming
    - Have a good breakfast
    - Leave books at home
    - Use the calculator on the system
    - Go with a positive attitude.
    - Get to the exam site EARLY

EXAM TIPS

- Relax before and during the exam
  - Take deep breaths
  - Stretch about every 40 minutes
  - If you get nervous, try to relax
  - Give yourself a goal and reward yourself
- Read each question carefully
- Be especially alert when double negatives are used
- Reread ALL questions containing negative words such as "not," "least" or "except"
- If a question is long and complex, read the final sentence, look at the options and then look for the subject and verb
- Check for qualifying words such as "all," "most," "some," "none," "highest-to-lowest" and "smallest-to-largest"
- Check for key words such as input, output, tool, technique, initiating, planning, executing, monitoring and controlling and closure
- Decide in your mind what the answer should be, then look for the answer in the options
- Reread the questions and eliminate options that are NOT correct
- The correct answer, if it's not simply a number, will include a PMI term
- Make sure you look at ALL the options
- Mark questions to come back to

TIME MANAGEMENT DURING THE EXAM

- Keep track of time (you have approximately 1 minute and 15 seconds for each question)
- Set up a time schedule for each question
- Allow time for review of the exam
- To stay relaxed, keep on schedule
- Answer all questions in order without skipping or jumping around
- If you are unsure, take a guess and mark the question to return to later; do not linger
- If you have memorized any formulas, use the scratch paper provided to write them down before you start the exam

- For questions involving problem solving:
  - Write down the formulas before solving
  - If possible, recheck your work in a different way (for example, rationalize)
- Subsequent questions may stimulate your memory and you may want to reevaluate a previous answer
- A lapse in memory is normal
- You will not know all the answers
- Take your time
- Do not be in a rush to leave the exam
- Before turning in the exam, verify that you have answered all questions

FAQS ABOUT THE EXAM

- Can you bring materials with you?
  NO
- What is the physical setting like?
  It is a small room or cubicle with a computer, chair, desk and trash can
- Can you take food or drink into the exam area?
  NO food or drink is allowed
- Can you take breaks during the exam?
  YES; you can go to the restroom; your clock is ticking all the time; you need to determine if you have time and need to take a break to clear your mind
- What are the time constraints?
  You have 4 hours (with an additional 15-minute tutorial and 15-minute survey)
- Are the exam questions grouped by knowledge area such as scope, time and cost?
  NO; the 200 questions are randomly scattered across the process groups and knowledge areas
- Can you take paper and pen into the exam area?
  NO; pencils and paper are supplied
- Can you see both the question and the answer on the same screen?
  YES

- Is there a way to mark out or eliminate options that you immediately know are not correct?
  NO; you can work only on a piece of scratch paper
- Is there a way to mark questions you are doubtful of?
  YES
- When you are done, can you review the exam?
  YES
- Can you review just the questions you marked as doubtful?
  YES
- Do you get immediate exam results?
  YES, if you are taking an online exam; after you are done, hit the SEND button; the computer will ask if you are sure; after you hit SEND, you will fill out an online evaluation of the exam process consisting of about ten questions; a testing center staff person will give you a detailed report of your results

MEMORIZATION TIPS FOR PERFORMANCE DOMAINS, PROCESS GROUPS, KNOWLEDGE AREAS AND PROCESSES

As stated in the PMP Examination Specifications, PMI defines the field of project management as consisting of six **Performance Domains:**
- Initiating
- Planning
- Executing
- Monitoring and Controlling
- Closing
- Professional Responsibility

In alignment with the first five performance domains are the five **Process Groups.** Each process group contains two or more processes. The process groups with their corresponding process counts are:

1

- Initiating (2)
- Planning (20)
- Executing (8)
- Monitoring and Controlling (10)
- Closing (2)

This yields a total of 42 processes. The process groups are discussed in detail in Chapter 3 of this study guide.

There are nine **Knowledge Areas**. Each of the processes, in addition to belonging to a process group, also belongs to a knowledge area. The knowledge areas with their corresponding process counts are:

- Integration (6)
- Scope (5)
- Time (6)
- Cost (3)
- Quality (3)
- Human Resources (4)
- Communications (5)
- Risk (6)
- Procurement (4)

EXAM TIP

Come up with your own creative phrases to remember the processes in each of the nine knowledge areas.

The individual processes are discussed in the knowledge area Chapters 4 through 12.

Table 3-1 of the *PMBOK® Guide* has a comprehensive chart that cross-references the individual processes, knowledge areas and process groups.

Many people like to use creative phrases that jog the memory to remember lists and sequences. Examples of memorable phrases follow for the five process groups and the nine knowledge areas.

Memorization Tip for the Five Process Groups:
Henry Initiated a committee named PEMCo to Close
down the railway line.
1. Initiating
2. Planning
3. Executing
4. Monitoring and Controlling
5. Closing

Memorization Tip for the Nine Knowledge Areas:
InSTantly aCQuaint HenRy with scope CReeP:
1. Integration
2. Scope
3. Time
4. Cost
5. Quality
6. Human Resources
7. Communications
8. Risk
9. Procurement

You may want to devise your own memorization tips
for processes in each of the knowledge areas. Here is an
example of a **Memorization Tip for the Project Scope
Management Processes:**
Henry used his tele**Scope** to **Collect** the **Require**d
Definitions and designs, **Creat**ing **WeBS** so intricate that
his work had to be **Verifi**ed and **Control**led in five **Steps.**
1. **Collect Requirements**
2. **Define Scope**
3. **Create WBS**
4. **Verify Scope**
5. **Control Scope**

1

FORMULAS, EQUATIONS AND RULES

Some formulas, equations and rules must be memorized to answer exam questions effectively. The most important items to remember are listed here. Most of these are discussed in more detail in the following chapters.

1. **Project Network Schedules**

   Network schedules are created after duration estimates and the relationships between the work packages have been determined. Following the path(s) from left to right makes a forward pass.
   - **Forward Pass**
     - Yields early start (ES) and early finish (EF) dates
     - Early finish = early start + duration
     - RULE: If there are multiple predecessors, use LATEST EF to determine successor ES

   After all paths have been given their forward path, they are traversed from right to left to make a backward pass.
   - **Backward Pass**
     - Yields late start (LS) and late finish (LF) dates
     - Late start = late finish - duration
     - RULE: If there are multiple successors, use EARLIEST LS to determine predecessor LF

   Once the forward and backward passes have been completed, the total float for the node can be calculated by:
   - Total float = late finish - early finish

2. Normal Distribution

The normal distribution, commonly known as the bell curve, is a symmetrical distribution, as shown in Figure 1-1. Each normal curve can be distinctly described using the mean and sum of the values The possibility of achieving the project objective in the mean time or cost is 0%, with a 50% chance of exceeding the mean and a 50% chance of beating the mean. Adding one or more standard deviations (σ) to the mean increases the chances of falling within the range. The probability of falling within 1σ, 2σ or 3σ from the mean is:

- $1\sigma = 68.27\%$
- $2\sigma = 95.45\%$
- $3\sigma = 99.73\%$

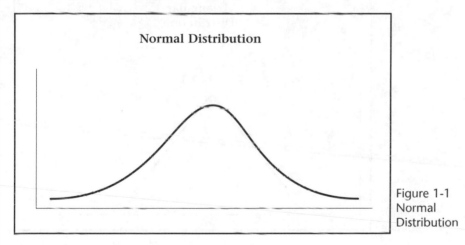

Figure 1-1
Normal
Distribution

3. Average or Triangular Distribution

When there are three possible values, each of which is equally likely, the distribution takes on the shape of a triangle, as shown in Figure 1-2.

- With A = lowest value, B = highest value and M = most likely value, variance for a task (V) (variance is not on the exam)
  - $V = [(A - B)^2 + (M - A)(M - B)]/18$
- Mean (μ)
  - $\mu = (A + M + B)/3$
- Standard deviation (σ)
  - $\sigma = \sqrt{V}$

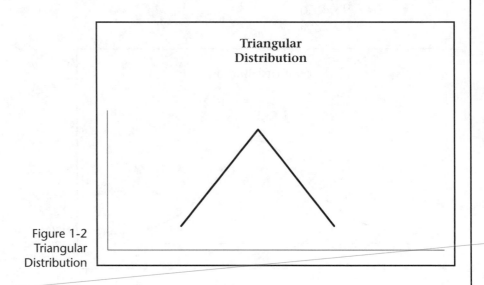

Triangular
Distribution

Figure 1-2
Triangular
Distribution

4. Weighted-Average or Beta/PERT Distribution

The beta distribution is like the triangular distribution except more weight is given to the most likely estimate. This may result in either a symmetrical or an asymmetrical (skewed right or skewed left) graph. An asymmetrical graph is shown in Figure 1-3.

- Where O = optimistic estimate, ML = most likely estimate and P = pessimistic estimate, variance for a task (V)
    - $V = \sigma^2$
- Mean (μ)
    - $(\mu) = [O + 4(ML) + P]/6$
- Standard deviation (σ)
    - $\sigma = (P - O)/6$

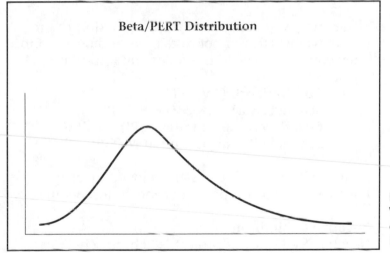

Beta/PERT Distribution

Figure 1-3
Weighted-Average
or Beta/PERT
Distribution

5. Statistical Sums

- The project **Mean** is the sum of the means of the individual tasks: $\mu_p = \mu_1 + \mu_2 + \ldots + \mu_n$

- The project **Variance** is the sum of the variances of the individual tasks: $V_p = V_1 + V_2 + \ldots + V_n$

- The project **Standard Deviation** is the square root of the project variance: $\sigma_p = \sqrt{V_p}$

1

6. **Earned Value Management**

Earned value management is used to monitor the progress of a project and is a tool and technique of processes in the integration, time, cost and communication knowledge areas. It uses three independent variables:
- **Planned Value (PV):** the budget or the portion of the approved cost estimate planned to be spent during a given period
- **Actual Cost (AC):** the total of direct and indirect costs incurred in accomplishing work during a given period
- **Earned Value (EV):** the budget for the work accomplished in a given period

These three values are used in combination to provide measures of whether or not work is proceeding as planned. They combine to yield the following important formulas:
- **Cost Variance (CV)** = $EV - AC$
- **Schedule Variance (SV)** = $EV - PV$
- **Cost Performance Index (CPI)** = EV/AC
- **Schedule Performance Index (SPI)** = EV/PV

Positive CV indicates costs are below budget.
Positive SV indicates project is ahead of schedule.

Negative CV indicates cost overrun.
Negative SV indicates project is behind schedule.

CPI greater than 1.0 indicates costs are below budget.
SPI greater than 1.0 indicates project is ahead of schedule.

CPI less than 1.0 indicates costs are over budget.
SPI less than 1.0 indicates project is behind schedule.

7. **Estimate at Completion**

Estimate At Completion (EAC) is the amount we expect the total project to cost on completion and as of the "data date" (time now). There are four methods listed in the *PMBOK® Guide* for computing EAC. Three of these methods use a formula to calculate EAC. Each of these starts with AC or actual costs to date and uses a different technique to estimate the work remaining to be completed, or ETC. The question of which to use depends on the individual situation and the credibility of the actual work performed compared to the budget up to that point.

- A **New Estimate** is most applicable when the actual performance to date shows that the original estimates were fundamentally flawed or when they are no longer accurate because of changes in conditions relating to the project:
  - EAC = AC + New Estimate for Remaining Work

- The **Original Estimate** formula is most applicable when actual variances to date are seen as being the exception and the expectations for the future are that the original estimates are more reliable than the actual work effort efficiency to date:
  - EAC = AC + (BAC - EV)

- The **Performance Estimate Low** formula is most applicable when future variances are projected to approximate the same level as current variances:
  - EAC = AC + (BAC - EV)/CPI
  A shortcut version of this formula is:
  - EAC = BAC/CPI

- The **Performance Estimate High** formula is used when the project is over budget and the schedule impacts the work remaining to be completed:
  - EAC = AC + (BAC - EV)/(CPI x SPI)

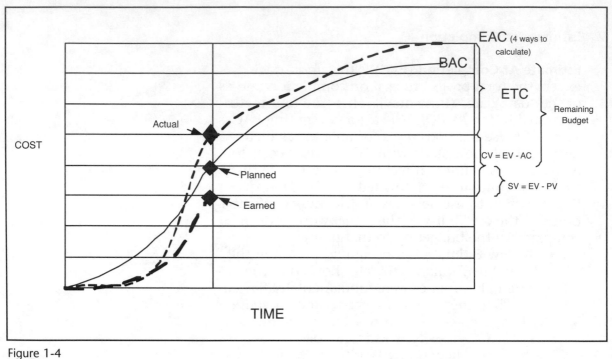

Figure 1-4
Earned Value
S-Curve

Formulas to be used with Figure 1-4 above include:
- CPI = EV/AC
- SPI = EV/PV

8. Remaining Budget

- RB = Remaining PV
  or
- RB = BAC - EV

9. Budget at Completion

- BAC = the total budgeted cost of all approved activities

10. Estimate to Complete

The estimate to complete (ETC) is the estimate for completing the remaining work for a scheduled activity. Like the FAC formulas above, there are three variations:
- ETC = an entirely new estimate
- ETC = (BAC - EV) when past variances are considered to be atypical
- ETC = (BAC - EV)/CPI when prior variances are considered to be typical of future variances

11. Communications Channels

- Channels = [n(n - 1)]/2
  where "n" = the number of people

12. Rule of Seven

In a control chart the "rule of seven" is a heuristic stating that if seven or more observations occur in one direction either upward or downward, or a run of seven observations occur either above or below the mean, even though they may be within the control lines, they should be investigated as if they have an assignable cause. The reason for this rule is that, if the process is operating normally, the observations will follow a random pattern and it is extremely unlikely that seven observations in a row would occur in the same direction above or below the mean.

The probability of any given point going up or down or being above or below the mean is 50-50 (i.e., 50%). The probability of seven observations being consecutively in one direction or above or below the mean would be calculated as 0.50^7, which equals 0.0078 (i.e., less than 1%).

SAMPLE STUDY SCHEDULE

Week/Day	Knowledge Area/ Domain	*PMBOK® Guide* Chapter	Study Guide Chapter	Goals
1	Framework	1 and 2	2	40 questions
2	Processes	3	3	40 questions
3	Integration	4	4	40 questions
4	Scope	5	5	40 questions
5	Time	6	6	40 questions
6	Cost	7	7	40 questions
7	Quality	8	8	40 questions
8	Human Resources	9	9	40 questions
9	Communications	10	10	40 questions
10	Risk	11	11	40 questions
11	Procurement	12	12	40 questions
12	Professional Responsibility		13	40 questions
13	Review	1 to 12	14	100 questions
14	Review	1 to 12	2 to 13	100 questions
15	Practice	1 to 12	2 to 13	200 questions

SAMPLE ASSESSMENT EXAM

Readers should give themselves 50 minutes to answer these 40 sample exam questions. This timing is similar to the average time per question used by PMI in the actual PMP exam.

1. Which of the following is not part of the project management plan?

   a) The staffing plan
   b) The work breakdown structure
   c) Performance measurement baselines for schedule and cost
   d) The project team members' contribution plan

2. Projects are typically initiated as a result of any of the following EXCEPT:

   a) The recommendation of the project manager
   b) The business need that will increase the organization's revenue
   c) A market demand for more technologically advanced products
   d) A social need identified by a feasibility study

3. Once the network diagram is laid out, the project manager will conduct a forward pass and a backward pass through the network. This will provide information on the _____ and identification of the _____.

   a) Slack for each activity, critical path
   b) Slack for each activity, high-risk activities
   c) Resource shortages, slack times
   d) High-risk activities, noncritical paths

4. The majority of firms utilizing project management may typically experience any of the following EXCEPT:

   a) Better control and customer relations
   b) Improved coordination and a reduction in organizational complexity
   c) Additional costs in rework and warranties
   d) Greater adherence to organizational policy and procedures

5. The project manager reviews work results of completed project scope activities and measures these against the:

   a) Requirements
   b) Project management plan
   c) Scope management plan
   d) Work breakdown structure

6. Of the six tools and techniques for the Control Cost process, which one integrates cost and schedule information as a key element of its approach?

   a) Earned value management
   b) Variance analysis
   c) To-complete performance index
   d) Performance reviews

7. When one large project has several smaller projects within it, these are known as:

   a) Projects or subprojects
   b) Programs or projects
   c) Operations or project portfolios
   d) Project life cycles or product life cycles

Notes:

8. One of the major problems facing project managers in acquiring staff is that functional managers are not willing to give up their best people, and even when they do, they do not give up control such as salary and promotion over their people. This is a disadvantage of the _____ organizational structure.

   a) Weak matrix
   b) Projectized
   c) Virtual
   d) Strong matrix

9. One key general management skill all project managers must have is good conflict management skills. Conflict within a team can be _____.

   a) One-sided
   b) An unnatural result of change
   c) Easy to address in any situation
   d) Positive or negative

10. The sequence of activities that cannot be delayed during the course of the project is referred to as the:

    a) Critical path
    b) Master schedule
    c) Slack line
    d) Action plan

11. Initial task(s) required to be performed by the project manager include all of the following EXCEPT:

    a) Budget and schedule preparation
    b) Selection of people to serve on the project team
    c) Getting to know the project's client
    d) Claims administration

Notes:

12. Cost of changes in requirements tends to:

   a) Increase as the project starts up and progresses
   b) Decrease as the project starts up and progresses
   c) Increase or decrease depending on the scope of the change
   d) Always require the project sponsor's approval

13. One purpose for risk management is:

   a) To make sure the schedule is met
   b) To increase the probability and impact of positive events
   c) Assessment of schedule change impacts
   d) Contingency planning

14. _____ is a bar chart that shows a distribution of values.

   a) Pareto
   b) Histogram
   c) Ishikawa
   d) Flowchart

15. Why use risk management?

   a) Some projects are easily delivered
   b) Planning only focuses on the past
   c) Uncertainty is often explicit and formal
   d) Projects can contain many surprises

16. To ensure control over the incidence and frequency of change requests, the project manager establishes a:

   a) Work breakdown structure
   b) Change control system
   c) Risk log
   d) Work procedure schedule

Notes:

17. A project is an endeavor with a well-defined purpose that is:

    a) Ongoing and repetitive
    b) Unique and temporary
    c) A combination of interrelated activities
    d) Started and ended on certain days during each month

18. You have just been notified that your customer has money problems and will not be able to pay for the upcoming milestone deliverables. As project manager you should:

    a) Tell everyone to stop working
    b) Release 90% of the project team
    c) Reduce the scope and begin administrative closure
    d) Shift these deliverables to the next phase to give the customer additional time to obtain funds

19. When planning a project, the team should take into account:

    a) Technical training requirements
    b) The overall strategic goals of the organization
    c) Project requirements, resources and schedules only
    d) The project manager's experience

20. Which of the following is the proper sequence of planning activities for a project?
    I.   Status report description
    II. Detailed task description
    III. Project deliverables decomposition
    IV. Product acceptance criteria
    V.   Budgets and schedules

    a) III, V, I, II, IV
    b) III, V, I, IV, II
    c) IV, III, II, I, V
    d) IV, II, V, I, III

Notes:

21. Which organizational structure provides the project manager with the highest degree of authority?

   a) Projectized
   b) Strong matrix
   c) Balanced matrix
   d) Functional

22. In a fixed price contract, who bears the greater burden of risk?

   a) The seller organization
   b) The buyer organization
   c) The project sponsor
   d) Both the buyer and the seller share the risk

23. The information from the work breakdown structure is used to derive all of the following EXCEPT:

   a) The project master schedule
   b) The project budget
   c) The project objectives
   d) Work package descriptions

24. A subcontractor is two weeks late in his deliverables and asks the project manager to accept these late deliverables in exchange for a reduction in his fee. This is an example of the _____ technique of conflict resolution.

   a) Forcing
   b) Problem solving
   c) Compromising
   d) Withdrawal

Notes:

25. As project manager, you notice that a team member is not performing well because he is inexperienced in the technology being utilized. What should be your best solution?

    a) Report the team member's bad performance to his functional manager
    b) Co-locate the team member right next to your office so you can check on his work
    c) Discuss a reward mechanism with the team member to encourage him to work harder
    d) Arrange for the team member to get training in the required technology

26. Primary objectives of project management include:

    a) Ensuring profitability, competitive advantages and gaining a leadership position
    b) Meeting project objectives in performance, time, cost and quality
    c) Upgrading the system, implementing new technology and facilitating operational change
    d) Solving business problems

27. Projects sometimes get authorized, even though they may not be profitable when fully costed, because the project can serve any of the following EXCEPT:

    a) As a means to develop new technology
    b) To improve the organization's competitive position
    c) As a means to broaden a product line or a line of business
    d) The personal interests of the executive team

28. The Estimate Costs process includes identifying and considering various costing alternatives; it requires you to use as inputs all of the following EXCEPT:

    a) Market conditions
    b) The work breakdown structure
    c) Resource rates
    d) Parametric estimating

Notes:

29. Good project objectives must be:

    a) General rather than specific
    b) Established without considering resource bounds
    c) Realistic and attainable
    d) Measurable, intangible and verifiable

30. A project is fully complete when:

    a) All work has been completed
    b) The customer has formally accepted the project results and deliverables
    c) Financial records for the project have been added to the project archives
    d) The project manager has arranged the project closure celebration

31. For effective communication, the message should be oriented to the _____.

    a) Sender
    b) Receiver
    c) Media
    d) Corporate culture

32. Slack or float is calculated by taking the difference between:

    a) Late finish and early finish of an activity
    b) Late finish and duration of an activity
    c) Early start and late finish of an activity
    d) Early start and late start of an activity

33. A work package is a:

    a) Deliverable at the lowest level of the work breakdown structure
    b) Task with a unique identifier
    c) Required level of reporting
    d) Task that can be assigned to one or more organizational units

Notes:

34. _____ is present in all projects.

    a) Knowledge
    b) Uncertainty
    c) Capital investment
    d) Contract closure

35. In the precedence diagramming method (PDM), common dependencies include:

    a) Start-to-node
    b) Finish-to-start
    c) Arrow-on-node
    d) Start-to-finish

36. Resource leveling is used when shared resources are available at certain times in limited quantities. It often results in:

    a) Project duration that is longer than the preliminary schedule
    b) Project duration that is shorter than the preliminary schedule
    c) No change to the project duration as the critical path is unchanged
    d) Fast tracking

37. Your project has fallen behind schedule and you are trying to get it back on track so you decide to crash some tasks. You will be most successful in completing the project on time and within budget by:

    a) Asking the customer which tasks could be crashed
    b) Crashing all tasks that are estimated to take more than five days
    c) Evaluating the risk impact of crashing tasks on the critical path
    d) Evaluating the cost and risk impact of crashing tasks with one or more days of float

Notes:

38. The output of the Perform Quality Control process that determines the correctness of deliverables is called:

    a) Recommended defect repair
    b) Quality control measures
    c) Validated defect repair
    d) Validated deliverables

39. The customer has asked for major changes that will incur significant costs. If the project is near completion, the project manager should:

    a) Ask the customer for a description of and reason for the changes
    b) Say no to the customer as the project is almost complete and less cost flexibility exists
    c) Meet with the project sponsor and determine if the changes should be made
    d) Meet with the project team to determine who can work overtime

40. Collecting information on how resources are being used to achieve project objectives is part of the _____ process.

    a) Report Performance
    b) Distribute Information
    c) Plan Communications
    d) Manage Stakeholder Expectations

Notes:

SAMPLE ASSESSMENT EXAM ANSWERS
with explanations and references are in
Chapter 15, Appendix A.

CHAPTER 2 | FRAMEWORK

2

PROJECT MANAGEMENT FRAMEWORK

Chapters 1 and 2 of the *PMBOK® Guide* provide a basic structure for the field of project management. These chapters provide an introduction to project management and the context or environment in which projects operate. Together, these two chapters describe the project management framework. Framework itself is not a knowledge area or a performance domain but it contains many important definitions and concepts that must be understood before attempting the remaining chapters of the *PMBOK® Guide*.

Framework questions on the PMP certification exam mainly cover definitions, concepts and approaches. You must be very familiar with PMI terminology. Projects, programs, project management, stakeholders, project and product life cycles, organizational structures and influences are among the topics covered.

> **EXAM TIP**
> Reference the Glossary of the *PMBOK® Guide* frequently to learn PMI terminology.

Things to Know

1. Know the various **Project Constraints**
2. How to define **Enterprise Environmental Factors**
3. The difference between a **Project** and **Product**
4. The **Project Life Cycle**
5. The relationship of **Project Life Cycles** to **Product Life Cycles**
6. The **Influence Curve**
7. **Organizational Process Assets**
8. The three primary **Forms of Organizational Structure**
9. The purpose of the **Project Management Office (PMO)**
10. The difference between **Projects**, **Programs** and **Portfolios**

Key Definitions

Co-location: project team members are physically located close to one another in order to improve communication, working relations and productivity.

Constraints: a restriction or limitation that may force a certain course of action or inaction.

Good Practice: a specific activity or application of a skill, tool or technique that has been proven to contribute positively to the execution of a process.

Enterprise Environmental Factors: external or internal factors that can influence a project's success. These factors include controllable factors such as the tools used in managing projects within the organization or uncontrollable factors that have to be considered by the project manager such as market conditions or corporate culture.

Operation: ongoing work performed by people, constrained by resources, planned, executed, monitored and controlled. Unlike a project, operations are repetitive; e.g., the work performed to carry out the day-to-day business of an organization is operational work.

Organizational Process Assets: any formal or informal processes, plans, policies, procedures, guidelines and on-going or historical project information such as lessons learned, measurement data, project files and estimates versus actuals.

Portfolio: a collection of programs, projects and additional work managed together to facilitate the attainment of strategic business goals.

Product Life Cycle: the collection of stages that make up the life of a product. These stages are typically introduction, growth, maturity and retirement.

Program: a group of related projects managed in a coordinated way; e.g., the design and creation of the prototype for a new airplane is a project, while manufacturing 99 more airplanes of the same model is a program.

2

Progressive Elaboration: the iterative process of continuously improving the detailed plan as more information becomes available and estimates for remaining work can be forecasted more accurately as the project progresses.

Project: work performed by people, constrained by resources, planned, executed, monitored and controlled. It has definite beginning and end points and creates a unique outcome that may be a product, service or result.

Project Life Cycle: the name given to the collection of various phases that make up a project. These phases make the project easier to control and integrate. The result of each phase is one or more deliverables that are needed and utilized in the next few phases. The work of each phase is accomplished through the iterative application of the initiating, planning, executing, monitoring and controlling and closing process groups.

Project Management: the ability to meet project requirements by using various knowledge, skills, tools and techniques to accomplish project work. Project work is completed through the iterative application of initiating, planning, executing, monitoring and controlling and closing process groups. Project management is challenged by competing and changing demands for scope (customer needs, expectations and requirements), resources (people, time and cost), risks (known and unknown) and quality (of the project and product).

EXAM TIP

Chapter 3 of the *PMBOK® Guide* is the standard for project management.

Project Management Information System: the collection of tools, methodologies, techniques, standards and resources used to manage a project. These may be formal systems and strategies determined by the organization or informal methods utilized by project managers.

Stakeholders: individuals and organizations who are involved in or may be affected by project activities. Examples of stakeholders include the project manager, team members, the performing organization, the project sponsor and the customer. PMI advocates that any discrepancies between stakeholder requirements should be resolved in favor of the customer. Therefore, the customer is one of the most important stakeholders in any project.

Standard: a document that describes rules, guidelines, methods, processes and practices that can be used repeatedly to enhance the chances of success.

Subproject: a component of a project. Subprojects can be contracted out to an external enterprise or to another functional unit.

PROJECT CONSTRAINTS

Projects are often performed under many constraints that could impinge on the project's successful or nonsuccessful completion. In addition, these constraints interact and require tradeoffs or decisions that must be made to fulfill project objectives.

For example, additional scope requirements will usually mean either more time to complete those requirements or more resources to work on these requirements, thereby increasing project cost as well as creating additional successful project teams. This was previously known as the triple constraint.

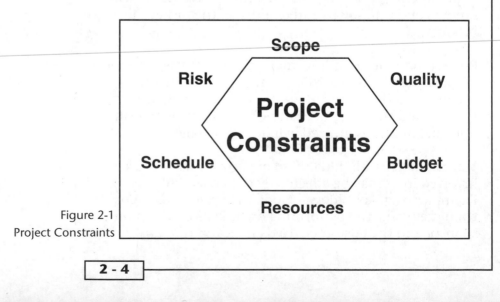

Figure 2-1
Project Constraints

The *PMBOK® Guide* Fourth Edition has now expanded the constraints to be balanced in managing a project to include the competing constraints of:
- Scope
- Quality
- Budget (Cost)
- Resources (Cost, Time)
- Schedule (Time)
- Risk

If one factor changes, one or more other factors are impacted, as depicted in Figure 2-1. In addition, **Enterprise Environmental Factors** may also constrain or limit the project team's ability to function.

ENTERPRISE ENVIRONMENTAL FACTORS

The workplace has changed tremendously in the last two decades, forcing organizations to compete in a global economy. Various internal and external factors can and often do contribute to, or detract from, a project's success.

Project teams are now geographically dispersed and the co-location of the project team members, although still a viable technique, is often no longer possible. With the advent of virtual teams (project teams that spend little or no time meeting face-to-face), the enterprise environmental factors and cultural norms, standard processes, common project management information systems and the organization's established communications channels are more important than ever.

Some best practices for project teams with one or more virtual team members to be successful are:
- Using web tools for virtual meetings to facilitate communications among team members and key stakeholders
- Being conscious of different time zones and cultures
- Using a **Virtual Team Room**, BLOGs, WIKIs or other collaboration tools for project deliverables and work products

2

- Being familiar with the organizational process assets and project management information systems and having both easily accessible
- Using a proven defined approach and documenting the adaptations (tailoring) of the process to fit the needs and requirements of the project
- Having frequent and regular contact with all stakeholders (virtual or face-to-face)
- Holding regularly scheduled team meetings to define requirements, discuss issues, review deliverables and make decisions
- Using multiple methods of communication, such as mail, e-mail, phone calls, phone conferences, virtual meetings, face-to-face meetings when possible and teleconferences

PROJECTS VERSUS PRODUCTS

A project is a temporary endeavor that is undertaken to create a unique product, service or result. When the outcome of a project is related to a product, the outcome of the project could be:
- The development of a new stand-alone product
- The addition of new functions or features to an existing product
- The development of a component or segment of a product or of an aspect of a product such as a prototype or installation at a new location

One product may have many separate projects associated with it, for example, the development of a new airplane. The product also sustains projects through all stages of its product life cycle, for example, a project to conduct market research to determine if there is a need for a long-range airplane that seats 600 passengers, to the final stage of retiring the airplane at the end of its life cycle.

PROJECT LIFE CYCLE

A project life cycle defines:
- The phases that a project goes through from initiation to closure (The *PMBOK® Guide* states that a project contains an initial phase, one or more intermediate phases and a final phase.)
- The technical work to be done in each phase
- The skills involved in each phase
- The deliverables and acceptance criteria for each phase
- How each phase will be monitored, controlled and approved before moving to the next phase

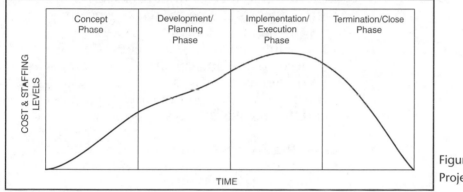

Figure 2-2
Project Life Cycle

A typical project life cycle may contain the following four phases, as shown in Figure 2-2:
- **Starting the Project (Concept Phase):** the problem to be solved is identified. Deliverables from this phase could be:
  - Feasibility studies that clarify the problem to be solved
  - Order of magnitude forecasts of cost
  - A project charter to grant permission for the project to proceed

- **Organization and Preparing (Development and Planning Phase):** what needs to be done is identified. Deliverables created here include:
  - The scope statement
  - A work breakdown structure (WBS)
  - A schedule baseline

- A determination of budgetary costs and a developed budget
- Identification of resources and team members with levels of responsibility
- A risk assessment
- A communications management plan
- The project management plan
- Control systems and methods for handling change control

- **Carrying Out the Work (Implementation and Execution Phase)**: actual work of the project is carried out. Deliverables include:
  - Execution results for work packages
  - Status reports and performance reporting
  - Procurement of goods and services
  - Managing, controlling and redirecting (if needed) of scope, quality, schedule and cost
  - Resolution of problems
  - Integration of the product into operations and the transferral of responsibility

- **Closing the Project (Termination and Close Phase)**: the product is finalized, evaluated and rejected or accepted. Deliverables include:
  - Formal acceptance
  - Documented results and lessons learned
  - Reassignment or release of resources

The starting or concept phase is (as its name implies) an initial phase of the project life cycle; the intermediate phases of the project life cycle are the development and planning and implementation and execution phases and termination and close is the final phase in the project life cycle.

Relationship of Project Life Cycles to Product Life Cycles

The life cycle of a project is only one aspect of the overall **Product Life Cycle**, as Figure 2-3 on the next page shows. A project can be initiated to determine the feasibility of a product in the introductory stage of a product life cycle. There may be a second project to address the design and development of the product once the feasibility study has determined the viability of the product.

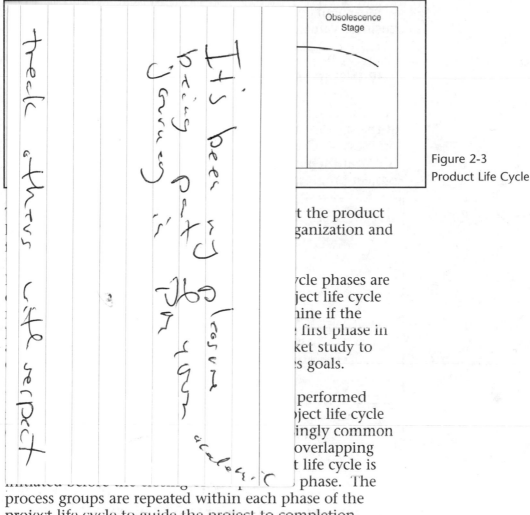

Figure 2-3
Product Life Cycle

t the product
ganization and

cle phases are
ject life cycle
ine if the
first phase in
ket study to
s goals.

performed
ject life cycle
ingly common
overlapping
t life cycle is
phase. The
process groups are repeated within each phase of the project life cycle to guide the project to completion. This overlapping of process groups within phases can be seen in the *PMBOK® Guide*'s Figure 2-5.

In today's rapidly changing environment, the iterative phase-to-phase relationship is becoming increasingly popular. In an iterative relationship, the project life cycle can be repeated in each phase of the project. As work progresses on the current phase and deliverables are produced, more information becomes available, thereby helping in planning the next phase. This **Progressive Elaboration** of the project's product or result requires working closely with the customer to prioritize requirements, minimize project risks and maximize business value.

THE INFLUENCE CURVE

The ability of a stakeholder to influence a change is high at the beginning of a project and decreases as the project progresses. Conversely, the impact or cost of a change is low at the beginning of a project and increases as the project progresses, as seen in Figure 2-4.

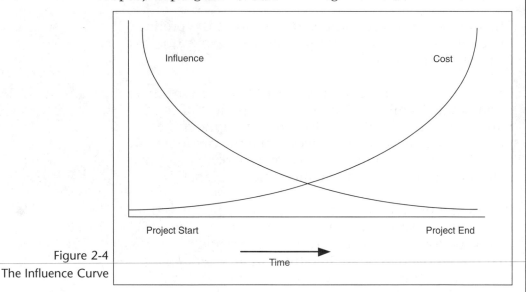

Figure 2-4
The Influence Curve

ORGANIZATIONAL PROCESS ASSETS

An organizational process asset can be any tangible property or resource of the organization that the project team has access to use, re-use, tailor or modify to support the project effort. The following are examples of situations in which a project manager utilized an organizational process asset:

- Using a schedule template for an IT project within the same organization as the starting point for the WBS development activities
- Using a prior quality control plan as the basis for another project's quality control plan
- Inserting current human resource guidelines for hiring and managing contractor resources for the project within the human resources plan
- Reviewing a prior project's lessons learned document to trigger thought and discussion on potential risks that could be encountered on the existing project

FORMS OF ORGANIZATIONAL STRUCTURE

PMI stresses the importance of **Organizational Structures** as the organizational structure will often constrain the availability of resources for a project. Become very familiar with Table 2-1 in the *PMBOK® Guide*, Organizational Influences on Projects.

Functional Organization

In a functional organization, each employee is in a hierarchical structure with one clear superior. Staff is grouped by specialty, such as accounting, marketing or engineering. The pros and cons of a functional organization are shown in Figure 2-5. Included in a functional organization is the use of a **Project Expeditor** or a **Project Coordinator**.

EXAM TIP

A functional organization is recognized by PMI as being the most prevalent type of organizational structure in place today. Therefore, on the exam, when a question compares organizations and the type of the second organization is not mentioned, assume it is a functional organization

PROS	CONS
• Flexibility in staff use	• Client is not the focus of activity
• Availability of experts for multiple projects	• Function rather than problem oriented
• Grouping of specialists	• No one fully responsible for the project
• Technological continuity	• Slow response to the client
• Normal advancement path	• Tendency to suboptimize
	• Fragmented approach to the project

Figure 2-5
Functional
Organization
Pros and Cons

Project Expeditor (PE): the PE is a facilitator who acts as the staff assistant to the executive who has ultimate responsibility for the project. This person has little formal authority. The PE's primary responsibility is to communicate information between the executive and the workers. This type of structure is useful in functional organizations where project costs are relatively low.

Project Coordinator (PC): the PC reports to a higher level in the hierarchy and is usually a staff position. A PC has more formal authority and responsibility than a PE. A PC can assign work to functional workers. This type of structure is useful in functional organizations in which project costs are relatively low compared to those in the rest of the organization.

Matrix Organization

Understand the different matrix organizations. The pros and cons of the matrix organization are listed in Figure 2-6.

PROS	CONS
• Project is the point of emphasis • Access to a reservoir of technical talent • Less anxiety about team future at project completion • Quick client response • Better firm-wide balance of resources • Minimizes overall staff fluctuations	• Two-boss syndrome • More time and effort needed to acquire team members • Functional managers may be reluctant to share top performers • Conflicts of authority between project manager and functional manager • Careful project monitoring required • Political infighting among project managers

Figure 2-6
Matrix Organization
Pros and Cons

Study the *PMBOK® Guide*'s:
- Figure 2-8 Weak Matrix Organization
- Figure 2-9 Balanced Matrix Organization
- Figure 2-10 Strong Matrix Organization
- Figure 2-12 Composite Organization

Matrix organizations have:
- High potential for conflict
- Team members who are borrowed from their functional groups and who are therefore caught between their functional manager and their project manager (but as projects draw to a close, these team members know they have a "home" with their functional groups)
- Team members who only see pieces of the project and may not see the project to completion
- An advantage in relatively complex projects where cross-organizational knowledge and expertise are needed
- Project managers whose authority and time on a project increases from weak matrix (lowest) to balanced matrix to strong matrix

Projectized Organization

In a projectized organization, team members are often co-located and the project manager has a great deal of independence and authority. Team members worry about their jobs as a project draws to a close. Figure 2-7 shows the pros and cons of the projectized organization.

EXAM TIP

PMI places enormous emphasis on the social, economic and environmental influences on projects. A key influence on the role and authority of the project manager is the various organizational structures. Anyone wishing to pass the PMP exam must understand the organizational influences and roles of functional, weak, balanced, strong matrix, projectized, project office, project expeditor and project coordinator types of organizational structures.

PROS	CONS
• One boss • Project manager has great deal of independence and authority • Team members are often co-located • Team members are treated as insiders • Most resources are involved in project work	• If not tracked closely, hourly costs may become inflated while specialists are waiting between assignments or are on call • Bureaucracy, standards, procedures, and documentation may result in an abundance of red tape

Figure 2-7
Projectized
Organization
Pros and Cons

Project Management Office (PMO)

The project management office is an additional layer of organization dedicated to helping project managers. Although most often found in matrixed or projectized organizations, they may exist in any type of organizational structure. Figure 2-8 shows the pros and cons of adding the PMO layer of organization.

PROS	CONS
• Emphasis on project management career paths • Less anxiety among project managers about next assignment at project completion • Centering of project management competencies • Standardization of the project management system • Centralized management	• Additional layer of hierarchy • Some of the adverse aspects of a matrix organization • All of the adverse aspects of a projectized organization • Lack of application knowledge by the project managers

Figure 2-8
PMO Pros and Cons

PROJECTS, PROGRAMS AND PORTFOLIOS

Projects are unique, one-time endeavors with a defined beginning and end. They have specific objectives to fulfill, which are achieved through coordination of interrelated tasks and activities.

Projects are not independent events within an organization. They are one piece of an overall strategic plan. The projects that an organization undertakes should facilitate the achievement of that strategic plan. They should be prioritized so that the most important projects are given every opportunity to succeed and should regularly be re-assessed as to their impact on an overall corporate vision.

A program is a collection of related projects that have a single focused objective. Managing projects in a "program" adds complexity and requires additional coordination between the projects within the program. However, program management can enhance the value of projects by coordinating seemingly independent activities to facilitate the achievement of objectives. Programs may include elements of related work outside of the scope of the discrete projects in the program.

A portfolio is a group of projects that are coordinated so that the organization can implement business strategy and organizational vision. The projects or programs in the portfolio may not be interdependent or directly related.

There usually isn't a lack of projects within organizations. Usually, projects are abundant. Every organization has a limited amount of time, money, staff, expertise, assets and other resources. The two that are most important are critical, specialized resources and money. There are always more "good" projects that could be selected than there are resources.

Each organization must choose. Successful organizations take the time to choose the mix of projects that helps them achieve their goals.

Portfolio Management is the pursuit of a balanced portfolio of projects. The balance comes from comparing several factors which may include:

- External market-driven costs versus internal cost reduction
- Enterprise versus business unit benefit
- Research and development versus existing product lines
- Short-term versus long-term goals
- High risks versus low risks

Portfolio management will aid in managing scarce resources. It benefits business units as they plan and execute projects. It provides senior management a way to compare projects across the organization and to consider new prospects that arise during the course of business. It assists in managing project and organization risks.

Organizations that manage portfolios of projects and programs have a greater capability to plan and predict their financial results. When projects and programs are

2

defined in terms of their contribution to the organization, senior management will make better decisions about the mix of projects and programs and their associated values.

Portfolio management helps all levels and business units communicate, which increases the probability the organization will have long-term financial success.

SAMPLE PMP EXAM QUESTIONS ON MANAGEMENT FRAMEWORK

Framework — Framework Questions

1. Projects create unique deliverables which include all of the following EXCEPT:

   a) Activities
   b) Products
   c) Services
   d) Results

2. The capability of a business to perform a service is an example of:

   a) A project scope statement
   b) A project deliverable
   c) A project objective
   d) A project milestone

3. An outcome or document from performing project management processes and activities is called a:

   a) Product
   b) Result
   c) Scope
   d) Report

4. One of the goals of portfolio management is to carefully select projects and programs that will:

   a) Centralize management of a program
   b) Meet the organization's strategic objectives
   c) Coordinate benefits of related projects
   d) Manage ongoing work directly

Notes:

5. Projects are typically authorized as a result of all of the following EXCEPT:

   a) Technological advance that could benefit the organization
   b) Legal requirement
   c) Market demand
   d) Project managers' prior experiences

6. A category of projects that is defined in terms of the product, the type of customer or the industry sector is a/an:

   a) Portfolio
   b) Program
   c) Application area
   d) Project

7. To provide better _____ of projects, projects can be divided into phases.

   a) Risk management
   b) Integration management
   c) Outsourcing
   d) Control

8. A phase-end review:

   a) Must be used to initiate the subsequent phase
   b) Can have an explicit goal of obtaining authorization to continue
   c) Includes a quality audit
   d) Can be delayed until project closure

9. An application area is defined as:

   a) Something that happens on occasion
   b) A category of projects that have common components
   c) A collection of projects or programs
   d) The process of making deeded information available to stakeholders

Notes:

10. PMI members adhere to:

    a) Customer quality assurance policies
    b) Federal, state, and local laws
    c) A "code of ethics"
    d) Good business practices

11. The primary purpose of the *PMBOK® Guide* is to identify that subset of the Project Management Body of Knowledge that is generally recognized as good practice. "Generally recognized" means:

    a) That the knowledge and practices described are applicable to most projects most of the time, and that there is widespread consensus about their value and usefulness
    b) Providing a general overview as opposed to an exhaustive description
    c) That the correct application of these skills, tools, and techniques can enhance the chances of success over a wide range of different projects
    d) That is it used as a reference to settle lawsuits arising from cost overruns

12. Projects can have intended and unintended _____ social impacts.

    a) Positive and/or negative
    b) Legal and/or illegal
    c) Team
    d) International

Framework — Planning Question

13. During the closing phase of a project, employees are concerned about their next assignment in which type of organizational structure?

    a) Projectized
    b) Strong matrix
    c) Balanced matrix
    d) Functional

Notes:

Framework — Executing Questions

14. What impact does a functional organization have on project team development if the team is totally within the functional department?

    a) Team development is simplified
    b) Team development becomes more complex
    c) Team development is not impacted
    d) Team development does not take place in functional organizations

15. General management skills provide much of the foundation for building project management skills. However, managing a project requires additional competencies of:

    a) Negotiating to acquire adequate resources
    b) Motivating and inspiring team members
    c) Effecting tradeoffs concerning project goals
    d) Understanding health and safety practices

2

ANSWERS AND REFERENCES FOR SAMPLE PMP EXAM QUESTIONS ON MANAGEMENT FRAMEWORK
Section numbers refer to the *PMBOK® Guide.*

1. A   Section 1.2
    Activities are performed to create a deliverable.

2. B   Section 1.2, Glossary
    Some projects are initiated to enable an organization to perform a service.

3. B   Section 1.2, Glossary
    A product is an artifact such as material or goods.

4. B   Section 1.4.1
    Portfolios and projects are selected based on the organization's specific goals.

5. D   Section 1.4.3
    A project could be authorized as a result of organizational needs, but not based on the past experiences of project managers.

6. C   Chapter 1, Glossary
    Application areas differ from industry to industry.

7. D   Section 2.1.3

8. B   Section 2.1.3.1
    Phase-end reviews are preferable but not required, so choice A is out; for choice C, a quality audit is not defined as part of a phase-end review; by definition, phase-end reviews are performed during the project life, so choice D is out.

9. B   Chapter 1, Glossary
    Choice A is the definition of an event; choice C is the definition of a portfolio; choice D is the definition of the distribute information process.

10. C   Section 1.1

11. A   Section 1.1

12. A   Section 1.2

13. A **Section 2.4.2**
A project-based organization derives its revenue from performing projects. Once the project is complete, there may not be another project to move to.

14. A **Section 2.4.2**
Team members are accountable primarily to the functional manager who should provide the appropriate support in delivering on projects.

15. C **Section 2.3**
Negotiating, motivating, maneuvering through politics are examples of general management and interpersonal skills.

CHAPTER 3 | PROCESSES

3

PROJECT MANAGEMENT PROCESSES, PROCESS GROUPS AND THE INTERACTION OF PROCESSES

PMI has created a standard which documents the processes needed to manage a project. These processes are based on best practices that are practiced on most projects, most of the time. However, PMI recognizes that not all of the processes need be, or even should be, applied to all projects all of the time. The project managers and their teams need to consider each process and determine if it is appropriate to their specific situation. This process is called **Tailoring** by PMI. PMI feels that the processes and interactions among processes described in the *PMBOK® Guide* should serve as a standard for project management. Various methodologies and tools can be used to implement the framework for project management within an organization. Variances from the *PMBOK® Guide* standard are documented as part of the organization's **Project Management Methodology**. The organization's project management methodology can, in turn, be tailored to fit the specific needs of the project based on customer requirements.

EXAM TIP

A diagram of the mapping of project management processes to the process groups and knowledge areas is found in the PMBOK Guide Table 3-1.

Things to Know

1. Project Management Processes and Process Groups
2. Project Management Process Interactions

Key Definitions

Input: a tangible item internal or external to the project that is required by a process for the process to produce its output.

Output: a deliverable, result or service generated by the application of various tools or techniques within a process.

Phase: one of a collection of logically related project activities usually resulting in the completion of one or more major deliverables. A project phase is a component of a project life cycle.

EXAM TIP

Be very familiar with *PMBOK®
Guide* Figures 3-1, 3-2, 3-5, 3-8,
3-29, 3-38 and 3-49.

Process: a collection of related actions performed to achieve a predefined desired outcome. The *PMBOK® Guide* defines a set of 42 project management processes, each with various inputs, tools, techniques and outputs. Processes can have predecessor or successor processes, so outputs from one process can be inputs to other processes. Each process belongs to one and only one of the five process groups and one and only one of the nine knowledge areas.

Process Group: a logical grouping of a number of the 42 project management processes. There are five process groups and all are required to occur at least once for every project. The process groups are performed in the same sequence each time: initiating, planning, executing, more planning and executing as required and ending with closing. The monitoring and controlling process group is performed throughout the life of the project. Process groups can be repeated for each phase of the project life cycle process groups and are not phases. Process groups are independent of the application area or the life cycle utilized by the project.

Tailoring: the adaptation of the standard processes and their constituent inputs and outputs to fit appropriately with the needs of the project. The degree of rigor applied to each process considered must also be determined. The project manager, together with the project team, is responsible for determining the amount of tailoring to be carried out and documenting the decisions made by the project team in a work reference model or other project document.

Technique: a defined systematic series of steps applied by one or more individuals using one or more tools to achieve a product or result or to deliver a service.

Tool: a tangible item such as a checklist or template used in performing an activity to produce a product or result.

PROJECT MANAGEMENT PROCESSES AND PROCESS GROUPS

The *PMBOK® Guide* defines five process groups required for any project. They are:

- **Initiating:** defining and authorizing the project (or phase of the project)
- **Planning:** defining objectives, refining them and planning the actions required to attain them
- **Executing:** integrating all resources to carry out the plan
- **Monitoring and Controlling:** measuring progress to identify variances and taking corrective action when necessary
- **Closing:** bringing the project or phase to an orderly end, including gaining formal acceptance of the result

The process groups are NOT project phases. In fact, it is not unusual to see all of the process groups represented within a single phase of a larger project.

In preparing for the PMP exam, take the time to read Chapter 3 of the *PMBOK® Guide* very carefully. PMI has put a lot of thought into the descriptions of the process groups, the interactions of the processes within them and the relationships of each process group to the other process groups.

Each process group contains a number of processes, as listed below, but PMI has also identified nine topic-related groupings for the processes called **Knowledge Areas**. The processes associated with a particular knowledge area all address a single topic. For example, the processes within the time knowledge area address defining and planning the project schedule. The *PMBOK® Guide* is organized around these knowledge areas: Chapters 4 through 12 define each of the processes within a knowledge area in detail, covering the knowledge areas of integration, scope, time, cost, human resources, quality, communications, risk and procurement. This study guide is organized the same way to facilitate the PMP exam candidate's study effectiveness.

The process group lists below show the process group, the processes in that group and, in parentheses, the knowledge area where that process is described.

Initiating Process Group

1. Develop Project Charter (Integration)
2. Identify Stakeholders (Communications)

Planning Process Group

1. Develop Project Management Plan (Integration)
2. Collect Requirements (Scope)
3. Define Scope (Scope)
4. Create WBS (Scope)
5. Define Activities (Time)
6. Sequence Activities (Time)
7. Estimate Activity Resources (Time)
8. Estimate Activity Duration (Time)
9. Develop Schedule (Time)
10. Estimate Cost (Cost)
11. Determine Budget (Cost)
12. Plan Quality (Quality)
13. Develop Human Resource Plan (Human Resources)
14. Plan Communications (Communications)
15. Plan Risk Management (Risk)
16. Identify Risks (Risk)
17. Perform Qualitative Risk Analysis (Risk)
18. Perform Quantitative Risk Analysis (Risk)
19. Plan Risk Responses (Risk)
20. Plan Procurements (Procurement)

Executing Process Group

1. Direct and Manage Project Execution (Integration)
2. Perform Quality Assurance (Quality)
3. Acquire Project Team (Human Resources)
4. Develop Project Team (Human Resources)
5. Manage Project Team (Human Resources)
6. Distribute Information (Communications)

7. Manage Stakeholder Expectations (Communications)
8. Conduct Procurement (Procurement)

Monitoring and Controlling Process Group

1. Monitor and Control Project Work (Integration)
2. Perform Integrated Change Control (Integration)
3. Verify Scope (Scope)
4. Control Scope (Scope)
5. Control Schedule (Time)
6. Control Costs (Cost)
7. Perform Quality Control (Quality)
8. Report Performance (Communications)
9. Monitor and Control Risks (Risk)
10. Administer Procurements (Procurement)

Closing Process Group

1. Close Project or Phase (Integration)
2. Close Procurements (Procurement)

PROJECT MANAGEMENT PROCESS INTERACTIONS

Each process has **Inputs**, **Tools**, and **Techniques** and **Outputs** as defined in the *PMBOK® Guide*. You must take the time to learn the flow of the processes within each process group, the relations of processes across process groups and how the outputs of one process become the inputs to other processes.

In order to help you understand how process groups flow and interact with one another, refer to Figure 3-1 and do Exercise 3-1, both on the following page.

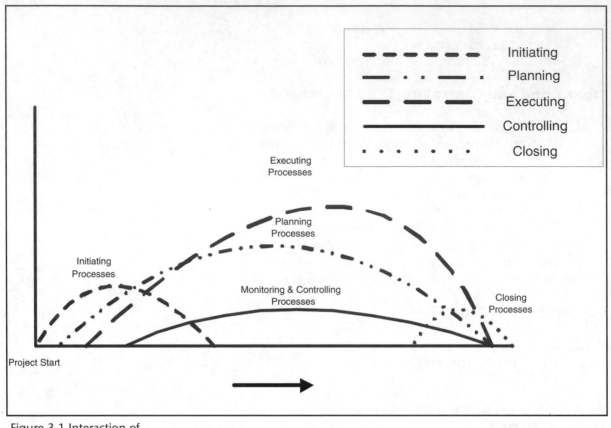

Figure 3-1 Interaction of
Process Groups (*PMBOK®
Guide* Figure 3-11)

Exercise 3-1

In the WAV files there are charts of the 42 processes with
the inputs, tools, techniques and outputs for each process.
Print out each chart, in color if possible, and cut out and
rearrange the processes for each one of the process groups.

HINT: See *PMBOK® Guide* Figures 4-1, 5-1, 6-1, 7-1, 8-1,
9-1, 10-1, 11-1 and 12-1.

The charts of each process will also make a very portable
quick reference you can use as a study aid.

SAMPLE PMP EXAM QUESTIONS ON MANAGEMENT PROCESSES

Processes — Framework Questions

1. The project manager is always responsible for:

   a) Ensuring that the project is highly profitable
   b) Hiring and firing members of the project team
   c) Selecting projects that can be accommodated
   d) Determining what processes are appropriate

2. When one large project has several smaller projects within it, this is known as:

   a) Project subprojects
   b) Program projects
   c) Operation project portfolio
   d) Project life cycle or product life cycle

Processes — Initiating Questions

3. Deliverable acceptance can be improved by:

   a) Assigning a PMP as a project manager
   b) Paying incentive premiums
   c) Letting the customer determine the deliverables
   d) Involving the stakeholders during initiation

4. Which process is primarily concerned with authorizing the project or project phase?

   a) Scope Initiation
   b) Develop Project Charter
   c) Project Planning Process
   d) Develop Project Scope

5. The initiating process group consists of which two processes?

   a) Develop Project Charter and Identify Stakeholders
   b) Develop a Scope Statement and Initiation
   c) Develop Project Charter and Initiation
   d) Initiation and Develop a Scope Statement

6. All of the following are inputs to the Develop Project Charter process EXCEPT:

   a) The contract
   b) Enterprise environmental factors
   c) The project statement of work
   d) The project charter

Processes — Planning Questions

7. Results of project iterations should always be documented as updates to:

   a) The project management plan
   b) The project statement of work
   c) The communication matrix
   d) The risk register

8. Significant changes occurring throughout the project life cycle can trigger:

   a) A rewrite of the project charters
   b) The need to revisit one or more of the planning processes or some of the initiating processes
   c) Assignment of a new project manager
   d) Cancellation of the project

9. Which definition defines the planning process group?

   a) It integrates people and other resources to carry out the project management plan for the project
   b) It defines and authorizes the project
   c) It formalizes the acceptance of the product, service or result of the project
   d) It defines and refines objectives, and plans the course of action required to attain the objectives and scope of the project

Notes:

Processes — Executing Question

10. _____ coordinate(s) people and other resources to carry out the plan.

   a) Resource planning
   b) Resource leveling
   c) Controlling processes
   d) Executing processes

Processes — Monitoring and Controlling Questions

11. The process which uses earned value management to aide in understanding variances in performance is called:

   a) Control Scope
   b) Control Costs
   c) Monitor and Control Risks
   d) Administer Procurements

12. As the project manager of a large residential construction project, you find that the developer has identified three new landscaping designs to the investors, even though the contract has been signed and construction has begun. In your estimate, all three designs would add $10,000 to $30,000 to the landscaping budget. You ask for a meeting with key stakeholders immediately to address this potential variance. You are exercising:

   a) Scope control
   b) Scope baselining
   c) Budget management
   d) Conflict management

Notes:

Processes — Closing Question

13. The process that provides the seller with formal
    written notice that a legal agreement has been
    completed is called:

    a) Claims Management
    b) Close Procurements
    c) Administer Contract
    d) Close Project or Phase

Notes:

3

3

**ANSWERS AND REFERENCES FOR SAMPLE
PMP EXAM QUESTIONS ON PROCESSES**
Section numbers refer to the *PMBOK® Guide.*

1. D   **Chapter 3**
        Choice A is out because projects don't have to
        be profitable; choice B is out because project
        managers may not have the authority to hire and
        fire; project managers don't always get to choose
        the projects they work on, so choice C is out.

2. A   **Section 3.2**
        Subprojects are typically referred to as projects
        and managed as such. They may be managed by
        a less-experienced project manager.

3. D   **Section 3.3**
        Choice A is out because having a PMP does not
        guarantee success; for choice B, some people and
        organizations are not motivated by dollars; for
        choice C, the customer may not know all the
        deliverables that may need to be produced.

4. B   **Section 3.3.1**
        Choices A, C and D are not processes defined
        within the *PMBOK® Guide.*

5. A   **Section 3.3**

6. D   **Section 3.3.1**
        The project charter is the output of the develop
        project charter process.

7. A   **Section 3.4**
        Iterations bring clarity to the different knowledge
        areas. Updating the project management plan is
        necessary in order to keep in step with the changes
        occurring on the project.

8. **B   Section 3.4**
    For choices A , C and D, although the project
    charter may be re-written, the project manager
    re-assigned or the project cancelled, the more
    accurate statement from PMI's standpoint is that
    the project manager should revisit various
    planning processes to determine what may need
    to change, if anything.

9. **D   Section 3.4**
    Choice A is the definition of the executing process
    group; choice B is the definition of the initiating
    process group; choice C is the definition of the
    closing process group.

10. **D   Section 3.5**
    This is the definition of the executing process
    group.

11. **B   Section 7.3**
    Earned value management (EVM) measures
    project performance in terms of dollars.

12. **A   Section 5.5**
    Before these new designs become a cost issue, the
    project manager must facilitate the discussion to
    determine if these requested changes will be in or
    out of scope.

13. **B   Section 12.4**
    Contracts are legally binding agreements and
    require formal closure.

CHAPTER 4 | INTEGRATION

4

INTEGRATION MANAGEMENT

The PMP certification exam addresses critical project management functions that ensure coordination of the various elements of the project. The *PMBOK® Guide* explains that the processes in project management are integrative in nature. They involve making tradeoffs among competing objectives to meet stakeholders' needs and expectations. Integration processes drive the associated knowledge area processes within each of the process groups and all process groups are addressed by one or more integration management processes. These processes interact with each other as well as with the other eight knowledge areas.

It is important to note that integration occurs within as well as outside the project. For example, project scope and product scope must be integrated and project work must be integrated with the ongoing other work of the organization (such as operations and deliverables from various technical specialties). One of the key tools or techniques used to integrate the processes and measure project performance is **Earned Value Management** (EVM). Earned value reports are introduced in this chapter and utilized for performance measurement in Time Management (Chapter 6), Cost Management (Chapter 7) and Communications Management (Chapter 10).

Interactions often have a domino effect and can be overt or subtle. Interactions engender tradeoffs and the project manager must be able to orchestrate these interactions as the project flows and changes throughout its life cycle. For example, increased resource usage in one area may adversely affect the schedule in another area. Complicating the picture is the fact that the project manager has to answer to many stakeholders and must constantly communicate upward, downward and laterally to ensure success. The integration management knowledge area of the PMP exam stresses how the different knowledge areas interact to continuously improve our ability to plan, perform and predict work.

EXAM TIP

Although this is the first knowledge area to be discussed (following the sequence of the *PMBOK® Guide*), we recommend that you revisit it after all other knowledge areas are reviewed.

4

Project integration management occurs throughout the project life cycle, from project start to close. The project manager faces many challenges that differ from those faced by functional or operational managers. The project manager must coordinate the integration of:

- Project work with ongoing operations
- Product and project scope
- Schedule, budget, metrics and reporting
- Skills, knowledge and deliverables from vendors, stakeholders and the performing organization
- Risks and staffing plans
- Performance and quality objectives

All six of the project integration management processes contain the tools and techniques of **Expert Judgment**. The Direct and Manage Project Execution process contains the additional tool of the **Project Management Information System (PMIS)** and the Perform Integrated Change Control process contains the technique of change control meetings. These tools and techniques must be defined, clearly understood and used in developing the project charter and other key documents of the project.

Things to Know

1. The six processes of integration management:
   - **Develop Project Charter**
   - **Develop Project Management Plan**
   - **Direct and Manage Project Execution**
   - **Monitor and Control Project Work**
   - **Perform Integrated Change Control**
   - **Close Project or Phase**
2. The purpose of a **Business Case**
3. **Project Statement of Work**
4. The importance of **Expert Judgment**
5. The contents of the **Project Charter**
6. The contents of the **Project Management Plan**
7. **Tailoring** and project management
8. The purpose of a **Project Management Information System (PMIS)**
9. **Configuration Management** and the **Change Control System**

10. The types of **Work Performance Information**
11. How to manage **Change Requests**

Key Definitions

These are used throughout the *PMBOK® Guide.*

Application Area: a category of projects that have unique components that may not be present in other categories of projects. For example, IT projects approaches are different from residential development projects.

Change Control: the procedures used to identify, document, approve (or reject) and control changes to the project baselines.

Change Management: the process for managing change in the project. A change management plan should be incorporated into the project management plan.

Enterprise Environmental Factors: external or internal factors that can influence a project's success. These factors include controllable factors such as the tools used in managing projects within the organization or uncontrollable factors that have to be considered by the project manager such as market conditions or corporate culture.

Expert Judgment: judgment based upon expertise appropriate to the activity. It may be provided by any group or person, either within the organization or external to it.

Organizational Process Assets: any formal or informal processes, plans, policies, procedures, guidelines and on-going or historical project information such as lessons learned, measurement data, project files and estimates versus actuals.

Progressive Elaboration: the progressive improvement of a plan as more specific and detailed information becomes available during the course of the project.

Project Management Information System: the collection of tools, methodologies, techniques, standards and resources used to manage a project. These may be formal systems and strategies determined by the organization or informal methods utilized by project managers.

Project Management Methodology: any structured approach used to guide the project team through the project life cycle. This methodology may utilize forms, templates and procedures standard to the organization.

DEVELOP PROJECT CHARTER PROCESS

This process is used to formally authorize a new project or validate an existing project for continuation into the next phase. Projects are initiated as a result of a problem to be solved, an opportunity or a business requirement. Therefore, many organizations often have more projects than resources to complete the projects. A method to select high priority projects must be used. One method is where projects are selected based on the business need and cost benefit analysis that are contained in the business case.

Business Case

An organization often has many identified projects; usually more projects exist than available resources can handle. Therefore, it is a good practice to follow a project selection and prioritization process where justification and cost benefit analyses of the project are evaluated. The business case is the document that justifies why the project should be accomplished. In some cases the customer or requesting organization writes the business case. Projects come about based on business needs such as:

- **Market Demand:** for the organization to stay in business, it must produce competitive products
- **Customer Request:** the sponsoring organization needs and will to pay for new functionality
- Legal or social requirements: Sarbanes-Oxley requirements and reports for accounting practices

It is important to review the business case at the end of each phase to ensure that the business need for the project still exists.

Project Statement of Work

An input to the Develop Project Charter process is the statement of work (SOW). The SOW is a narrative description of the products or services to be delivered by the project. Since the products or services can be delivered by either an internal or an external organization, the SOW is also an important artifact of the project procurement management knowledge area. PMI calls a SOW for external organizations a contract statement of work. A SOW generally includes:

- The **Business Need** or reasons the product or service is required
- The description of the product scope or product requirements with as much detail as possible to support project planning and estimates
- The **Strategic Plan** and how the project supports the organization's strategic goals to facilitate the project selection decision-making process

Expert Judgment

The expert judgment tool and technique may be available in many forms. Subject matter experts may exist within the organization to provide experts in assessing the information on hand and providing recommendations and guidance. Expert judgment may also come from outside organizations or groups.

The **Delphi Technique** is a form of expert judgment in which opinions are obtained from a panel of experts who work independently and anonymously. It is often used in risk management but can also be used to gain consensus on project selection, scope of work, estimates and technical issues.

Many people within the organization can be considered "experts." A project manager may be an expert when it comes to orchestrating and coordinating all the efforts of the project. The quality assurance manager may be the expert in determining the best types of tests that will ensure a high quality product. It is up to the project manager to assess the needs of the project and consult with or involve "experts" throughout the project life cycle to ensure a successful project result.

The Project Charter

The project charter is an important document that establishes a project. It:

- Contains the **Business Need**, purpose and justification for the project
- Includes the **Product Requirements**
- Should contain the assigned project manager and/or his or her **Authority** level for the project
- Could be the signed **Contract** when procurement processes are used
- Defines the **Goals** and **Objectives** of the project (sets the project direction)
- Is approved by key stakeholders
- Shows organizational, environmental and external **Constraints** and **Assumptions**
- Contains the summary **Budget** and milestone schedule

PMI recognizes the iterative nature of projects and the use of **Progressive Elaboration** in the development of the project. The develop project charter process demonstrates that when projects are initiated, not all information is available in a detailed form. The objective of this process is to get the project initiated and to assign resources to explore the detailed needs of the project. The **Project Charter** might be considered a "1st draft" of the understanding of project requirements. The project charter is an input to the planning processes of develop project management plan, collect requirements and define scope to help define the project management plan, the requirements and the project scope statement.

Some aspects critical to the measurement of success of the project are outlined in the project charter. These key aspects are:

- Purpose and project objectives
- Project sponsor or authority
- Project description and requirements
- **Success Criteria**
- **Acceptance Criteria**
- **Identified Risks**
- Initial WBS, preliminary milestones and summary budget
- **Project Manager Assignment** (with responsibility and authority level)

CASE STUDY: THE LAWRENCE RV GARAGE PROJECT

This case study will be used throughout this study guide. You will be asked to prepare various documents relating to the case as you go through the initiating, planning, executing and monitoring and controlling processes. Since this study guide is organized following the presentation of topics in the *PMBOK® Guide*, the exercises are not necessarily in the order in which they would be completed in a real project. Although this case study is not on the exam, it is provided here to strengthen your understanding and application of project management disciplines and techniques.

Examples of each of the documents you need to provide for a project are provided for you to compare with your results. There are no right or wrong documents; you will develop different levels of detail in your answers and the examples provided simply demonstrate our interpretation of one approach. We have used Microsoft Project Standard 2002 to create some of the examples. Any of the currently available project management software packages will provide similar results.

4

Case Study Overview

The goal of the Lawrence RV Garage Project is to build an RV garage on the property of Mr. and Mrs. Lawrence. They have been parking their RV and their son's boat in their backyard in a fenced, gated area. However, their city has passed a new ordinance that prohibits residents with RVs, boats, off-road vehicles or utility trailers from storing or parking such vehicles on their property or on the street for more than 72 hours. These vehicles must now be parked or stored in a "building suitable for that purpose." Mr. and Mrs. Lawrence have decided to build an RV garage.

They hired an architectural firm to develop the plans and specifications for the garage. These have been completed, along with all the working drawings and a bill of materials, and the architect has also agreed to be Mr. and Mrs. Lawrence's project manager, helping them select a contractor and working with the contractor's project manager.

Acme Construction and Engineering (ACE) has won the bid to build the garage. You have been appointed to be the project manager for ACE. You were not involved with the bidding process.

The garage is designed to be big enough to hold a motor home or travel trailer and a boat. It is 50 feet long and 30 feet wide with two 14-ft.-high by 12-ft.-wide roll-up doors for the RV and boat and a standard 3-ft. side door. There are two windows on the side of the garage that has the standard door, three windows on the side with no door and two windows in the back wall. Inside there are to be lights and electrical outlets to be used when working on the RV or boat. The plans also show RV hookups inside (water, electric and sewer) and there should also be a drain in the floor. There should be a small bathroom (commode and sink only) in the back corner of the garage and a utility sink adjacent to the bathroom.

The exterior walls are to be stucco and the roof is to be asphalt shingles to match the existing house. Walls should be of 2X6 construction to allow for greater insulation.

Since there is an existing home, utilities are already present. The architect has submitted the plans to the city but they have not yet been approved and a permit has yet to be issued.

Case Study Exercise

Exercise 4-1: Create a project charter for the Lawrence RV Garage Project. It really should be written by the general manager for the contractor but she has asked you to write the draft and then the two of you will polish it together.

DEVELOP PROJECT MANAGEMENT PLAN PROCESS

The Develop Project Management Plan process integrates all the **Subsidiary Plans** from the various knowledge areas into one cohesive whole. This complete, consistent and coherent document is the project management plan. It is crucial that the project manager and the project team spend sufficient time in creating the project management plan because this document serves to reduce project uncertainty, improve the efficiency of work, provide a better understanding of the project objectives and provide a basis for monitoring and controlling. This key document also serves as a communication and educational tool for stakeholders on the project.

PMI emphasizes the four concepts of planning:
- Planning begins during the starting phase of a project
- Planning does not end until the project is finished
- Planning is an intellectual process that runs through all the other processes of the project

- Planning is iterative; as the project proceeds, the project team must plan, replan and plan again

In planning a project, first the project objectives are clearly defined and a WBS is created to define the work in more detail; this WBS is used to schedule the work with resources assigned to obtain a time-phased budget. This time-phased budget is used to obtain the planned value S-curve as seen in Figure 4-1.

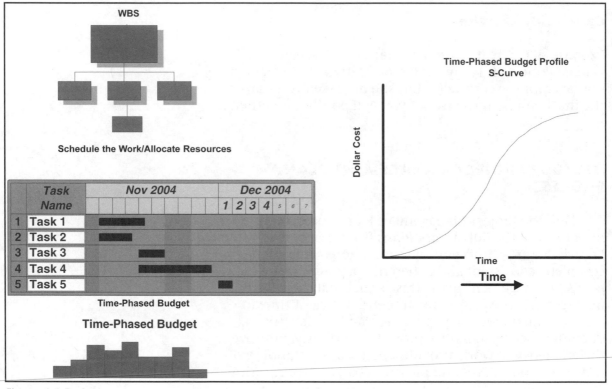

Figure 4-1 Project Scope and Time Definitions of Cost

The Project Management Plan

A project management plan is more than just a set of instructions. It is not just a WBS or an output of MS Project™. Planning is an analytical exercise whose objective is to eliminate crisis by preventing anything from falling through the cracks. Creating it is an **Iterative Process** used to guide project execution. It is a collection of documents that identify the project assumptions and decisions The project management plan provides both a standard communication tool throughout the lifetime of the project and a verification and agreement on objectives and requirements from the stakeholders. The plan is documented and approved by both the customer and the sponsor. All baselines for tracking, control, analysis, communications and integration elements are incorporated into the project management plan.

The project management plan is a key document that integrates outputs from all the other planning processes to form a consistent, comprehensive document to guide the execution and control of the project.

The key elements of the project management plan may ultimately include:
- The selected **Project Life Cycle** to be used
- The project management approach or strategy to be used by the definition of the selected processes and tools and techniques
- How a standard process could be tailored
- How project work will be managed and executed
- How changes will be monitored and controlled
- How **Configuration Management** will be performed
- How the integrity of performance baselines will be maintained, including **Requirements Traceability**
- How the project will be closed
- The description of other phases or related projects in multiphase or multiprogram environments
- The level of frequency and techniques for communicating with stakeholders
- The schedule or milestone chart of key management reviews for progress, issue resolution and decisions
- **Subsidiary Management Plans**, including the following plans and their definitions:
  - **Scope Management Plan:** provides guidance on how project scope is defined, documented, verified, managed and controlled; it is created before performing the five processes of scope management

> **EXAM TIP**
> Know the key elements of the project management plan.

4

- **Requirements Management Plan**: tracks how requirements are managed, analyzed, documented, prioritized and traces changes to requirements through the project life cycle
- **Schedule Management Plan**: describes how changes to the schedule will be managed
- **Cost Management Plan**: describes how cost variances will be managed based on the needs of the stakeholders
- **Quality Management Plan** and **Process Improvement Plan**: describe how the project management team will implement its quality policy
- **Human Resource Plan**: describes how and when human resources will be brought into and taken off the project team
- **Communications Management Plan**: addresses the collection, distribution, access to and updates of project information
- **Risk Management Plan**: documents procedures to manage risk throughout the project
- **Procurement Management Plan**: describes how procurement processes will be managed

Tailoring

Tailoring is a form of modification to accommodate unique situations. Since no two projects are identical and each project brings with it new challenges and risks, the project manager must consider how standard or unique a project is and determine whether or not tailoring is needed.

In our discussion of utilizing organizational process assets for our project, it is expected that these resources are available to be used, re-used or modified to accommodate the uniqueness of a project. This is a form of tailoring.

A project manager may also have significant experience in a particular type of project, such as software implementations, but each project has different stakeholders with different needs; therefore, there could be many unique attributes which need to be considered. A project manager must make tailoring decisions and balance the project constraints as well as meet the acceptance criteria of the deliverables by the key stakeholders.

DIRECT AND MANAGE PROJECT EXECUTION PROCESS

Project execution consists of the primary processes whereby the project management plan is put into action. Most of the project resources and costs are expended in this process. Important inputs to this process are the project management plan, the **Enterprise Environmental Factors** and the organizational process assets as these inputs influence how the project team carries out its work.

In order for the project management plan to be executed, work is assigned to resources by the project manager and then monitored for completion of deliverables and work results. Therefore, the key outputs of this process are **Deliverables**, requested changes and work performance information. Since project activities are performed by people, the project manager must understand the organizational structure and individual motivations of the people working on the project. These skills are addressed within the Develop Project Team process of the human resource management knowledge area.

Project Management Information System (PMIS)

The project management information system is a tool or technique of the Direct And Manage Project Execution process. This system can include both manual and automated systems used to gather, integrate and disseminate the outputs of the develop project management plan processes. It is used by the project management team to create and control changes to the project management plan. The PMIS can contain many subsystems, such as project management scheduling software, information/progress reporting systems, web links to related systems and a configuration management system.

4

Configuration Management

Configuration management (CM) is a systematic procedure that refers to change management. CM protects both the customer from unauthorized changes by project staff and the project staff from new or undocumented requirements changes from the customer. A configuration management system:
- Is a collection of formal documented procedures used to apply direction and control compliance of products and components with project requirements
- Is a subsystem of the project management information system
- Includes the processes that define how project deliverables and documents are controlled, changed and approved
- In many areas includes the change control system

The purpose of CM is to ensure compliance to stated requirements by:
- Defining the process by identifying and documenting the characteristics of the configurable items (project products or components)
- Controlling and managing change requests to characteristics of configurable items
- Ensuring the integrity and consistency of the items as defined by the requirements and approved modifications by the use of internal or external audits

Change Control System

The change control system is also a collection of formal documented procedures that define how project change requests are submitted, validated, recorded, approved or rejected, communicated and worked within the project. In many areas the change control system is a subset of the configuration management system.

Work Performance Information

Work performance information is an output of the Direct And Manage Project Execution process and are used to identify problems and issues so that corrective action can be taken. As the product of the project is created, performance against project baselines must be monitored and reported. **Performance Reports** and work results are addressed in many knowledge areas of the *PMBOK® Guide*. It is important to know the various types of reports for the exam.

Typical reports used are:
- Status or **Progress Reports** (daily, weekly, etc.)
- **Trend Analysis**
- **Variance Analysis**
- **Exception Reports**
- **Earned Value Reports**
- **Schedule Reports** that consist of:
  - Gantt charts
  - Milestone charts
  - Network diagrams
- **Cost Reports** that consist of:
  - S-curves
  - Histograms
  - Expenditure tables

MONITOR AND CONTROL PROJECT WORK PROCESS

As the work of the project is carried out, deliverables or work results are created. Issues arise or changes come about in the form of change requests. The project manager and team continuously monitor performance by comparing actual performance against the project management plan and determine if corrective or preventive actions are necessary. In some cases defects may be found which may require rework. As a result of any of the above issues, one or more change requests are created. These change requests will impact project deliverables and may increase project costs and schedules. In some cases a mid-project evaluation may be needed.

Mid-Project Evaluations are conducted while project work is still in progress. The main purpose of such evaluations is to determine if objectives are still relevant and if these objectives are being met. **Lessons Learned** should also be documented at this time instead of waiting for the project to be completed.

A third party or people outside the team should be used to conduct mid-project evaluations so that results are less biased. Mid-project evaluations, however, often cause stress and conflict within the project team for the following reasons:

- Evaluations can be disruptive, take time away from project work, require review meetings to be scheduled and result in significant changes
- The evaluation could generate the impression in project team members that they are not to be trusted (i.e., that "Big Brother is watching")
- The evaluation could be arbitrary or inconsistent, making the evaluation results misleading, skewed or invalid
- Management may misuse evaluation results to identify and punish poor performance
- Management may use evaluation results to support personal agendas or gains
- Identification of significant problems would result in drastic changes
- The project could be terminated

However, mid-project evaluations can prove extremely beneficial if conducted well. Such evaluations may involve project participants who enter or leave a project at phase transitions. Those departing can provide useful insights based on intimate experience with the project. Those arriving could provide "fresh eyes" and new methods for achieving project objectives. An enterprise quality assurance function, a corporate audit department or a project office with proven processes and experienced staff may help mid-project evaluations be more readily accepted.

Managing Change Requests

In the *PMBOK® Guide 4th Edition*, PMI consolidated several change request topics into the overall concept of managing change requests. Change requests are an output of the Monitor And Control Project Work process. They can come in several forms, such as corrective action, preventative action or defect repair. Change requests may be necessary to ensure the quality delivery of the project or product scope. In other cases, change requests are additions to the agreed-upon scope and should be, once documented and approved, adjustments to the project baseline.

PERFORM INTEGRATED CHANGE CONTROL PROCESS

Changes are inevitable in projects. The Perform Integrated Change Control process coordinates changes across the entire project by determining that a change has occurred, managing the change when it does occur and ensuring that changes are controlled and agreed upon. Through the use of a change control system, the project manager is able to be in control and make necessary adjustments to ensure the project's success.

The Perform Integrated Change Control process works hand-in-hand with the Report Performance process in communications management to integrate the subsidiary change control processes found in the scope, time, cost, quality, risk and procurement knowledge areas.

Within the Perform Integrated Control process there is a tool and technique called **Change Control Meetings.** In these change control meetings, members of the **Change Control Board (CCB)** follow the change control process to ensure the requested changes to the project and product scope are properly considered and documented. Both the CM and Change Control processes are integrated with the overall project management information system.

4

CLOSE PROJECT OR PHASE PROCESS

The Close Project Or Phase process is one of the two processes in the closing process group, the other process being the Close Procurements process described in project procurement management (Chapter 12). There are many questions about the similarities and differences between these two processes. Know that the Close Procurements process supports the Close Project Or Phase process as it also verifies the acceptance of project deliverables. The Close Project Or Phase process includes the step-by-step activities needed to conclude the project (or phase), such as:

- Project's product, service or results transition to production or the next phase as needed to satisfy the exit criteria of the project or phase
- **Organizational Process Assets** updates

SAMPLE PMP EXAM QUESTIONS ON INTEGRATION MANAGEMENT

Integration — Planning Questions

1. The knowledge area that includes all the processes and activities needed to identify, define, combine, unify and coordinate project management activities is:

   a) Project scope management
   b) Executing process group
   c) Project integration management
   d) Project schedule management

2. You are asked to take on a project that is in trouble. In re-planning the project you should place the highest priority on:

   a) Schedule, as the project is already behind schedule
   b) Quality, cost, or schedule, depending on the project objectives
   c) Cost, then schedule, then quality
   d) Quality, as with good quality, cost and schedule come back inline

3. A narrative description of products to be supplied by the project is the:

   a) Project scope statement
   b) Charter
   c) Statement of work
   d) Contract

4. As you start a new project for a new organization, you must consider the organization's standard processes, which are known as:

   a) Enterprise environmental factors
   b) Organizational process assets
   c) Tools and techniques
   d) Perform quality assurance

Notes:

Integration — Initiating Questions

5. Some of the activities performed by all project management teams are to analyze and understand the scope, create a project management plan, prepare a work breakdown structure, execute the project in accordance to the project management plan, measure and monitor status and analyze project risks. These activities show the importance of:

   a) Project risk management and using decision models
   b) Knowledge of the current marketplace conditions, company culture and project risks
   c) Using human resource management processes and personnel administration rules
   d) Project integration management

6. The tool and technique known as "expert judgment" in the initiating process group is used to:

   a) Determine corrective actions needed on the project
   b) Define detailed project deliverables
   c) Prepare the project charter
   d) Communicate the project scope to stakeholders

7. A project scheduling software application can be considered part of an organization's:

   a) Enterprise environmental factors
   b) Request for proposal
   c) Project management methodology
   d) Organizational process assets

Notes:

Integration — Executing Questions

Notes:

8. Performing actions to execute the project management plan is part of the _____ process.

   a) Direct and Manage Project Execution
   b) Manage Project Team
   c) Perform Integrated Change Control
   d) Administer Procurements

9. Any unique and verifiable product, result or capability is:

   a) A deliverable
   b) An activity attribute
   c) An objective
   d) A schedule activity

10. Each week, your project team provides you with schedule progress, the extent to which quality standards are being met and resource utilization details. These are all examples of:

    a) Earned value analysis
    b) Work performance information
    c) Monte Carlo simulation
    d) Quality audits

Integration — Monitoring and Controlling Questions

11. The Monitor and Control Project Work process is concerned with:

    a) Comparing actual project performance against the project management plan and providing forecasts to updated current cost information
    b) Comparing projected project performance with the budget baseline
    c) Completing the work defined in the project management plan
    d) Having a comprehensive list of all schedule activities

12. All of the following change management activities can be performed as part of the Perform Integrated Change Control process EXCEPT:

    a) Identifying that a change has occurred
    b) Reviewing and approving requested changes
    c) Implementing approved changes
    d) Identifying that a change needs to occur

13. The role and responsibilities of the change control board must be:

    a) Clearly defined within the configuration control and change control procedures
    b) Published on the PMO website
    c) Detailed enough for someone to understand his or her job fully
    d) Outlined in the project charter

14. When you have completed the Perform Integrated Change Control process, what will you do next?

    a) Recommend defect repair
    b) Implement approved change requests
    c) Recommend preventative actions
    d) Rebaseline the schedule

Integration — Closing Questions

15. All of the following are organizational process asset updates within the Close Project Or Phase process EXCEPT:

    a) Final product
    b) Project files
    c) Historical information
    d) Formal acceptance documents

Notes:

4

ANSWERS AND REFERENCES FOR SAMPLE PMP EXAM QUESTIONS ON INTEGRATION MANAGEMENT

Section numbers refer to the *PMBOK® Guide*.

1. C   **Chapter 4**

2. B   **Chapter 1**
   PMI emphasizes the overall importance of quality management in projects.

3. C   **Section 4.1.1.1**
   Choice A is out because the project scope statement defines the project deliverables and the work required to create those deliverables; for choice B, the project SOW is an input to the charter; for choice D, a contract can define the SOW which in term is the input to the project charter and subsequently the scope statement.

4. B   **Section 4.1.1.5**

5. D   **Section 4**
   Key activities performed that demonstrate the integrative nature of projects and project management.

6. C   **Section 4.1.2.1**
   Expert Judgment is a tool and technique in the Develop Project Charter process.

7. A   **Section 4.2.1.3**
   A project management information system (PMIS) is a standardized set of automated tools that are used by the project manager and project team. It is considered an enterprise environmental factor.

8. A   **Section 4.3**

9. A   **Section 4.3.3.1**
Choice B is out because activity attributes describe schedule activities, such as successors and predecessors; for choice C, objectives are something for which work is to be directed, a strategic position to be attained, or a result to be obtained; choice D is out because schedule activities are performed in order to create a project deliverable.

10. B   **Section 4.3.3.2**
For choice A, earned value analysis is a tool and technique of the control costs process; choice C is out because a Monte Carlo simulation is a tool and technique of the develop schedule process; for choice D, quality audits are structured, independent reviews of compliance to project policies, processes, and procedures.

11. A   **Section 4.4**

12. C   **Section 4.5**
Choice C is correct because implementing approved changes is part of the direct and manage project execution process.

13. A   **Section 4.5**

14. B   **Section 4.5.3.1**
Choices A and C are inputs to the perform integrated change control process; for choice D, schedule changes may NOT be the result of the change control process, so choice B is the best answer.

15. A   **Section 4.6**
Choice A is the final product, not an organizational process asset.

4

CASE STUDY SUGGESTED SOLUTION

Exercise 4-1
Project Charter for the Lawrence RV Garage Project

This project has as its goal to build a recreational vehicle (RV) and boat garage on the property of Mr. and Mrs. David Lawrence in Anytown, United States. The garage will be built according to the architectural plans and specifications provided by the owners.

The major deliverables are the garage structure, including a finished interior, and a driveway connecting to the existing driveway per the plans and specs.

The garage is being built to comply with new city codes that require boats and/or RVs stored for more than 72 hours to be enclosed in a structure suitable for that purpose.

This project is scheduled to start on or about May 20, 2004 and should be completed within 120 calendar days. The initial budget is $37,500.

The project sponsors are Mr. and Mrs. Lawrence. Their project manager is Scott Hiyamoto, who is also the architect. The project manager for Acme Construction and Engineering (ACE) is [Your Name Here]. Mr. Hiyamoto is acting as the agent of the Lawrences and has full authority to make decisions on their behalf. Mr. and Mrs. Lawrence will direct all their communications through Mr. Hiyamoto. Mr./Ms. [Your Name Here] is acting as the agent for ACE and has full authority to make decisions on its behalf. All employees of ACE and all of its subcontractors, and their employees, will direct all their communications through Mr./Ms. [Your Name Here].

Signed

Susan Ruzicka, General Manager Acme Construction & Engineering	David E. Lawrence Property Owner
[Your Name Here] Acme Construction & Engineering	Scott Hiyamoto, Managing Partner Hiyamoto, Kwame, & Blum, LLP

CHAPTER 5 | SCOPE

5

SCOPE MANAGEMENT

Project scope management questions on the PMP certification exam cover diverse yet fundamental project management topics. Defining and managing the scope or the amount of work of the project is an important aspect of project management. There must be an understanding of how the project scope is broken down into smaller, more manageable, components and how these components are controlled. The requirements management plan, the updated and refined scope statement, work breakdown structures (WBSs), scope verification and scope changes are the topics covered.

The role of the project manager includes defining the work, making sure that only the work of the project is being completed and preventing additional work (scope creep) not defined in the project. PMI does not advocate "gold plating" or giving the customer more than what was asked for.

In the project context, the term "scope" may refer to:
- Product scope, which consists of the features and functions of a product or service, with results measured against the product requirements
- Project scope, which describes the work that must be done to deliver a product, service or result with completion being measured against the project management plan

Project scope management is concerned with defining and controlling both what is and what is not included in the project.

Things to Know

1. The five processes of scope management:
   - **Collect Requirements**
   - **Define Scope**
   - **Create WBS**
   - **Verify Scope**
   - **Control Scope**

> **EXAM TIP**
> PMI places enormous emphasis on the tool or technique of decomposition, which is breaking down the major project deliverable into smaller, more manageable elements. These elements are further subdivided until the deliverables are specific enough to support the planning, executing, monitoring and controlling and closing process group activities. The resulting collection of elements that define the total scope of the project is called the work breakdown structure (WBS).

5

2. The importance of the **Requirements Management Plan** and **Requirements Traceability Matrix**
3. What is **Product Analysis**
4. The purpose and contents of the **Project Scope Statement**
5. All aspects of the **WBS**
6. The **Code of Accounts** (and how it differs from the **Chart of Accounts**)
7. The purpose of **Control Accounts**
8. The differences between **Verify Scope** and **Perform Quality Control**
9. Controlling **Scope Changes**

Key Definitions

Chart of Accounts: the financial numbering system used to monitor project costs by category. It is usually related to an organization's general ledger.

Code of Accounts: the numbering system for providing unique identifiers for all items in the WBS. It is hierarchical and can go to multiple levels, each lower level containing a more detailed description of a project deliverable. The WBS contains clusters of elements that are child items related to a single parent element; for example, parent item 1.1 contains child items 1.1.1, 1.1.2 and 1.1.3.

Control Account: the management control point at which integration of scope, budget and schedule takes place and at which performance is measured.

Decomposition: the process of breaking down a project deliverable into smaller, more manageable components. In the create WBS process, the results of decomposition are deliverables, whereas in the define activities process project deliverables are further broken down into schedule activities.

Planning Package: a component of the work breakdown structure that is below the control account to support known uncertainty in project deliverables. Planning packages will include information on a deliverable but without any details associated with schedule activities.

Requirements Traceability Matrix: a matrix for recording each requirement and tracking its attributes and changes throughout the project life cycle to provide a structure for changes to product scope. Projects are undertaken to produce a product, service or result that meets the requirements of the sponsor, customer and other stakeholders. These requirements are collected and refined through interviews, focus groups, surveys and other techniques. Requirements may also be changed through the projects' configuration management activities.

Rolling Wave Planning: a progressive elaboration technique that addresses uncertainty in detailing all future work for a project. Near-term work is planned to an appropriate level of detail; however, longer term deliverables are identified at a high level and decomposed as the project progresses.

Scope Baseline: the approved detailed project scope statement along with the WBS and WBS dictionary.

Work Breakdown Structure (WBS): a framework for defining project work into smaller, more manageable pieces, it defines the total scope of the project using descending levels of detail.

WBS Dictionary: houses the details associated with the work packages and control accounts. The level of detail needed will be defined by the project team.

Work Package: the lowest level of a WBS; cost estimates are made at this level.

COLLECT REQUIREMENTS PROCESS

This process defines the activities needed to determine and define the features and functions that meet the needs and expectations of the sponsor, customer and other stakeholders. It uses the **Project Charter** and **Stakeholder Register** as input and many tools and techniques to elicit and document stakeholder needs into **Product Requirements** (for example, product specifications, performance, quality, security, etc.) or **Project Requirements** (business guideline, project management practices, delivery schedules, etc.). As individual requirements are gathered, they are combined into the requirements documents and reviewed with stakeholders. The requirements documentation must meet the business need for the project. Once the requirements documentation has been reviewed and approved as complete, consistent, traceable and clear, it is baselined.

Requirements Management Plan

The requirements management plan is an important document that is used with the requirements documentation to assist the project manager in communication, thereby lessening possible future issues of managing the requirements baseline, project changes, conflict issues and project risks. The requirements management plan:

- Describes how requirements will be managed
- Describes how requirements changes will be identified and classified
- Describes how requirements changes will be integrated, tracked, reported and approved
- Defines the requirements prioritization process
- Discusses metrics to measure the product
- Details the attributes to be tracked in the requirements traceability matrix

Requirements Traceability Matrix

A requirement traceability matrix is an output of the Collect Requirements process and is critical to controlling scope creep in that it looks at each requirement of the project and links those requirements directly back to a specific project objective. Managing requirements tightly ensures that the project will stay focused on the delivery of the project objectives. Those that do not will most likely experience excessive change requests and a high potential for scope creep.

DEFINE SCOPE PROCESS

Although a high level description of the project and product was prepared in the Develop Project Charter process, it is refined here with additional information about the project and the product, service or result of the project.

Product Analysis

Managing a project that affects or creates a product has different considerations than those projects that produce a service or result. Considerations of material purchases, marketing and integration with customer environments are a few. For example, a project that has been initiated to enhance the design of a riding lawnmower product line must consider the full bill of materials and product design to determine the specific changes that are necessary to the bill of materials to ensure the product produced will meet the market expectations.

Project Scope Statement

The project scope statement is the basis for future project decisions and is critical to project success. It provides the basis for agreement on project scope between the project team and the customer. The **Scope Statement** contains enough information to allow stakeholders to document their agreement on the:
- Project's **Objectives** and characteristics of the product service or results
- Project's **Deliverables**
- Project exclusions
- Project's **Constraints** and **Assumptions**
- Product **Acceptance Criteria**

A detailed project scope statement:
- Provides documentation for future project decisions
- Can have multiple levels as project work goes through decomposition
- Is refined or revised to reflect approved changes to the requirements of the project

- Is referred to in some organizations as the scope of work or statement of work (SOW)

In order to ensure project success, project **Objectives** must be defined. Good objectives should be clear, defined well and feasible. PMI advocates project objectives that follow the SMART guideline. That is, objectives must be:
- **S**pecific — clear with no ambiguity
- **M**easurable — with quantifiable indicators of success
- **A**ssignable — with responsibility resting on an individual or organization
- **R**ealistic — achievable within the constraints
- **T**imely — with specific duration and due dates

Case Study Exercise

Exercise 5-1: Once the project charter from Exercise 4-1 has been accepted by the stakeholders, you need to develop a scope statement for the Lawrence RV Garage Project. It should be detailed enough so that all stakeholders know what is being done but since there are architectural drawings already existing, you will not need to describe every board.

CREATE WBS PROCESS

In order to understand further and define the work of the project, it must be broken down into smaller, more manageable components. The resulting deliverable-oriented hierarchical structure is known as the **Work Breakdown Structure** (WBS). The lowest levels of the WBS are the planned units of work the project team must execute in order to achieve the project objectives and results.

The Work Breakdown Structure

The WBS provides input to other planning processes such as the Control Scope, Define Activities, Estimate Costs, Determine Budget and Plan Procurements processes.

The WBS, WBS dictionary and the **Scope Statement** are outputs of the Create WBS process. Any work not defined in the WBS is outside the scope of the project, therefore the WBS is the foundation of the project and contains the building blocks of project work. The WBS:
- Breaks the project into smaller pieces, those at the lowest level being known as work packages
- Defines the total scope of the project using descending levels of detail
- Is deliverable oriented
- Contains items that are assigned unique identifiers (i.e., **Code of Accounts**)

The benefits of using a WBS are that it:
- Facilitates communication and a common understanding of project scope
- Provides a framework for project identification
- Brings focus to project objectives
- Forces a breakdown of project work into smaller work packages that are more easily assigned and tracked
- Creates work packages that are small enough for more accurate estimates
- Identifies holes or weak areas of project scope requirements
- Facilitates performance measurement
- Clearly defines responsibilities
- Facilitates progress status reporting, problem analysis and the tracking of time, cost and performance
- Allows for improved handling of change control requests
- Is available for reuse with appropriate modifications for similar projects

The following are some guidelines for developing a WBS:
- Utilize the project team for help
- Identify higher levels before breaking down into more detailed levels
- Know that some components will break down into more detailed levels than others
- Work down toward tangible deliverables (work packages), keeping in mind that:

- The effort to produce the deliverable can be confidently estimated
- The types of skills required for the deliverable can be evaluated
- Required resources can be determined
- Costs can be determined and confidently estimated
- The deliverable can be easily tracked

Some examples of names of WBS levels are:

- **Program:** a grouping of programs and projects all linked to a common objective or goal
- **Project:** the summation of all work to be completed to achieve a unique product, service or result
- **Control Account:** a summary level of the WBS used to categorize and measure progress
- **Work Package:** the lowest-level item of the WBS. Cost estimates are made at this level; it is sometimes stipulated that a work package is not more that 80 hours of effort. Work packages assist in risk identification and may be broken down further during the activity definition process into schedule activities and even smaller tasks
- **Planning Package:** a known set of work that will need to be performed without the specific details on schedule activities
- **Schedule Activity:** a further subdivision of the work package
- **Task:** work not necessarily listed in the WBS and is the lowest level of effort on the project

EXAM TIP
Know the difference between a planning package and a work package.

Key outputs of the Create WBS process are the WBS, of course, but also the WBS dictionary and the project scope statement. These three items are combined and called the **Scope Baseline**. The scope baseline is a component of the project management plan.

Control Accounts

An important aspect of the WBS are control accounts which are management control points where the integration of scope, schedule and cost takes place and where performance is measured. Management control of projects at every work package level can be very time consuming, so PMI advocates the use of selected management points of the WBS. Therefore, a control account could control one or more work packages. The advantages of control accounts are:

- All **Earned Value** performance measurement in a project should take place at this level
- It is the building block of **Performance Measurement**
- The sum of the control accounts will add up to the total project value

There is no recommended standard for the appropriate dollar size of a control account. Some organizations define a rule of thumb, such as 300 hours — but it should be whatever is manageable.

In the example in Figure 5-1 on the following page, the control account is placed at the section level (2.2.1, 2.2.2, etc.) and individual or small group efforts at the subtask or work package level are rolled up to the control account plan to be managed by the project manager and reported to stakeholders. This avoids micromanaging of individual team members and smoothes out minor variances from the plan.

Case Study Exercise

Exercise 5-2: After the scope statement from Exercise 5-1 has been approved, develop the WBS to show the breakdown of the work that needs to be done to deliver the complete Lawrence RV Garage Project.

5

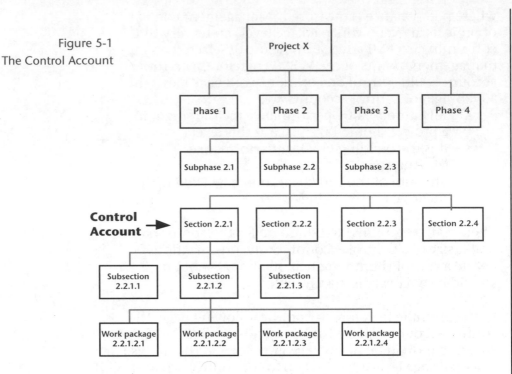

Figure 5-1
The Control Account

VERIFY SCOPE PROCESS

The Verify Scope process is the process of getting formal acceptance of completed project deliverables from stakeholders who may be the project sponsor, clients or customers. In order to confirm work was completed correctly and satisfactorily, verify that the scope:

- Involves the review of work results by conducting audits, reviews and inspections
- Is similar to the **Perform Quality Control** process as both involve checking work products
- Is different from the Perform Quality Control process because it focuses on the acceptance criteria of the deliverables (i.e., the scope of work) instead of the validation of the deliverables
- Is often performed after the Perform Quality Control process but the two processes can be performed in parallel
- Determines whether work results conform to requirements

- Documents the formal acceptance and signoff of deliverables
- Could generate change requests for defect repair
- Can be repeated at the end of each project phase

Verification is typically determined through a predefined process of inspection that should have been agreed upon as part of the scope statement and requirements management plan.

Verify Scope versus Perform Quality Control

At the end of every project, the project manager and the project team will go through an exercise of obtaining customer acknowledgement that the project delivered upon its objectives. The acceptance criteria which were developed during the development of the project charter, scope statement and project plan will be used in determining the final outcome of the project, success or failure.

The process for verifying scope is very different from the process that will be discussed in Chapter 8, the Perform Quality Control process. The Perform Quality Control process is focused on the lower levels of the WBS and ensures that each component of the project is being delivered according to the detailed requirements or specifications. Theoretically, as each level of deliverables is validated as part of the perform quality control process, the likelihood of a successful scope verification will increase, but will not be guaranteed.

CONTROL SCOPE PROCESS

The Control Scope process monitors the status of both project and product requirements. It also manages changes to the requirements baseline and the scope baseline. Frequently, a **Scope Change** also requires adjustments to project objectives, cost, time and quality. Therefore, a scope change usually means updates to the project management plan, project documents and organizational process assets updates. In most cases

5

replanning is necessary. **Change Requests** and **Work Performance Measurements** are other outputs of the Control Scope process.

Controlling Scope Changes

A key responsibility of the project manager is to ensure that an appropriate change management process be in place for the project. A change management process is implemented for the sole purpose of reviewing and determining whether or not requested changes are considered within the scope or outside the scope of the project. Typically a change management process includes an entity called a **Change Control Board** (CCB) whose responsibility it is to review and either approve or deny change requests.

A CCB should include membership of the project team and other key stakeholders, including the customer. The CCB's purpose is to objectively evaluate the requests being submitted and determine an action to be taken.

A strong Change Control process reduces the risk of scope creep.

SAMPLE PMP EXAM QUESTIONS ON SCOPE MANAGEMENT

Scope — Planning Questions

1. The product scope can:

   a) Include subsidiary components each with their own product scope
   b) Be the same as project scope
   c) Define the reason the project is being initiated, such as a social need
   d) Define the work that needs to be accomplished to deliver the product

2. Brainstorming and mind mapping are examples of what tool and technique?

   a) Group creativity techniques
   b) Product analysis
   c) Stakeholder analysis
   d) Product acceptance criteria

3. A key input to the Define Scope process is:

   a) Requirements documentation
   b) The work breakdown structure dictionary
   c) The project scope statement
   d) The risk register

4. You are asked by your sponsor to describe how the formal verification and acceptance of the project deliverables will be obtained. The document that should include this information is the:

   a) Executive sponsor sign-off
   b) Contract
   c) Project scope management plan
   d) Communications management plan

Notes:

5. _____ represent verifiable products, services or results.

   a) Work breakdown structure components
   b) Project scope statements
   c) Change requests
   d) Identified risks

6. The information from the work breakdown structure is used to derive all of the following EXCEPT:

   a) The project's master schedule
   b) The project budget
   c) Work component descriptions
   d) The project objectives

7. A work breakdown structure dictionary will include detailed descriptions of work packages and _____.

   a) Planning tasks
   b) Control accounts
   c) Risk responses
   d) Deliverable instructions

8. The scope management plan should include:

   a) Project deliverables, justification and objectives
   b) How the project scope will be managed and controlled
   c) A description of how project scope will be managed, the project's product and all supporting details
   d) A description of how scope changes will be integrated, corrective actions and lessons learned

Notes:

Scope — Monitoring and Controlling Questions

9. A member of your team brings ideas for enhancements to the scope of work to a team meeting. These suggestions will add work to the project that is beyond the requirements of the project charter. As project manager, you point out that only the work required for the project should be completed by the team or the project could miss its goals. You are:

    a) Performing integrated change control
    b) Collecting requirements
    c) Verifying scope
    d) Managing risk

10. Documenting the completed deliverables that have been accepted is an output of the _____ process.

    a) Verify Scope
    b) Create WBS
    c) Perform Quality Assurance
    d) Administer Procurements

11. During a project meeting, two team members are arguing about when the Verify Scope process should be done, and they come to you for your opinion. You tell them that the Verify Scope process should be done:

    a) Only once, during planning
    b) Every time a deliverable is produced
    c) At the end of each project phase
    d) At the very end of the project to obtain formal acceptance

Notes:

5

12. Your project is nearing completion and you have scheduled a deliverable review meeting with your customer for next week as part of the Verify Scope process. The Verify Scope process includes:

    a) Obtaining the stakeholders' formal acceptance of the project's deliverables
    b) Organizing and defining the total scope of the project
    c) The project deliverables
    d) Assuring that all requested changes and recommended corrective actions are completed

13. Deliverables are one of the inputs to the Verify Scope process. This is because the key purpose of the Verify Scope process is to ensure:

    a) The project will be completed on time
    b) The acceptance of the work results
    c) The correctness of the work results
    d) That a scope change has occurred

14. The system which defines items requiring formal change control and the process for controlling changes to such items is known as the:

    a) Contingency reserves system
    b) Procurement administration system
    c) Configuration management system
    d) Integrated change control system

15. A tool and technique of the Verify Scope process is inspection. Which one of the following is an output of the Verify Scope process?

    a) Work results
    b) Accepted deliverables
    c) Scope changes
    d) Deliverables

Notes:

5

5

ANSWERS AND REFERENCES FOR SAMPLE PMP EXAM QUESTIONS ON SCOPE MANAGEMENT
Section numbers refer to the *PMBOK® Guide.*

1. A   **Chapter 5**
    Choice B is most likely not the answer since product scope references the features and functionality, while project scope looks at how the product will be delivered; for choice C, product scope addresses features and functionality of the product being delivered (this is the definition of the project charter); choice D is the definition of project scope.

2. A   **Section 5.1.2.4**
    For choice B, product analysis includes techniques such as value engineering, or functional analysis; for choice C, stakeholder analysis identifies the influence and interests of the various stakeholders; for choice D, product acceptance criteria are defined within the project scope statement.

3. A   **Section 5.2.1.2**

4. C   **Section 5.2.3.1**
    The scope management plan identifies the verification and acceptance criteria for the project.

5. A   **Section 5.3.2.1**

6. D   **Section 5.3.3**
    Project objectives should already have been defined as part of the scope statement, an output of the Define Scope process.

7. B   **Section 5.3.2**
    Although deliverable instructions are probably included in the WBS dictionary, the WBS dictionary's purpose is to detail the work packages and control accounts.

8. B   **Section 5.5.1.1**
    It is easy to remember that the scope management plan is from the planning process group. Choice

D is incorrect as it contains outputs from a controlling process. Choices A and C list some of the contents of the scope statement.

9. A   **Section 5.5**
The answer cannot be B as the product requirements and project charter already exist. It is not C, since you are not accepting any completed deliverables. Choice D is not the best answer.

10. A   **Section 5.4**

11. C   **Section 5.4**
The Verify Scope process is performed more than once. However, it is not tied to the WBS for each deliverable, making C the best answer.

12. A   **Section 5.4.3.1**
Choice B is WBS creation; for choice C, the project deliverables are used in the Verify Scope process, but it is not the verification process; choice D is the Control Scope process.

13. B   **Section 5.4.3.1**
The main purpose of the Verify Scope process is to obtain stakeholders' "formal acceptance." The verify scope process differs from the Quality Control process, which is concerned with the correctness of work results.

14. C   **Section 5.5.1.1**
For choice A, contingency reserves address the additional funds or time needed to minimize the risk of overruns; choice B, Administer Procurements, is the process of managing the contract and the relationship between the buyer and seller. A certain amount of configuration management will be used by the contract administrator; choice D is too broad, making choice C the better answer.

15. B   **Section 5.4.3.1**
The primary focus of the Verify Scope process is acceptance of work results/deliverables.

5

CASE STUDY SUGGESTED SOLUTIONS

Exercise 5-1
Scope Statement for the Lawrence RV Garage Project

As stated in the project charter, the goal of this project is to build a recreational vehicle (RV) and boat garage on the property of Mr. and Mrs. David Lawrence in order to comply with a new city ordinance regarding RV and boat parking.

The garage is designed to be big enough to hold a motor home or travel trailer and a boat, with room at the back for miscellaneous storage and a small workshop area. It is 50 feet long and 30 feet wide with 2 14-ft.-high by 12-ft.-wide roll-up doors for the RV and boat and a standard 3-ft. side door. There are 2 windows on the side of the garage that has the standard door, 3 windows on the side with no door and 2 windows in the back wall. Wall height is 16 ft. The roof is to use engineered trusses, manufactured by an approved supplier. Inside there are to be lights and electrical outlets to be used when working on the RV or boat. The interior is to be heated and air conditioned. The plans also show RV hookups inside (water, electric and sewer) and there should also be a drain in the floor. There should be a small bathroom (commode and sink only) in the back corner of the garage and a utility sink adjacent to the bathroom.

The exterior walls are to be stucco and the roof is to be asphalt shingles to match the existing house. Walls should be of 2X6 construction to allow for greater insulation.

Since there is an existing home, utilities are already present. The garage will have its own electric service and its own hot water heater. The architect has submitted the plans to the city but they have not yet been approved, and a permit has not yet been issued.

The major deliverables are the garage structure, including finished interior, and a driveway connecting to the existing driveway per the site plan. No landscaping is included in the specifications.

5

This project is scheduled to start on or about May 20, 2004 and complete within 120 calendar days. The initial budget is $37,500.

Assumptions: the plans will be approved by the city as submitted. The plans will be approved by June 1, 2004. The plans and specifications, which are attached by reference, are complete and sufficient to plan, execute and complete this project. Anything not included in the plans and specifications is explicitly outside the scope of this project.

Constraints: construction permits for residential units, including detached garages, state that construction must be complete within 185 days from the issue date. The owner states that any change order resulting in an increase of $1,000 from the baseline cost, or when accumulated change orders exceed $2,000, a formal review of the proposed change or changes must be held with the owners, architect and general contractor all present.

Attached by reference:

Site plan
Foundation and slab plan
Framing plan
Electrical plan
Plumbing plan
Heating, ventilating and air conditioning plan
Door and window specifications
Exterior finish plan
Interior finish plan
Roof truss engineering specifications
Driveway specifications
Bill of materials

Exercise 5-2
WBS List for the Lawrence RV Garage Project

WBS	Task Name
0	Lawrence recreational vehicle garage
1	Project management
1.1	Finalize plans and develop estimates
1.2	Sign contract and notice to proceed
1.3	Apply for permits
1.4	Execute and control project
1.4.1	Track progress
1.4.2	Weekly status meeting
2	Site work and foundation
2.1	Clear and grub lot
2.2	Install temporary power service
2.3	Install underground utilities
2.4	Excavate for foundations
2.5	Install forms and rebar
2.6	Pour concrete for foundation and slab
2.7	Cure concrete
2.8	Strip forms
2.9	Perform foundation/slab inspection
2.99	Foundation complete
3	Framing
3.1	Install mudsills
3.2	Frame walls
3.3	Frame corners
3.4	Install roof trusses
3.5	Complete roof framing
3.6	Conduct framing inspection
3.99	Framing complete
4	Exterior
4.1	Install wall sheathing
4.2	Install roof decking
4.3	Install felt, flashing and shingles
4.4	Hang exterior doors
4.5	Install windows
4.6	Wrap exterior
4.7	Apply brown coat
4.8	Cure brown coat 7 days
4.9	Apply finish coat
4.99	Exterior complete

WBS List for the Lawrence RV Garage Continued

5	Interior
5.1	Finish rough-in plumbing
5.2	Rough-in electrical
5.3	Rough-in HVAC
5.4	Rough-in communication (phone, cable, computer, alarm)
5.5	Utility inspections
5.6	Place wall insulation
5.7	Place ceiling insulation
5.8	Install drywall on walls
5.9	Install drywall on ceilings
5.10	Tape and float drywall
5.11	Prime all walls and ceilings
5.12	Paint all walls and ceilings
5.13	Install bath and storage cabinets
5.14	Complete plumbing
5.15	Complete electrical
5.16	Complete communications (phone, cable, computer, alarm)
5.17	Complete HVAC
5.99	Interior complete
6	Grounds work
6.1	Grade for driveway and sidewalk
6.2	Setup driveway and sidewalk forms
6.3	Lay out driveway rebar
6.4	Pour concrete driveway and sidewalks
6.5	Cure concrete
6.6	Remove forms
6.99	Grounds complete
7	Final acceptance
7.1	Complete final inspection for certificate of occupancy
7.2	Cleanup for occupancy
7.3	Perform final walk-through inspection
7.4	Complete punch list items
7.99	Project complete

5

TIME

CHAPTER 6 | **TIME**

6

TIME MANAGEMENT

Time management is that portion of project management concerned with the project schedule. It includes defining the project activities, ordering the activities in their logical sequence, estimating the effort and duration of each activity and building an overall project schedule. Time management also includes managing the schedule once the project is under way, since the actual amount of time it takes to complete activities does not always match the estimates.

The PMP certification exam focuses time questions heavily around the precedence diagramming method (PDM), the critical path method (CPM), critical chain method and three-point estimating. You must be familiar with the differences between these four techniques and the appropriate circumstances for their use. The exam will test your knowledge of how CPM networks are constructed, how schedules are computed, what the critical path is and how networks are used to analyze and solve project scheduling, resource allocation and resource leveling issues. The exam may also contain some rather elementary scheduling exercises. Variance analysis and earned value calculations can also appear in time management knowledge area questions.

Things to Know

1. The six processes of time management:
   * **Define Activities**
   * **Sequence Activities**
   * **Estimate Activity Resources**
   * **Estimate Activity Durations**
   * **Develop Schedule**
   * **Control Schedule**
2. **Activity Attributes** and their relationship to the **WBS Dictionary**
3. The three types of **Dependencies**
4. The **Precedence Diagramming Method** (PDM)
5. Definitions of **Finish-to-Start**, **Start-to-Start**, **Finish-to-Finish** and **Start-to-Finish** logical relationships

6. **Lags** and **Leads**
7. Estimating tools and techniques for activity duration estimating:
    *   **Expert Judgment**
    *   **Analogous Estimating**
    *   **Quantitatively-Based** or **Parametric Estimating**
    *   **Three-Point Estimating** or **Triangular Distribution**
    *   **Reserve Analysis**
8. Difference between **Weighted-Average** and **Critical Path Method** (CPM) estimating techniques
9. The **Critical Path Method** and the **Critical Path Method Schedule Development**
10. How to perform a **Forward Pass** and a **Backward Pass**
11. Definitions of **Float, Total Float, Slack** and **Free Float**
12. The purpose of **Resource Leveling**
13. The **Critical Chain Method**
14. Performing **Reserves Analysis** as part of schedule development
15. **Crashing** and **Fast Tracking** techniques and how to apply them
16. The impact of **Resource Constraints** on a project schedule and how to **Finalize Resource Requirements**
17. **Earned Value** terms and formulas (these will be needed in several other sections too):
    *   **PV** or planned value
    *   **AC** or actual cost
    *   **EV** or earned value
    *   **CV** or cost variance
    *   **SV** or schedule variance
    *   **CPI** or cost performance index
    *   **SPI** or schedule performance index

Key Definitions

Activity Attributes: similar to a WBS dictionary because they describe the detailed characteristics of each activity. Examples of these attributes are description, predecessor and successor activities and the person responsible.

Contingency Reserve: a dollar or time value that is added to the project schedule or budget that reflects and accounts for risk that is anticipated for the project.

Crashing: using alternative strategies for completing project activities (such as using outside resources) for the least additional cost. Crashing should be performed on tasks on the critical path. Crashing the critical path may result in additional or new critical paths.

Critical Path: the path with the longest duration within the project. It is sometimes defined as the path with the least float (usually zero float). The delay of a task on the critical path will delay the completion of the project.

Fast Tracking: overlapping or performing in parallel project activities that would normally be done sequentially. Fast tracking may increase rework and project risk.

Float: the amount of time that a schedule activity can be delayed without delaying the end of the project. It is also called **Slack** or **Total Float**. Float is calculated using a **Forward Pass** (to determine the early start and early finish dates of activities) and a **Backward Pass** (to determine the late start and late finish dates of the activities). Float is calculated as the difference between late finish date and early finish date. The difference between the late start date and the early start date always produces the same value for float as the preceding computation.

Hammock: summary activities used in a high-level project network diagram.

Lag: the amount of time a successor's start or finish is delayed from the predecessor's start or finish. In a finish-to-start example, activity A (the predecessor) must finish before activity B (the successor) can start. If a lag of three days is also defined, it means that B will be scheduled to start three days after A is scheduled to finish.

Lead (negative lag): the amount of time a successor's start or finish can occur before the predecessor's start or finish. In a finish-to-start example, activity A (the predecessor) must finish before activity B (the successor) can start. A lead of three days means that B can be scheduled to start three days before A is scheduled to finish.

Logical Relationships: there are four logical relationships between a predecessor and a successor:
- **Finish-to-Start**, in which the predecessor must finish before the successor can start. This is the most common relationship and the default for most software packages
- **Finish-to-Finish**, in which the predecessor must finish before the successor can finish
- **Start-to-Start**, in which the successor can start as soon as the predecessor starts
- **Start-to-Finish**, in which the predecessor must start before the successor can finish (This is the least used and some software packages do not even allow it.)

Predecessor: the activity that must happen first when defining dependencies between activities in a network.

Project Network Schedule Calculations: there are three types of project network schedule calculations: a forward pass, a backward pass and float. A forward pass yields early start and early finish dates, a backward pass yields late start and late finish dates, and these values are used to calculate total float.

Schedule Activity: an element of work performed during the course of a project. It is a smaller unit of work than a work package and the result of decomposition in the Define Activities process of project time management. Activities can be further subdivided into tasks.

Scheduling Charts: there are four types of scheduling charts: the Gantt chart, the milestone chart, the network diagram and the time-scaled network diagram.

EXAM TIP

The most common relationship is the finish-to-start relationship. Use other relationships when there is a need for schedule compression.

6

- A **Gantt Chart** is a bar chart that shows activities against time, although the traditional early charts did not show task dependencies and relationships, modern charts often show dependencies and precedence relationships; these popular charts are useful for understanding project schedules and for determining the critical path, time requirements, resource assessments and projected completion dates
- A **Milestone Chart** is a bar chart that only shows the start or finish of major events or key external interfaces (e.g., a phase kickoff meeting or a deliverable); it consumes NO resources and has NO duration; these charts are effective for presentations and can be incorporated into a summary Gantt chart
- A **Network Diagram** is a schematic display of project activities showing task relationships and dependencies; the precedence diagramming method (PDM) is useful for forcing the total integration of the project schedule, for simulations and "what if" exercises, for highlighting critical activities and the critical path and for determining the projected completion date
- A **Time-Scaled Network Diagram** is a combination of a network diagram and a bar chart; it shows project logic, activity durations and schedule information

Standard Deviation: the measurement of the variability of the quantity measured, such as time or costs, from the average. It is important to memorize these percentages.
- $\pm 1\sigma = 68.27\%$
- $\pm 2\sigma = 95.45\%$
- $\pm 3\sigma = 99.73\%$

This means that when you have $\pm 3\sigma$, 99.73% of all possible values fall within this range.

Statistical Terms: the primary statistical terms are the project mean, variance and standard deviation.
- The project **Mean (μ)** is the sum of the means of the individual tasks
- The project **Variance** is the sum of the variances of the individual tasks
- The project **Standard Deviation (σ)** is the square root of the project variance

Successor: the activity that happens second or subsequently to a previous activity when defining dependencies between activities in a network.

Triangular Distribution or **Three-Point Estimating**: takes the average of three estimated durations — the optimistic value, the most likely value and the pessimistic value. By using the average of three values rather than a single estimate, a more accurate duration estimate for the activity is obtained.

Weighted Three-Point Estimates, or **Beta/PERT**: program evaluation and review technique (PERT) uses the three estimated durations of three-point estimating but weighs the most likely estimate by a factor of four. This weighted average places more emphasis on the most likely outcome in calculating the duration of an activity. Therefore, it produces a curve that is skewed to one side when possible durations are plotted against their probability of occurrence.

What-If Scenario Analysis: a technique used to assess the feasibility of the project schedule should unexpected events occur. This analysis is useful for preparing contingency and response plans to mitigate the impact of identified risk events and could involve simulations of various project durations using different sets of project assumptions. The most common simulation method is the **Monte Carlo Analysis** technique.

DEFINE ACTIVITIES PROCESS

This process involves the identification of the specific activities that must be performed in order to produce the deliverables of the WBS **Work Packages**. Therefore, the key inputs are the approved detailed scope statement, **WBS** and **WBS Dictionary** (included in the scope baseline), the **Enterprise Environmental Factors** and the **Organizational Process Assets**. Each of the WBS work packages is then broken down (decomposed) into smaller components called activities. These activities comprise the **Activity List**. Note that **Decomposition** is the tool and technique used in the Create WBS process as well.

The primary difference between decomposition in the Define Activities process and decomposition in the Create WBS process is the final output. In the Create WBS process, the results are deliverables; in the Define Activities process, the results are activities. In some areas, the WBS and activity list are developed concurrently but in every case, by further breaking down the work, the scope is further refined and could result in WBS updates.

Activity Attributes and their Relationship to the WBS Dictionary

Activity attributes describe the characteristics of each activity planned within the work package. Similar to the WBS dictionary, the activity attributes typically include descriptions, predecessor and successor tasks, the person or department responsible for the task and any other assumptions that may have been made in detailing what it takes to complete the activity. Figure 6-1 on the next page shows how activity attributes relate to the WBS dictionary.

WBS ID: 1.1.3
Description: Riding lawn mower tires procurement

Responsibility: Procurement Department – Sue Adams

Schedule:
    Milestone: Required no later than 3/3/2010
    Predecessor: Riding lawn mower design
    Successor: Chassis assembly
Schedule Activities:
    1. Request for Proposal distributed
    2. Vendor selected
    3. Finalize purchase contract and place order
    4. Receive and inspect receipt

Resources Required:

Cost Estimates:

Quality Requirements:

Acceptance Criteria:

Receive and inspect receipt (WBSID 1.1.3)
Description: The tires that are purchased for the lawn mower are expected to be delivered by the vendor and will be inspected by the shipping/receiving department of XYZ company.

Responsible Person: John Mark, Shipping Manager

Schedule:
    Predecessor: Finalize purchase contract and place order
    Successor: Chassis assembly

Acceptance Criteria:
    1. Order received must include 100% of purchase quantity. Will not accept a partial shipment.
    2. Tires must be certified to meet production specification X.44.673

Figure 6-1
WBS Dictionary and
Activity Attributes

SEQUENCE ACTIVITIES PROCESS

The four processes of Sequence Activities, Estimate Activity Resources, Estimate Activity Durations and Develop Schedule are so closely linked that some projects combine the four processes into a single process to come up with the project schedule. The Sequence Activities process involves organizing project tasks in the order they must be performed. For example, one cannot start the lawn mower until the ignition component is operational, and one cannot attach wheels until they are received from the supplier. This organization is accomplished by using the activity list and product description to determine the immediate predecessor(s) and successor(s) of each task. In addition, **Mandatory Dependencies** (hard logic), **Discretionary Dependencies** (preferred or soft logic), **External Dependencies** and **Milestones** must be considered.

Network Diagramming

Project schedule **Network Diagrams** are an important output of the Sequence Activities process. The main technique used is the precedence diagramming method (PDM). PDM is used for critical path determination. The network diagram may show that activity refinements are necessary, and it may result in updates to the activity list. There are many exam questions on critical path as well as on float, duration estimates and forward and backward passes.

- In the **Precedence Diagramming Method (PDM)**, also called **Activity-on-Node (AON)**, boxes or circles are used to represent activities while arrows show the sequence of workflow. Four types of dependencies or logical relationships are used — **Finish-to-Start**, **Finish-to-Finish**, **Start-to-Start** and **Start-to-Finish**. Finish-to-start is the most common. Know how to calculate duration and elapsed time for simple PDM networks. PDM can also show lead (i.e., negative lag) and lag times.

Lags and Leads

Lags and leads are used for different purposes. A lag is used when there is a waiting period between a predecessor and a successor activity. Pouring concrete is a good example. When the activity of pouring concrete is complete, there is a waiting period before any of the next activities can be performed on that concrete. Assuming a three-day lag, the schedule relationship would be depicted as in Figure 6-2 on the following page.

Leads are typically used when some acceleration is needed on the project schedule. In a software development project, for instance, ideally all training materials should be started after the completion of software testing. To accelerate the schedule by two days, the training material task could start two days earlier withing testing being fully complete. The schedule relationship would be depicted as in Figure 6-3, also on the following page.

6

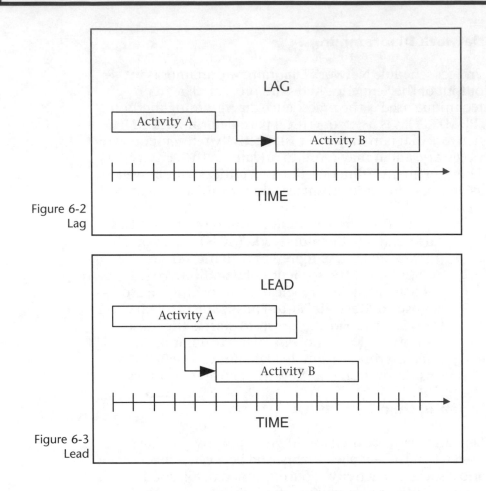

Figure 6-2
Lag

Figure 6-3
Lead

ESTIMATE ACTIVITY RESOURCES PROCESS

Once the project schedule **Network Diagram** is available, resources are assigned. Resources come in several forms: people, equipment, materials, facilities and money. One of the key components of determining an accurate schedule for any project is the ability to determine accurately the type of resources (by description, quantity and availability) needed to perform work activities. These resource estimates can then be used to estimate project costs. Therefore, the Estimate Activity Resources process is very closely tied to the Estimate Costs process in the next chapter.

The *PMBOK® Guide* breaks down estimating into two steps. The first is estimating resources from a skill and availability standpoint (which is the Estimate Activity Resources process) and the second is estimating the duration of each work package based on the decisions made in the Estimate Activity Resources process.

The **Activity List**, **Activity Attributes** and **Resource Calendar** are key inputs to the Estimate Activity Resources process. By assigning resources and estimates to each activity — which then are rolled up to work packages within the WBS — a more detailed and accurate schedule is produced. The primary outputs of this process are the activity resource requirements, the updates to project documents and the **Resource Breakdown Structure**. The resource breakdown structure is a hierarchical structure of the identified resources broken out by category and type. It is a useful document for managing resource utilization information.

ESTIMATE ACTIVITY DURATIONS PROCESS

Once the project tasks have been organized in the order that they are to be performed and the resources identified, Estimate Activity Durations is the process of defining the number of work periods that will be needed to complete the individual activities. In estimating the duration of the task, it is necessary to know the resource requirements and capabilities, factors influencing elapsed time and any historical information of similar tasks. The project team must decide if the types of estimates should be deterministic (if a single estimate is used and the duration is known with a fair degree of certainty) or probabilistic (if the task duration is uncertain, a three-point estimating technique or weighted average is used).

Primary tools and techniques in this process are the various estimating methods. In obtaining the duration estimates of the tasks, activity refinements may be necessary and updates may need to be made to the activity attributes.

6

Estimating Tools and Techniques

Expert Judgment (such as the **Delphi Technique**): one or more subject matter experts are used as a source for obtaining estimates. If subject matter experts lack historical information or experience, the risk of inaccurate estimates is increased.

Within time management the project manager may consult with a senior resource (an "expert") in order to obtain good work effort estimates rather than have inexperienced team members provide them.

Analogous Estimating (or **Top-Down Estimating**): obtained by comparing the current project activities to previous project activities and using the actual duration of the previous similar activity as the basis for the current activity. The degree of similarity affects accuracy. This technique should be used early in the estimating cycle when there is not much detail known about the activity. Analogous estimating is considered to be a form of expert judgment.

Quantitatively-Based Estimating (sometimes called **Parametric Estimating**): the quantities of the units of work are multiplied by a productivity unit rate to obtain an estimated activity duration. These estimates are based on historical information that has been codified. An example is the creation of a training manual in terms of pages per day. A junior writer may produce two pages per day while a senior writer may produce five pages per day. A software development example may be the number of lines of code produced per day by various levels of programmers.

Three-Point Estimating: a technique to reflect risk in the estimates that are provided for both time and cost. The two formulas that are typically used to adjust for risk are triangular and Beta/PERT weighted average.

- Triangular mean (μ) = [(A + M + B)]/3
  where A = lowest value, M = most likely value
  and B = highest value
- Variance (V)
  V = σ^2 or
  V = [(A - B)^2 + (M - A)(M - B)]/18

- PERT or weighted average mean where
  A = lowest value, M = most likely
  and B = highest value
  (μ) = [A + 4(ML) + B]/6
- Standard deviation (σ)
  σ = (B - A)/6

DEVELOP SCHEDULE PROCESS

The Develop Schedule process utilizes the duration estimates for each task in order to determine the start and finish dates for each task. By traversing the longest path within the project, the **Critical Path** can be determined and the project schedule is developed. Therefore, necessary inputs to the Develop Schedule process are the **Network Diagrams** with **Duration Estimates**, **Resource Requirements**, **Activity List**, **Resource Calendars**, the **Project Scope Statement**, **Enterprise Environmental Factors** and **Organizational Process Assets**.

In order to produce the project schedule, schedule network analysis is used to calculate early and late start and finish dates without regard for resource availability and limitations. Schedule network analysis uses various analytical techniques such as the CPM, the **Critical Chain Method**, **What-If Scenario Analysis**, **Resource Leveling**, **Schedule Compression** and scheduling tools. Loops and open-ended nodes in the network diagram are adjusted before the analytical technique is applied.

Float, or **Slack**, is also a concept you must understand. You must know how it presents challenges and opportunities to project schedulers.

The project schedule, schedule baseline and updated schedule management plan are the primary outputs of the Develop Schedule process.

Critical Path Method Schedule Development

When calculating the critical path for a project, you start with the network diagram and duration estimates to determine:
- Float
- Early start date (ES)
- Early finish date (EF)
- Late start date (LS)
- Late finish date (LF)

TASK ID	
Duration	Float
ES	EF
LS	LF

Figure 6-4
Matrix for a
Network Diagram

These variables are formatted into a simple matrix for each task of the network diagram, as shown in Figure 6-4.

The network diagram is traversed from left to right in a **Forward Pass** to determine ES and EF:
- Start time of the project is zero (0)
- ES = EF of the immediate predecessor
- EF = ES plus duration
- A successor starts when ALL its predecessors are complete
- Project finish date = EF of the final task

Figure 6-5 on the following page illustrates the results of the forward pass. Once the forward pass is complete, begin the **Backward Pass** by traversing the network diagram from right to left to determine LF and LS of each task:
- Project LF = EF of the final task of the project
- LS = LF minus duration
- LF = the earliest LS of ALL its successors

Once LF and EF are known, **Float** can be calculated:
- Float = LF - EF

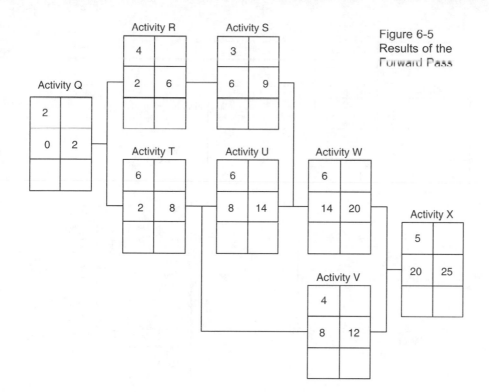

Figure 6-5
Results of the
Forward Pass

The results are shown in Figure 6-6 on the following page. Note that both activities R and S in the example each have a **Total Float** of five days. The combined duration of activity R and S is seven days, while the combined duration of activity T and U (on the critical path) is twelve days and activity W (also on the critical path) is the successor to both activities U and S. Since **Free Float** is defined as the amount of time an activity can be delayed without delaying the start of an immediate successor; the free float for activity R is zero days, which allows activity S to have a free float of five days.

In CPM analysis a finish-to-start relationship is used exclusively. Once the network diagram is completed and the schedule activity relationships are known, a **Gantt Chart** can be developed. Gantt charts are generally used to monitor schedule progress. Other relationships besides finish-to-start can be reflected along with leads and lags. A sample Gantt chart is shown in Figure 6-7.

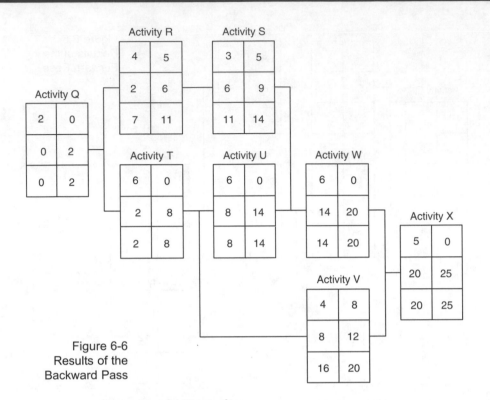

Figure 6-6
Results of the
Backward Pass

Case Study Exercises

Exercise 6-1: Using the WBS for the Lawrence RV Garage Project developed in Chapter 5, Exercise 5-2, create a network diagram showing the dependencies of the various WBS items. Use the activity-on-node (AON) technique. Also include your estimates for how many days each activity will take. All estimates should be in whole days.

Exercise 6-2: Draw a Gantt chart based on the precedence diagram from Exercise 6-1 for the Lawrence RV Garage Project.

Resource Constraints

In many cases projects are resource constrained, which limits optimal scheduling. Two methods that can be used to facilitate scheduling with limited resources are **Resource Leveling** and the **Critical Chain** method. In general these methods typically lengthen the schedule.

	Task Name	Start	Finish	Duration	Jul 2005
1	Activity Q	6/13/2005	6/14/2005	2d	
2	Activity R	6/15/2005	6/20/2005	4d	
3	Activity S	6/21/2005	6/23/2005	3d	
4	Activity T	6/15/2005	6/22/2005	6d	
5	Activity U	6/23/2005	6/30/2005	6d	
6	Activity V	6/23/2005	6/28/2005	4d	
7	Activity W	6/30/2005	7/7/2005	6d	
8	Activity X	7/8/2005	7/14/2005	5d	

Figure 6-7
Gantt Chart

Finalizing Resource Requirements

The output of the Develop Schedule process is an official set of plans for the project that includes:
- The project schedule
- The baselines
- Schedule data which may include a resource requirement histogram, such as in Figure 6-8 on the following page
- Project document updates

The steps to be taken for assigning people to work each schedule activity in a work package and detailed into a Gantt chart are:
- Assign resources to each activity, one resource at a time
- For each time period, sum up the resources required
- Develop a **Resource Histogram**

Resource Leveling

Resource leveling is a schedule network analysis technique that is performed after the critical path has been determined to address specific delivery dates and take into account resource availability or to keep resource usage at a constant level during specified time periods of the project. The resulting schedule often has an altered critical path and could result in the project taking longer to complete.

EXAM TIP

Resource requirement updates could lengthen a project schedule. If an activity requires three people working for four calendar weeks but only two people are available, it will take six calendar weeks to complete the project, all other factors being equal.

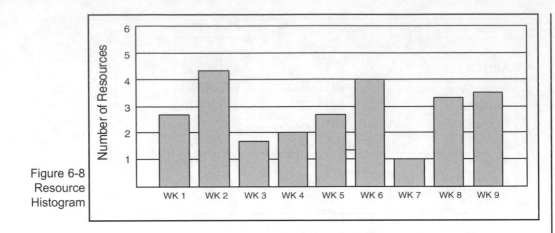

Figure 6-8
Resource
Histogram

The resource leveling technique reviews the project schedule for either over- or under-allocation of resources. There may be times when more resources are needed than are available, which could occur for equipment, people or subject matter experts. There may be individual resources that are assigned to one or more tasks during a time period that exceeds the individual's available time.

Resource usage is evaluated at the project level by preparing a resource histogram to determine total resources used in each time period. The project manager may try to eliminate spikes and gaps in total resource usage within the histogram, as shown in Figure 6-9 on the facing page. Resource leveling is used to reschedule concurrent activities where individuals have one or more constraints. It may result in extending the duration of the project.

Figure 6-9 shows a histogram of a project where there are 3.5 resources available. You can see that there are two work periods where there are not enough resources for the work to be performed, while in the other periods there are ample resources

Critical Chain Method

The critical chain method is a schedule network analysis technique that is performed after the critical path has been determined to take into account resource availability. If a resource is unavailable for any period of time, the resulting schedule often has an altered critical path.

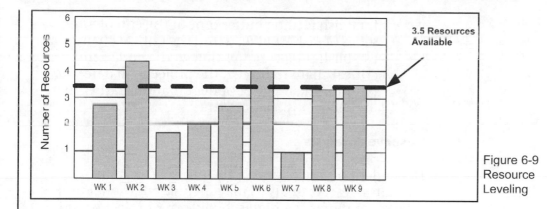

Figure 6-9
Resource
Leveling

The critical chain method is an alternative to the critical path method. It views the project as a system instead of a network of independent tasks. While the **Critical Path** is determined by task dependency relationships, the critical chain adds resource dependencies to define a resource-limited schedule. The longest sequence of resource-leveled tasks is the critical chain.

The critical chain method tries to adjust for problems in estimating and managing tasks that result from poor multi-tasking, estimates with too much contingency for uncertainty, work that expands to fill the available time, waiting until the latest possible time to start and lack of prioritization.

The critical chain method includes techniques that:
- Focus on the project end date, not individual task completion
- Use an estimate for tasks at the 50% confidence level, so that half the tasks will be earlier than the estimate and half the tasks will be later
- Level the tasks throughout the whole project to determine the critical chain
- Eliminate multi-tasking on significant tasks while focusing on critical chain tasks
- Create project, feeding and resource buffers for project uncertainties instead of building contingency into individual tasks; uncertainty is determined by comparing the difference between estimates at a high confidence level (90% - 95%) and the 50% confidence level

- Establish feeding buffer time at the end of a series of tasks that feed into the critical chain
- Establish project buffer time at the end of the critical chain to protect the project end date
- Monitor the usage of buffer durations rather than individual task performance

Reserve Analysis

Dependent on the nature of the project duration estimates, reserve analysis may include additional time reserves or buffers. A high schedule risk project would contain a bigger contingency reserve than a project with little schedule risk. A key aspect of the **Critical Chain** method uses feeding buffers and an overall project buffer to protect target dates along the critical chain from slippage. These **Contingency Reserves** or **Buffers** should be analyzed regularly and adjusted as more project data become available.

Schedule Compression

Schedule compression is a special case of schedule network analysis where the project schedule is shortened without changing the project scope. **Crashing** and **Fast Tracking** are two techniques supported by PMI as ways to accelerate the project schedule without changing the project scope. Both techniques require an understanding of network diagrams.

Both crashing and fast tracking can result in increased costs and can increase the risks of achieving the shorter project schedule. Simulations such as Monte Carlo analysis are also used to calculate the probable results for the total project.

As a project manager you must recognize that there are always tradeoffs to schedule compression. You may have to bring in extra resources or more expensive resources in order to perform schedule activities in shorter time frames or in parallel.

Depending upon **Risk Tolerances** and the **Constraints** and **Assumptions** in your scope statement, the choice of where to compress the schedule will usually become obvious.

Figure 6-10 shows an example of opportunities to compress the schedule project depicted in Figures 6-5 through 6-9.

Possible Opportunity	Schedule	Cost	Risk
Reduce Activity W 3 days by hiring an expert	Reduce 3 days		Low
Break Activity W into 2 equal activities and hire another resource at the current rate	Reduce 3 days		High
Reduce Activity T 2 days by working over the weekend	Reduce 2 days		Medium

Figure 6-10 Schedule Compression

CONTROL SCHEDULE PROCESS

The Control Schedule process involves the handling of factors that could impact the project schedule. It involves:
- The review and approval processes of changes that lead to schedule changes
- Determining the size and impact of the change
- Managing the actual schedule change

Changes to the project schedule could come in the form of a change request or in response to project performance or nonperformance needing corrective action. **Variance Analysis** is a key technique of schedule control. Comparing actual start and finish dates to planned dates provides early problem determination.

Although **Earned Value Management** (EVM) is not discussed in detail in project time management, it is very much a part of variance analysis and many exam questions could utilize earned value concepts in this knowledge area.

Earned Value Terms and Formulas

Earned value management is a technique that describes plans and performance in terms of monetary amounts to calculate both the cost and schedule status of a project that has started. Since costs are the basis of all the calculations, even schedule information is stated in cost units. Also, remember that EVM is always as of a specific date (the data date).

Three dimensions of EVM are planned value, actual cost and earned value.

- **Planned Value (PV)** is the sum of the approved cost estimates for activities scheduled to be performed during a given period
- **Actual Cost (AC)** is the amount of money actually spent in completing work in a given period
- **Earned Value (EV)** is the sum of the approved cost estimates for activities completed during a given period

Variables monitored are cost and schedule variances, the cost and schedule performance indices and budget and estimate at completion.

- **Cost Variance (CV)** is earned value (EV) minus actual cost (AC). It is the difference between the budgeted cost of the work completed and the actual cost of completing the work. A negative number means the project is over budget.
  - CV = EV - AC

- **Schedule Variance (SV)** is earned value (EV) minus planned value (PV). It represents the difference between what was accomplished and what was scheduled. A negative number means the project is behind schedule.
  - SV = EV - PV

- **Cost Performance Index (CPI)** is earned value (EV) divided by actual cost (AC). It is the ratio of what was completed to what it cost to complete it. Values less than 1.0 indicate we are getting less than a dollar's worth of value for each dollar we have actually spent. CPI measures cost efficiency.
  - CPI = EV/AC

- **Schedule Performance Index (SPI)** is earned value (EV) divided by planned value (PV). It is the ratio of what was actually completed to what was scheduled to be completed in a given period. Values less than 1.0 mean the project is receiving less than a dollar's worth of work for each dollar we were scheduled to spend. SPI measures schedule efficiency.
  - SPI = EV/PV

6

SAMPLE PMP EXAM QUESTIONS ON TIME MANAGEMENT

Time — Planning Questions

1. The deliverable which sets the format and establishes criteria for developing and controlling the project schedule is the:

    a) Quality management plan
    b) Schedule management plan
    c) Cost management plan
    d) Schedule baseline

2. Project deliverables, constraints and assumptions are considered _____ during the Define Activities process.

    a) Explicitly
    b) Implicitly
    c) Critical
    d) Unimportant

3. Milestones can be:

    a) Required for every project
    b) Required by contract
    c) Unrealistic
    d) Also known as a work package

4. In utilizing the precedence diagramming method (PDM), the most common logical relationship is:

    a) Start-to-node
    b) Finish-to-start
    c) PERT dependency
    d) Start-to-finish

Notes:

5. In order to expedite the preparation of the network schedule, _____ are commonly used.

   a) Checklists
   b) Activity lists
   c) Templates
   d) Dependencies

6. All of the following are tools and techniques of the Estimate Activity Resources process EXCEPT:

   a) Expert judgment
   b) Analogous estimating
   c) Alternatives analysis
   d) Bottom-up estimating

7. You are the project manager of a critical project. A key resource, John, just told you that he will be going on vacation for three weeks in the middle of the project. This fact should be included in the:

   a) Resource calendar
   b) Scope statement
   c) Activity attributes
   d) Schedule baseline

8. The technique which can improve duration estimates by considering the amount of risk in the original estimate is:

   a) Reserve analysis
   b) Three-point estimating
   c) Rolling-wave planning
   d) Decomposition

Notes:

9. Slack or float is calculated by taking the difference between:

   a) Late finish and early finish of an activity
   b) Late finish and duration of an activity
   c) Early start and late finish of an activity
   d) Early finish and late start of an activity

10. The two categories of time constraints that need to be considered in the Develop Schedule process are:

   a) Constraints and assumption
   b) Analogous and parametric
   c) Imposed dates and dictated milestones
   d) Leads and lags

Task	Duration	Predecessor	Cost	Crash Cost	Max crash days
A	3	-	$1,500	$300/day	0
B	5	A	$1,000	$200/day	2
C	4	A	$2,400	$300/day	2
D	3	B	$1,100	$100/day	1
E	2	C	$500	$100/day	0

11. Given the table above, what is the cost of crashing this project to nine days?

   a) $6,500
   b) $300
   c) $500
   d) $6,200

12. In crashing a task, you would focus on:

   a) As many tasks as possible
   b) Non-critical tasks
   c) Accelerating performance of tasks on critical path
   d) Accelerating performance by minimizing cost

Time — Monitoring and Controlling Questions

13. The Control Schedule process is concerned with all of the following EXCEPT:

    a) Determining the current status of the project schedule
    b) Determining if the project schedule has changed
    c) Identifying and analyzing newly arising risks on the project
    d) Managing the actual changes

14. You are the project manager for a business process improvement project for a strategic business process, and a key resource on the project has been asked to work on another project by the CEO of the company for the next two weeks. This key resource is scheduled to start work on key deliverables in two weeks. Your response to this request should be:

    a) Communicate to the CEO that the key resource is critical to the success of the project and that he or she cannot have the resource for the two weeks
    b) Ask the key resource to turn down the CEO's project
    c) Identify the issue as a risk and add two weeks to the project as a contingency plan
    d) Assuming the CEO's project will, in fact, take only two weeks, the project manager does not have to change the schedule

Notes:

Task	PV	AC	EV
1	10,000	8,000	9,000
2	12,000	10,000	11,000

15. Using the table above, what is the schedule variance for task 1?

   a) 1,000
   b) 2,000
   c) -1,000
   d) -2,000

Notes:

ANSWERS AND REFERENCES FOR SAMPLE PMP EXAM QUESTIONS ON TIME MANAGEMENT

Section numbers refer to the *PMBOK® Guide*.

1. B   Chapter 6

2. A   Section 6.1.1.1
   It is very important to identify clearly the expectations of deliverables during activity definition in order to accurately estimate the resources and costs.

3. B   Section 6.1.3.3
   The answer is an example of a mandatory milestone. For choice A, milestones do not have to be developed for every project; for choice C, although not uncommon, milestones should be defined as realistically as possible; choice D is out because milestones and work packages are not the same.

4. B   Section 6.2.2.1
   The precedence diagramming method is an example of a schedule network technique.

5. C   Section 6.2.2.4
   Choice A is out because checklists are addressed as part of risk management, and could be considered a type of "template"; for choice B, activity lists are inputs to the Sequence Activities process; for choice D, dependencies will help define the schedule but are not something that will help expedite schedule preparation.

6. B   Section 6.3.2
   Analogous estimating is a tool and technique of the Estimate Activity Duration process.

7. A   Section 6.5

8. **B** **Section 6.4.2.4**
   Choice A incorporates additional time for contingency; choice C is a form of progressive elaboration; choice D is the subdivision of project work into smaller, more manageable components.

9. **A** **Section 6.5.2.2**
   The critical path method requires calculating slack or float to determine the path with least scheduling flexibility.

10. **C** **Section 6.5.2.7**
    A dictated milestone is a form of imposed date or specified schedule objective.

11. **B** **Section 6.5.2.7**
    First the critical path and project duration must be calculated. A CPM diagram can be drawn and the critical path calculated. The diagram shows the project duration to be 11 days, and the critical path to be ABD. Since A cannot be reduced, then only B and D can be affected in order to reduce the schedule to 9 days. The Cost would be $300, 1 day from B and 1 day from D.

12. **C** **Section 6.5.2.7**
    Only by accelerating the performance of the critical path tasks can one shorten the project duration. Accelerating performance of non-critical tasks does not affect project duration.

13. **C** **Section 6.6**
    Choice C is the definition of the Monitor And Control Risks process.

14. D   **Section 6.6.2**
Choice A may be a career-limiting move. Choice B may be a career-limiting move for the resource. For choice C, identification as a risk is a good thing, but at this time there may not be any need to add schedule contingency. You may want to look at some resource contingency. For choice D, it appears that the schedule won't have to be impacted, but you'll want to keep an eye on the progress.

15. C   **Section 6.6.2.2**
Schedule Variance (SV) =
$$\text{Earned Value - Planned Value}$$
$$SV = \$9,000 - \$10,000$$
$$SV = -\$1,000$$

6

CASE STUDY SUGGESTED SOLUTIONS

Exercise 6-1
Network Diagram for the Lawrence RV
Garage Project

This example uses the phases of the project as tasks to show dependencies.

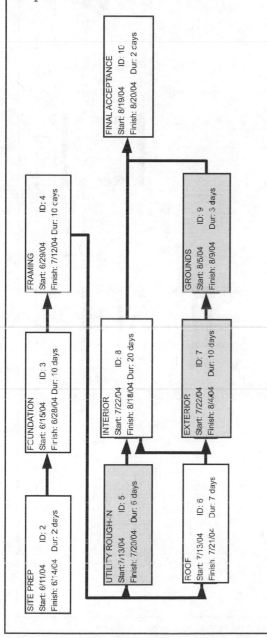

Exercise 6-2
Gantt Chart for the Lawrence RV Garage Project

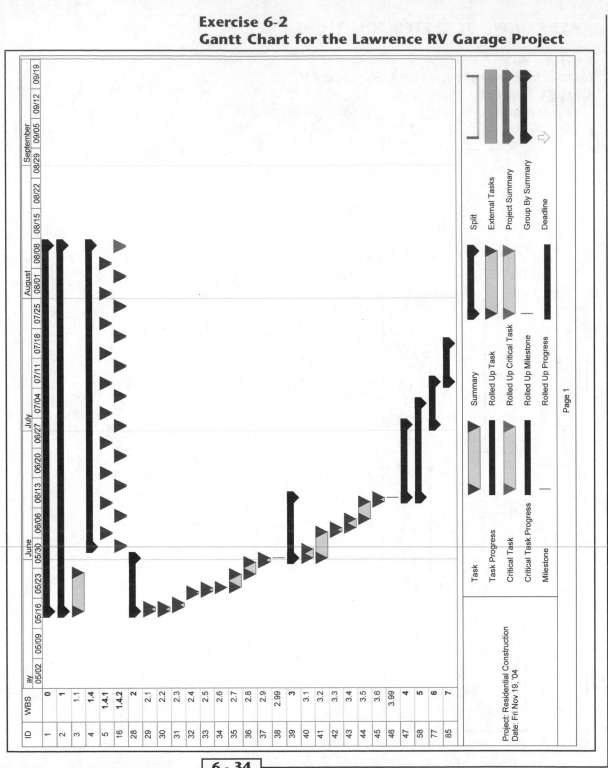

COST

COST MANAGEMENT

Project cost management questions on the PMP certification exam do not require you to be a math whiz. The questions address cost management from a project manager's perspective, which is much more general. However, these questions are NOT easy.

This section addresses a broad range of cost issues such as financial projections, cost estimating and budgeting, earned value, creating and interpreting S-curves and forecasting. This is probably the section people spend the most time studying.

In addition, performance reporting, earned value analysis and communications are integrated into questions on cost. Formulas you will need to know are fairly simple, but you must know them. You must also understand and be able to evaluate performance using earned value formulas and variance analysis.

Cost management is a three-step process comprised of estimating costs, determining a budget and controlling costs.

Things to Know

1. The three processes of cost management:
    - **Estimate Costs**
    - **Determine Budget**
    - **Control Costs**
2. What is **Life Cycle Costing**
3. The difference between **Estimate Costs** and **Pricing**
4. The tools and techniques for the estimate costs process:
    - **Analogous Estimating**
    - **Parametric Estimating**
    - **Bottom-Up Estimating**
    - **Three-Point Estimating**
5. Know **Cost Estimating Techniques**
6. **Reserve Analysis** and **Funding Requirements**
7. **Cost Performance Baseline**
8. How to create an **S-Curve**
9. How to **Crash** with time and/or cost tradeoffs

> **EXAM TIP**
> Crashing should be focused on activities on the critical path.

10. The earned value terms and formulas:
    - **PV** or planned value
    - **AC** or actual cost
    - **EV** or earned value
    - **CV** or cost variance
    - **SV** or schedule variance
    - **CPI** or cost performance index
    - **SPI** or schedule performance index
    - **BAC** or budget at completion
    - **EAC** or estimate at completion
    - **ETC** or estimate to complete
    - **VAC** or variance at completion
    - **TCPI** or to-complete performance index
11. The **Profitability Measures (ROS, ROI, PV, IRR, BCR** and the **Payback Method)**

Key Definitions

Contingency Reserve: a dollar or time value that is added to the project schedule or cost that reflects and accounts for risk that is anticipated for the project. It can be applied at the work-package level.

Crashing Costs: costs incurred as additional expenses above the normal estimates to speed up an activity.

Direct Costs: costs incurred directly by a project.

Fixed Costs: nonrecurring costs that do not change if the number of units is increased.

Indirect Costs: costs that are part of doing business and are shared among all ongoing projects.

Management Reserve: a dollar value, not included in the project budget, that is set aside for unplanned changes to project scope or time that are not currently anticipated.

Opportunity Costs: costs of choosing one alternative over another and giving up the potential benefits of the other alternative.

Percent Complete: the amount of work completed on an activity or WBS component.

Sunk Costs: money already spent; there is no more control over these costs. Since these are expended costs they should not be included when determining alternative courses of action.

Variable Costs: costs that increase directly with the size or number of units.

Cost Management General Concepts

Project cost management focuses on the cost of the resources needed to complete a project. The *PMBOK® Guide* emphasizes **Life Cycle Costing** as a way to get a broader view of project costs. Life cycle costing includes acquisition, operation, maintenance and disposal costs. Project decisions should take into consideration life cycle costing. For example, a project manager may purchase a proprietary technology because he or she realizes, in considering life cycle costing, that the purchase will decrease future maintenance support and training.

ESTIMATE COSTS PROCESS

There is often confusion between **Cost Estimating** and **Pricing**. In the Estimate Costs process, costs of key resources are estimated. The project team also considers the tradeoffs between scope, time and cost and evaluates the overall impact of cost on the project. Pricing is a business decision about what the customer or client should be charged for the product or service produced by the project. Cost is part of the pricing decision but only one component.

Tools and techniques used in cost estimating are analogous estimates, parametric estimates, bottom-up estimates, three-point estimating, reserve analysis and vendor bid analysis. The outputs of this process are the cost estimates for each schedule activity, the basis for estimates and updates to project documents.

Types of Estimates

Analogous Estimating is based on actual costs of previous, similar projects and on comparing them to current project work packages. The degree of similarity between the prior project and the current project affects the accuracy of the estimate. Also, remember to consider changes in labor rates, purchased resources and overhead since the prior project. Analogous estimating takes less time and costs less than other types of estimates.

Parametric Estimating is based on the statistical relationship between historical information and other variables. An example used in home construction is the cost per square foot. This number remains about the same no matter how big the house. Software development companies may base their parametric estimates on lines of code and function points.

Bottom-Up Estimating is based on a very detailed WBS that allows the estimator to estimate each work package more accurately. When the individual work package estimates are rolled up, they become the project estimates. This technique requires detailed specifications as well as a good understanding of the cost components for each work package.

Three-Point Estimating is used to take risk into account. One method is Beta/PERT, which estimates optimistic (O), pessimistic (P) and most likely (ML) values for costs. The Beta/PERT technique may be used to calculate expected activity cost using the formula:

- Expected Cost = $(O + 4ML + P) / 6$

Cost Estimating Techniques

Reserve Analysis is a key technique for estimating costs since estimates are highly sensitive to the expected monetary value of risk events. Risk assessment is used to determine the appropriate level of contingency reserves. Take note of the risk analysis discussed in Chapter 11.

Vendor Bid Analysis can occur when the project or items within the project are procured. The team may be required to estimate and analyze what the project or procured item should cost.

Ranges of Estimates are on an order of magnitude. As more detailed planning information becomes available, cost estimates should be revised. These revisions may occur at the end of a major phase as well. When starting the project, a rough order of magnitude (ROM) estimate may have a range of ± 50%. Detailed planning may allow the project manager to reduce the range to ± 10%.

EXAM TIP

Projects can only be estimated with 100% certainty at the conclusion of the project.

DETERMINE BUDGET PROCESS

Once the cost estimates for each activity are available, the Determine Cost Budget process involves aggregating the values to create the authorized cost performance baseline. This cost baseline is used to measure project performance.

Reserve Analysis

Reserve analysis is conducted during the Determine Cost Budget process as well as during the Estimating Cost process. Both contingency and management reserves may be determined, but they are not part of the cost performance baseline.

- **Contingency Reserves** are allowances established to account for uncertainty and potential risk events
- A **Management Reserve** may be established for unplanned changes to cost

Funding Requirements and Funding Limit Reconciliation

Similar to home construction or remodeling projects, funds for construction are released as certain milestones are achieved. PMI recognized that many organizations have limited resources and expenditures which must be managed. Based on funding limits that may be set by the customer, finance, the group or another department, work schedules may have to be adjusted or reconciled to accommodate the payment schedule.

Cost Performance Baseline

The cost performance baseline is the authorized budget at completion (BAC) spread over the project schedule. It is the plan used for comparing progress and controlling project costs. Cumulative costs are shown as an S-curve.

S-Curves

S-curves are a graphical representation of accumulated budgeted costs over time. Typically, costs rise gradually early in the project, accelerate during execution and taper off as a project closes, creating a curve that resembles an "S" as shown in Figure 7-1.

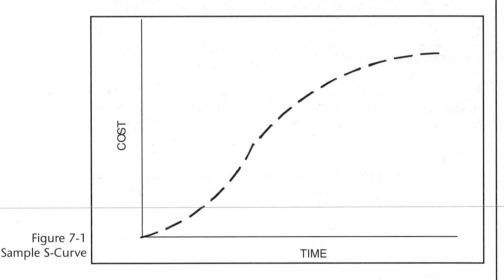

Figure 7-1
Sample S-Curve

An example of the data that would generate an S-curve would be the weekly labor costs to create project deliverables such as the WBS, project schedule and histogram. Next, add in any material costs and factors for overhead items. Figure 7-1 is an example of an S-curve like one that would be generated from the data in Figure 7-2.

Activity	Week 1	Week 2	Week 3	Week 4	Week 5
Q	400				
R	600	200			
S		600			
T	600	600			
U		200	800		
V		200	400		
W			200	1,000	
X					1,000
Total Labor	1,600	1,800	1,400	1,000	1,000
Material	1,000	1,000	1,000	1,000	1,500
Overhead (10% of labor)	160	180	140	100	100
Total Budget	2,760	2,980	2,540	2,100	2,600
Cumulative Budget	2,760	5,740	8,280	10,380	12,980

Figure 7-2
S-Curve data

Case Study Exercise

Exercise 7-1: Using the schedule from the previous exercises and the data below for the Lawrence RV Garage Project, develop an S-curve diagram.

Work Package	Labor	Materials and Equipment	Total
Project Management	$5,000		$5,000
Site Prep	$500	$500	$1,000
Foundation	$1,000	$1,500	$2,500
Framing	$2,500	$7,500	$10,000
Utilities			
Plumbing (subcont.)			$800
Electrical (subcont.)			$1,100
HVAC (subcont.)			$1,800
Roof (subcont.)			$4,500
Stucco (subcont.)			$500
Insulation (subcont.)			$550
Drywall	$350	$1,950	$2,300
Painting	$250	$250	$500
Interior Finish	$150	$450	$600
Driveway and Walks	$300	$1,200	$1,500
Acceptance	$225		$225
TOTALS	$10,275	$13,350	$32,875

CONTROL COSTS PROCESS

Projects often operate under many constraints, but of all the constraints, cost is one of the most difficult to control. As changes occur, adjustments and contingency plans can be established to maintain time, quality, risk and scope objectives. Costs however are nearly always negatively affected as schedules slip or scope increases. In addition, if unforeseen costs are incurred, adjusting or absorbing these changes to stay on budget is extremely difficult.

In order to counteract these forces, it is important to ensure that any changes that impact project costs are approved, that these changes are identified quickly and that the changes are controlled as they occur.

PMI advocates the use of **Earned Value Management (EVM)** to integrate scope, schedule and resources. EVM promotes common understanding by using common metrics and it helps assess the magnitude of cost variations quickly. It also accurately reflects the variations associated with schedule and costs separately. EVM provides a consistent methodology for measuring performance across projects.

Crashing with Time and/or Cost Tradeoffs

In Chapter 6 on time management, crashing was discussed as a strategy to compress the project schedule without reducing project scope. Crashing requires using alternative strategies for completing project activities (such as using outside resources) for the least additional cost. Figure 7-3 on the following page recalls the schedule compression table in Figure 6-10, but with the cost component added.

In order to control crashing costs, the following steps should be followed:
- Isolate the critical path; crashing should be performed on activities on the critical path
- Calculate cost for the estimated duration of each activity
- Calculate crash cost per time unit for each activity

- Begin with those activities in which the crash cost per time unit saved is the lowest
- Continue with the next lowest crash cost per time unit saved activity until the desired reduction in project schedule is achieved
- Note that crashing the critical path may result in additional or new critical paths where additional crashing of activities must occur

Possible Opportunity	Schedule	Cost	Risk
Reduce Activity W 3 days by hiring an expert	Reduce 3 days	Increase $2,000 for the 3 days	Low
Break Activity W into 2 equal activities and hire another resource at the current rate	Reduce 3 days	Increase $600 for the 3 days	High
Reduce Activity T 2 days by working over the weekend	Reduce 2 days	Increase $400 for the 3 days	Medium

Figure 7-3
Schedule
Compression
with Cost
Component

7

Earned Value Terms and Formulas

Some of these are the same terms and formulas used in time management, but in cost management, there are additional terms that facilitate cost management and forecasting.

Three dimensions of EVM are planned value, actual cost and earned value. These are the earned value terms:

- **Planned Value (PV)** is the sum of the approved cost estimates for activities scheduled to be performed during a given period
- **Actual Cost (AC)** is the amount of money actually spent in completing work in a given period
- **Earned Value (EV)** is the sum of the approved cost estimates for activities completed during a given period

There are many techniques to measuring earned value, which represents work accomplished. A simple percent complete formula may not be determined accurately, so other techniques may be more appropriate. Some techniques to use with non-recurring tasks are:

- **Milestones With Weighted Values:** specific milestones are defined and each milestone is given a specific value that will be earned upon completion; this is used for longer activities that exceed normal review points
- **Fixed Formula:** a percentage of the project is earned when the activity starts and the remaining percentage is earned when the activity is complete; for example 25%/75% or 50%/50%; this is used for shorter work packages
- **Percent Complete:** a subjective estimate of the percentage of work that has been earned for the given time frame; this is appropriately used for longer activities when work packages are specific and measurable
- **Percent Complete With Milestone Gates:** a subjective estimate of percentage of work that has been earned up to a milestone gate; additional value cannot be earned until the activity is completed; this is used for longer activities

Variables monitored are cost and schedule variances, the cost and schedule performance indices and budget and estimate at completion. These are the earned value formulas:

- **Cost Variance (CV)** is earned value (EV) minus actual cost (AC); it is the difference between the budgeted cost of the work completed and the actual cost of completing the work; a negative number means the project is over budget
  - $CV = EV - AC$

- **Schedule Variance (SV)** is earned value (EV) minus planned value (PV); it represents the difference between what was accomplished and what was scheduled; a negative number means the project is behind schedule
  - $SV = EV - PV$

- **Cost Performance Index (CPI)** is earned value (EV) divided by actual cost (AC); it is the ratio of what was completed to what it cost to complete it; values less than 1.0 indicate we are getting less than a dollar's worth of value for each dollar we have actually spent; CPI measures cost efficiency
  - $CPI = EV/AC$

- **Schedule Performance Index (SPI)** is earned value (EV) divided by planned value (PV); it is the ratio of what was actually completed to what was scheduled to be completed in a given period; values less than 1.0 mean the project is receiving less than a dollar's worth of work for each dollar we were scheduled to spend; SPI measures schedule efficiency
  - $SPI = EV/PV$

EXAM TIP

According to Fleming and Koppelman (pages 23 to 24), CPI and SPI may be used to determine the efficiency of the project when the project is at least 20% complete. That is, a project that is 10% over budget after 20% of the work is complete will probably overrun the entire project budget by at least 10%.

7

Forecasting

There are a number of techniques to use for forecasting the remaining work, or **Estimate to Complete** (ETC), to arrive at the **Estimate at Completion** (EAC).

- **Budget At Completion (BAC)** is the estimated total cost of the project when completed and could be considered the project baseline

- **Estimate to Complete (ETC)** is the estimated additional costs to complete activities or the project

- **Estimate At Completion (EAC)** is the amount we expect the total project to cost on completion and as of the "data date" (time now); there are four methods listed in the *PMBOK® Guide* for computing EAC; three of these methods use a formula to calculate EAC; each of these starts with AC or actual costs to date and uses a different technique to estimate the work remaining to be completed, or ETC; the question of which to use depends on the individual situation and the credibility of the actual work performed compared to the budget up to that point

- A **New Estimate** is most applicable when the actual performance to date shows that the original estimates were fundamentally flawed or when they are no longer accurate because of changes in conditions relating to the project:

  EAC = AC + New Estimate for
        Remaining Work

- The **Original Estimate** formula is most applicable when actual variances to date are seen as being the exception and the expectations for the future are that the original estimates are more reliable than the actual work effort efficiency to date:

  EAC = AC + (BAC - EV)

- The **Performance Estimate Low** formula is most applicable when future variances are projected to approximate the same level as current variances:

  EAC = AC + (BAC - EV)/CPI

  A shortcut version of this formula is:

  EAC = BAC/CPI

- The **Performance Estimate High** formula is used when the project is over budget and the schedule impacts the work remaining to be completed:

  EAC = AC + (BAC - EV)/(CPI x SPI)

- **Variance at Completion (VAC)** is the difference between the total amount the project was supposed to cost (BAC) and the amount the project is now expected to cost (EAC)
  - VAC = BAC - EAC

Percent Spent is the ratio of actual cost to project budget:
- AC/BAC

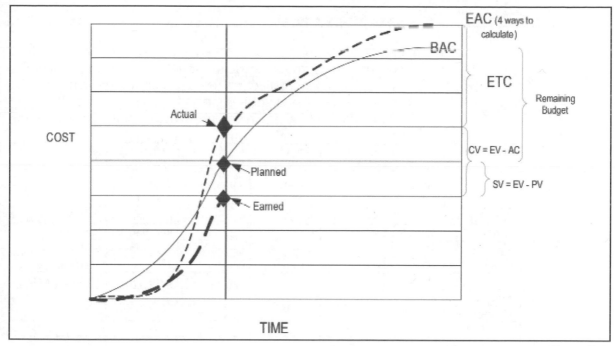

Figure 7-4
Earned Value
S-Curve

Figure 7-4 demonstrates the various earned value terms
and calculations on a project S-curve.

To Complete Performance Index (TCPI)

Another technique for forecasting is to determine the cost
performance that must be attained to meet the BAC or
EAC. Based on the BAC, the formula is:
- TCPI = (BAC - EV)/(BAC - AC)

If the EAC has been approved, it will be used instead of the
BAC. The formula based on the EAC is:
- TCPI = (BAC - EV)/(EAC - AC)

Case Study Exercise

Exercise 7-2: After the garage is framed, the roof installed and the plumbing, electrical and HVAC are in, the owner asks for a formal project review. You are tasked with creating the earned value reports for the Lawrence RV Garage Project based on the following actuals-to-date data.

Phase	Actual Start Variance	Actual End Variance	Actual Duration Variance	Actual Resources Variance	Actual Materials Costs Variance	Notes
Site Prep	+4	+4	Per plan	Per plan	Per plan	Permit delay
Foundation	+6	+7	+1	Per plan	Per plan	Rain delay
Framing	+8	+9	+1	Per plan	Per plan	Materials delay
Utilities	+12	+12	Per plan	Per plan	+8%	Materials delay
Roof	+13	+12	-1	Per plan	Per plan	Materials delay
Interior						
Exterior						
Grounds						
Acceptance						

Profitability Measures

Many projects require an evaluation of the projected profits or returns for the dollars expended. There are a variety of ways to measure profit:

- **Return on Sales (ROS)** measures the ratio of profit to total sales
  - ROS = Gross Profit/Total Sales or
  - ROS = Net Profit/Total Sales
- **Return on Investment (ROI)** measures the ratio of profit to total investment or to total assets, in which case it is called **Return on Assets (ROA)**
  - ROI = Net Profit/Total Investment
  - ROA = Net Profit/Total Assets

- **Present Value (PV)** (not to be confused with planned value) is the value today of future cash flows, based on the concept that payment today is worth more than payment in the future because we can invest the money today and earn interest on it
  - $PV = M/(1+ R)^t$ where M = amount of payment t years from now, and R is the interest rate (also known as the discount rate)
  - For example: if we think we can get 2% interest for the next 2 years, how much must we invest now in order to have $1,000 2 years from now?
    $PV = 1,000/(1 + 0.02)^2$
    $\qquad = 1,000/1.0404$
    $\qquad = 961.17$
  - For **Net Present Value (NPV)** (as of a cash flow), add up the PVs over the number of years
- **Internal Rate of Return (IRR)** is the percentage rate that makes the present value of costs equal to the present value of benefits
- **Benefit Cost Ratio (BCR)** is just that, a ratio of benefits to costs. As an example, an organization may establish that the BCR should be >1.3 before considering the project
  - $BCR = PV(revenue)/PV(cost)$
- **Payback Method** is the amount of time it takes to earn back the investment cost; organizations set criteria for acceptable payback periods

SAMPLE PMP EXAM QUESTIONS ON COST MANAGEMENT

Cost — Planning Questions

1. You are the project manager on a construction project. Your company typically captures costs based on the phase of the project, such as initial contract, materials ordering (pre-construction), construction or interior. The customer wants you to capture costs based on certain deliverables such as design, foundation, structure and roof. What should you do next?

   a) Develop a combined structure
   b) Meet the customer's request
   c) Determine the cost of complying with the customer's request
   d) Continue as your company always has

2. You are planning how you will manage cost on your medical device project. Which of the following should be considered?

   a) Project statement of work, business case and project charter
   b) Work performance information, change requests and expert judgment
   c) Quality metrics, process analysis and checklists
   d) Level of accuracy, control thresholds and reporting formats

3. The project budget should include all costs:

   a) For all resources that will be charged to the project
   b) For the project and related projects
   c) For contingencies for identified risks
   d) For bonuses for the project team

Notes:

4. Factors that are considered to be real, certain or true are:

   a) Constraints
   b) Estimates
   c) Assumptions
   d) Deadlines

5. The use of parametric estimating is most reliable when:

   a) Performed on each work package and summed
   b) The model includes a significant amount of historical data
   c) All risks have response strategies defined
   d) Using the experience of other similar projects

6. As the project manager on a medical research project, you begin estimating the costs for the project. The project sponsor on the project, who has worked on similar projects before, tells you that the project should cost approximately $1 million. However, your team developed an estimate using a parametric model and came up with an estimate closer to $3 million. The estimate you should use is:

   a) $1 million
   b) $3 million
   c) $1.5 million
   d) $4 million

7. During your status review meetings with the project team, an issue was identified that would increase the testing necessary. As the project manager, you make the formal request to your sponsor to add more resources to resolve the issue in order to stay on schedule. The sponsor agrees which allows you to:

   a) Request funds from management reserves
   b) Slip the schedule
   c) Report the resource issue as closed
   d) Go over budget on the specific tasks that need the resources

Notes:

8. The project cost baseline should include all of the following EXCEPT:

   a) Interest charges
   b) Management contingency reserve
   c) Corporate allocations
   d) Equipment costs

9. The cost management process that aggregates the estimated costs of individual work packages is the:

   a) Determine Budget process
   b) Control Costs process
   c) Cost Planning process
   d) Estimate Costs process

10. Project funding requirements can be:

    a) Incremental and non-continuous
    b) Non-conservative estimates
    c) Real or imaginary
    d) Also called management reserves

Cost — Monitoring and Controlling Questions

11. Your project shows that the planned expenditure rate is 100 work units per week for each of eight weeks. What is the planned value (PV) at the end of four weeks?

    a) 400 work units
    b) 300 work units
    c) 800 work units
    d) There is insufficient information to make a judgment

Notes:

Task	PV	AC	EV
1	95	100	95
2	150	130	110
3	130	130	130
4	80	60	70

12. Based on the table above, which task is on schedule and within budget?

   a) Task 1
   b) Task 2
   c) Task 3
   d) Task 4

13. After the fifth month on her project, a project manager finds that the cumulative actual expenditures totaled $120,000. The planned expenditures for this length of time were $100,000. How is the project doing?

   a) It is ahead of schedule
   b) It is in trouble because of a cost overrun
   c) It will finish within the original budget
   d) The information is insufficient to make an assessment

14. Your project data shows that, at some point in the time during execution, the earned value (EV) is $10,000 and the actual cost (AC) is $7,500. The cost variance (CV) is:

   a) There is insufficient data to make a determination
   b) -$2,500
   c) 1.333
   d) $2,500

Notes:

15. Your project cumulative CPI is 0.65, but in your assessment you determine that a certain purchase of equipment was the key driver to this result. In calculating ETC, you decide to utilize the formula:

   a) ETC based on typical variances
   b) ETC based on atypical variances
   c) ETC based on new estimate
   d) ETC based on contingency reserves

Notes:

ANSWERS AND REFERENCES FOR SAMPLE PMP EXAM QUESTIONS ON COST MANAGEMENT

Section numbers refer to the *PMBOK® Guide*.

1. **C   Section 7**
   Choice C is the best answer because accommodating the customer's request may require a change in cost.

2. **D   Section 7**
   Choice D shows some components of a cost management plan.

3. **A   Section 7.1**
   For choice B, related projects will have their own project budget; choice C is out because contingency reserves are separate from the project budget; for choice D, depending upon your organizational process assets, bonuses for the project team may or may not be included.

4. **C   Section 7.1.1 and the Glossary definition of "assumptions"**
   For choice A, constraints are limitations and may be real or perceived; for choice B, estimates are uncertain but hopefully educated guesses; for choice D, deadlines are a type of constraint.

5. **B   Section 7.1.2.3**
   The more data provided to parametric models, theoretically the more accurate the model will be. For choice A, summing up each work package is bottom-up estimating; for choice C, the completion of the plan risk responses process is not required to produce a parametric estimate; choice D is the definition of analogous estimating.

6. **B   Section 7.1.2.3**
   Project team knowledge is useful, but far less reliable than documented performance.

7. **A   Section 7.2.2.2**
Management reserves are funds set aside for addressing unplanned changes in project scope. For choice B, by definition you are asking for more resources and work to be performed to keep the schedule on track, so a schedule slip is not a correct answer; for choice C, the issue is not closed until funds have been allocated and approved; choice D is not always the case; you may be able to re-baseline these schedule activities.

8. **B   Section 7.2.2.2**
Management contingency reserves are typically excluded from the project cost baseline the project manager will have responsibility to manage.

9. **B   Chapter 7**
All of the answers are cost management processes except cost planning.

10. **A   Section 7.2.3.2**
Choice B is out because funding requirements are based on the project budget, which should be realistic; for choice C, funding requirements are a "real" plan for how funds will be utilized; choice D is out because management reserves are included in the project funding requirements planning.

11. **A   Section 7**
The PV is the cumulative expenditure over the specified time as follows:

Weeks	1	2	3	4	5	6	7	8
WU/WK	100	100	100	100	100	100	100	100
CUM	100	200	300	400	500	600	700	800

12. C   Section 7.3.2.1
SPI = 1, CPI = 1

13. D   Section 7.3.2.1
The earned value or the value of the work physically accomplished needs to be known.

14. D   Section 7.3.2.1
CV = EV - AC
CV = $10,000 - $7,500
Choice C is the CPI.

15. B   Section 7.3.2.5
A cost performance index of less than one indicates a cost overrun trend; however if the key driver to the index result is a one-time (atypical) event, you can utilize the formula ETC = (BAC - EV).

7

CASE STUDY SUGGESTED SOLUTIONS

Exercise 7-1
S-Curve for the Lawrence RV Garage Project

This diagram was generated in Excel using the following data:

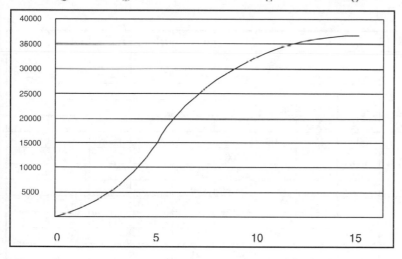

Week	1	2	3	4	5	6	7	8	9	10	11	12	13
Phase													
PM	384	384	384	384	384	384	384	384	384	384	384	384	384
Site	1,000												
Foundation	800	1,700											
Framing		7,000	1,000	1,000	1,000								
Utilities			500	1,000	2,500								
Roof						4,500							
Stucco							2,300	2,200					
Insulation									550				
Drywall									1,500	800			
Paint											500		
Interior												600	
Grounds									300	1,200			
Acceptance													225
Weekly Totals	2,184	9,084	1,884	2,384	3,884	4,884	2,684	2,884	3,634	1,184	884	984	609
Cumulative Totals	2,184	11,268	13,152	15,536	19,420	24,304	26,988	29,872	33,506	34,690	35,574	36,558	37,167

Exercise 7-2
Earned Value Reports for the Lawrence RV Garage Project

Using the information in this exercise, we extrapolated the following data:

Week	1	2	3	4	5	6	7	8	9	10	11	12	13
Phase													
PM	384	384	384	384	384	384	384	384	384	384	384	384	384
Site		1,000											
Foundation		800	1,500	200									
Framing				7,000	1,000	1,000							
Utilities					500	1,150	2,500						
Roof								4,500					
Stucco							2,300	2,200					
Insulation									550				
Drywall									1,500	800			
Paint											500		
Interior												600	
Grounds								300	1,200				
Acceptance													225
Weekly Totals	384	2,184	1,884	7,584	1,884	2,534	5,184	7,384	3,634	1184	884	984	609
Actuals	*384*	*2,184*	*1,884*	*7,584*	*1,884*	*2,534*	*2,884*	*4,884*					
Cumulative Actuals	384	2,568	4,452	12,036	13,920	16,454	19,338	24,222	24,222	24,222	24,222	24,222	24,222

These data yielded the EVT results below, based on the cumulative numbers and the planned numbers from Exercise 7-1.

Week	1	2	3	4	5	6	7	8	9	10	11	12	13
Cum EVT													
PV	2,184	11,268	13,152	15,536	19,420	24,304	26,988	29,872	33,506	34,690	35,574	36,558	37,167
EV	384	2,568	4,452	12,036	13,920	16,304	19,188	24,072					
AC	384	2,568	4,452	12,036	13,920	16,454	19,338	24,222					
SV	-1,800	-8,700	-8,700	-3,500	-5,500	-8,000	-7,800	-5,800					
SVI	0.176	0.228	0.339	0.775	0.717	0.671	0.711	0.806					
CV	0	0	0	0	0	-150	-150	-150					
CVI	1.000	1.000	1.000	1.000	1.000	0.991	0.992	0.994					

Looking at the schedule variance (SV), we can see that we fell behind right away in the first week. We picked up over the next three weeks, then slipped even more for two weeks and have regained some in the last two weeks. We are currently at about 80% of where we had planned to be at this time.

Cost variance (CV) is better. In fact, for the tasks we completed, we were right on target for the first five weeks. In week six we went over budget, but have not yet had any additional budget slippage. We are getting about 99 cents worth of value for every dollar spent.

QUALITY

CHAPTER 8 | QUALITY

8

QUALITY MANAGEMENT

The quality management questions on the PMP certification exam are straightforward — especially if you know definitions of terms and understand statistical process control. You are not required to solve quantitative problems but there are questions on statistical methods of measuring and controlling quality.

An emphasis on customer satisfaction and continuous improvement is likely to be on the exam; how tools such as Pareto analysis and cause-and-effect diagrams are used may also be on the exam.

To pass, you must know the differences among the three quality processes: Plan Quality, Perform Quality Assurance and Perform Quality Control.

Many organizations use these terms interchangeably; however PMI specifically defines each in terms of the process group in which it is performed. The following chart summarizes the three processes as defined by PMI and questioned within the PMP exam.

Process	Plan Quality	Perform Quality Assurance	Perform Quality Control
Primary Activity	Plan	Implement/Manage	Measure/Monitor
Explanation	Determine what the quality standards for the project will be and document how the project will be measured for compliance.	Use the measurements to see if the quality standards will be met; validate the standards.	Perform the measurements and compare to specific quality standards; identify ways of eliminating the problem in the future.
Process Group	Planning	Executing	Monitoring and Controlling

Things to Know

1. The three processes of quality management:
   - **Plan Quality**
   - **Perform Quality Assurance**
   - **Perform Quality Control**
2. **Quality Management General Concepts**
   - **Quality** vs. **Grade**
   - The **Impact of Poor Quality**
   - The **Legal Implications of Quality**
   - **Market Expectations** regarding quality
   - Where **Responsibility for Quality** lies
   - **Prevention Over Inspection**
   - **Quality Policy**
   - **Quality Objectives**
3. **Quality Approaches**
4. The importance of **Process Improvement**
5. The concept of **Cost of Quality (COQ)**
6. The contents of the **Quality Management Plan**
7. The **Quality Audit**
8. Quality theories
   - **Deming**
   - **Crosby**
   - **Juran**
   - **Taguchi**
9. The basic tools of quality:
   - **Cause and Effect Diagrams**
   - **Control Charts**
   - **Flowcharts**
   - **Histograms**
   - **Pareto Charts**
   - **Run Charts**
   - **Scatter Diagrams**
   - **Statistical Sampling**
   - **Inspections**

Key Definitions

Capability Maturity Model Integration (CMMI): defines the essential elements of effective processes. It is a model that can be used to set process improvement goals and provide guidance for quality processes.

EXAM TIP

The project quality management knowledge area of the *PMBOK® Guide* mainly discusses product quality over process quality.

8

Grade: the category or level of the characteristics of a product or service.

Lean Six Sigma: a business improvement methodology that strives to achieve the fastest rate of improvement on quality, process speed and customer satisfaction while lowering costs and invested capital.

Malcolm Baldrige: the national quality award given by the United States' National Institute of Standards and Technology. Established in 1987, the program recognizes quality in business and other sectors. It was inspired by Total Quality Management (TQM).

Organizational Project Management Maturity Model (OPM3®): focuses on the organization's knowledge, assessment and improvement elements.

Process Quality: specific to the type of product or service being produced and the customer expectations, the level of process quality will vary. Organizations strive to have efficient and effective processes in support of the product quality expected. For example, the processes associated with building a low-quality, low-cost automobile can be just as efficient, if not more so, than the processes associated with building a high-quality, high-cost automobile.

Product Quality: specific to the type of product produced and the customer requirements, product quality measures the extent to which the end product(s) of the project meets the specified requirements. Product quality can be expressed in terms that include, but are not limited to, performance, grade, durability, support of existing processes, defects and errors.

Project Quality: typically defined within the project charter, project quality is usually expressed in terms of meeting stated schedule, cost and scope objectives. Project quality can also be addressed in terms of meeting business objectives that have been specified in the charter. Solving the business problems for which the project was initiated is a measure of quality for the project.

8

Quality: the degree to which a set of inherent characteristics satisfies the stated or implied needs of the customer. To measure quality successfully, it is necessary to turn implied needs into stated needs via project scope management.

Quality Objective: a statement of desired results to be achieved within a specified time frame.

Quality Policy: a statement of principles for what the organization defines as quality.

Six Sigma: is an organized process that utilizes quality management for problem resolution and process improvement. It seeks to identify and remove the causes of defects.

Warranties: assurance that the products are fit for use or the customer receives compensation. It could cover downtime and maintenance costs.

Quality Management General Concepts

Quality and **Grade** are different. Grade is a way to distinguish between products with the same functional use but different technical attributes. For example, a Grade One bolt has a certain strength while a Grade Three bolt of the same size is stronger and a Grade Five bolt is stronger still. The Grade One bolt, though of low grade, can still be of high quality (no defects, of proper size, etc.)

Regardless of the organization, the **Impact of Poor Quality** can be significant; it can result in higher costs to the entity or the customer, less customer satisfaction, lower team morale and greater risk of project failure.

In addition to the benefits organizations gain from implementing quality programs, there are **Legal Implications of Quality** that must be addressed when developing the quality management plan:
- Criminal liability
- Fraud or gross negligence
- Civil liability
- Criminal or civil liability, even if following orders

- Lawsuits against the company
- Appropriate corporate actions

In determining what preventative measures to take to avoid nonconformance costs, the project manager must take into consideration the **Market Expectations** of the project's product by reviewing the customer's product expectations on the following criteria:

- Salability: a balance of quality and cost
- Producibility or constructability: the ability of the product to be produced with available technology and workers at acceptable cost
- Social Acceptability: the degree of conflict between the product or its process and the values of society
- Operability: the degree to which a product can be safely operated
- Availability: the probability that the product, when used under given conditions, will perform satisfactorily; the two key parts of availability are:
- Reliability: the probability that the product will perform, without failure, under given conditions for a set period of time
- Maintainability: the ability of the product to be restored to its stated performance level within a specified period of time

EXAM TIP

Be sure to read the PMP test questions on responsibility for quality carefully, in order to determine to whom in the organization the question refers.

8

The organization as a whole has a **Responsibility for Quality**, and PMI recommendations may not be what your organization practices. The PMI position is:

- The project manager has the ultimate responsibility for the quality of the product of the project (In reality, the project manager may delegate work but must retain responsibility.)
- The team member has the primary responsibility for quality at the task or work package level
- The primary responsibility for establishing design and test criteria resides with the quality engineer

Whoever is responsible for quality within an area of expertise must identify quality problems, recommend solutions when problems occur, implement solutions and, if the process is nonconforming, limit further processing.

8

EXAM TIP

PMI emphasizes that quality should be planned into the project, not inspected in.

For many years, the determination of quality relied heavily on **Inspection** methods. Over the years, it has been determined that the costs of inspection can become so high that it is better to spend money on **Prevention** to keep problems from ever occurring. The current views of PMI subscribe to the notion that quality must be planned in and not inspected in. In reaching this conclusion, PMI researched many key quality experts from the past several decades. The exam could include questions on specific theories or experts' opinions. See the quality theories section in this chapter.

Organizations may have a statement defining the principles for quality within the organization. This is generally known as the **Quality Policy** of the organization.

PMI does not advocate developing a quality policy from scratch. Most organizations have a quality policy endorsed by senior management which can be adopted or adjusted to fit the needs of the project. If the project spans more than one key organization in a joint partnership, a project quality policy may need to be developed.

The quality policy does NOT define how quality will be achieved. When organizations create quality policies, they do so to promote consistency, to provide specific guidelines for important matters and to help outsiders better understand the organization. For example, some companies consider quality as the ability to produce products very inexpensively and want to be considered the low-cost leader, while others prefer to offer the most options or features for a higher price. Successful quality policies are drafted by specialists, approved by top management and understood by and adhered to by the entire organization.

Quality Objectives are written for the project by the project team. In writing quality objectives, it is important to realize the perspective from which they are being written. For customers, quality is typically defined by the ability of the project's product to be fit for use. From a project perspective, adherence to specifications will define quality. Whether defining objectives from the customer's or the project's perspective, it is important to define goals specifically through stated quality objectives and ensure that they are communicated well and understood by all stakeholders.

Quality Approaches

There are many non-proprietary approaches to quality such as total quality management and continuous improvement, which have been popular in Japan, and Six Sigma and Lean Six Sigma in the United States.

Although there is no explicit definition of **Total Quality Management** (**TQM**), most definitions include providing quality products at the right time and at the right place, thereby meeting or exceeding customer requirements. Kerzner has defined seven primary strategies for TQM (pages 806 to 809):

- Solicit improvement ideas from employees
- Encourage teams to identify and solve problems
- Encourage team development
- Benchmark every major activity in the organization
- Utilize process management techniques
- Develop staff to be entrepreneurial and innovative in dealing with customers and suppliers
- Implement improvements in order to qualify for ISO 9000

Continuous Improvement Process (**CIP**) or **Kaizan** is another approach to quality. Kaizan is the Japanese word for a sustained gradual change for improvement. It differs from innovation, which consists of sudden jumps that plateau and mature over time before the next jump. The **Plan-Do-Check-Act** cycle developed by Deming is the basis for CIP. The Japanese also came up with the concept of providing materials only when they are needed in manufacturing environments. This concept is known as **Just In Time (JIT)**. TQM and **Six Sigma Initiatives** help to improve project management processes as well as project management products.

PLAN QUALITY PROCESS

The Plan Quality process is performed in conjunction with all other project planning. The Plan Quality process includes:

- Identifying which **Quality Standards** are relevant to the project and product and determining how to satisfy them
- **Benchmarking** past projects to find ideas for improvements and to establish quality performance measures
- Using **Cost Benefit Analysis** to compare the benefits and the costs of quality
- **Flowcharting** a process or system to show how various components interrelate (used to help determine potential future quality problems and establish quality standards)
- Having a **Design of Experiments** with "what if" scenarios to determine which variables will have the most influence on project outcomes, thereby improving quality

Process Improvement

PMI emphasizes the importance of continually assessing the gap between the current position of the organization and the desired goals or capabilities to be achieved. This continual activity of planning and implementing processes within the organization to improve is known as process improvement. Therefore, process improvement is an analytical approach that focuses on activities that provide value to the organization. There are many well-known process improvement models available, such as **CMMI**, **Malcolm Baldrige** and **OPM3®**. Each of these models is based on the premise that process improvement is a continuous strategy based on ongoing incremental betterment within an organization. This continuous process improvement provides an iterative means for ongoing incremental improvement of all processes, including project management processes. The document that details the activities to analyze processes in order to improve value is the **Process Improvement Plan**.

Cost of Quality (COQ)

Conformance is the ability for the product of the project to meet requirements. A project manager has options when planning a project. He or she can implement quality processes to increase the likelihood that the products will meet requirements, or the project manager can inspect the product, determine if it meets requirements and take corrective action if it does not.

PMI advocates the Deming approach, described further below, that says approximately 85% of the costs of quality are the direct responsibility of management. These costs can be broken up into two categories: the costs of conformance and the costs of nonconformance.

Costs of Conformance	Costs of Nonconformance
Quality training	Rework
Studies	Scrap
Surveys	Inventory costs
Validation and audits	Warranty costs

Costs of conformance can be categorized as prevention costs, such as the use of high-quality parts and documented process and appraisal costs, which assess quality at various stages of the project to increase the likelihood of conformance.

Costs of nonconformance can be categorized as internal or external failures.
- **Internal Failures** are the costs associated with scrapping or reworking the product before it reaches the end customer
- **External Failures** are those that have reached the customer. External failures include costs associated with handling and resolving customer concerns

Quality does not happen because a plan is created. In order to implement a quality plan successfully, training the organization should be at the top of the priority list.

Quality Management Plan

A quality management plan is a key output of the Plan Quality process. It should describe how the project management team will implement its quality policy and will provide input to the overall project management plan. A good quality management plan will specifically address each of the following:
- Design control
- Document control
- Purchased material control
- Material identification and control
- **Inspections**
- Test control
- Measuring and testing equipment control
- Corrective actions
- Quality assurance records
- **Quality Audits**
- **Process Improvements**

PERFORM QUALITY ASSURANCE PROCESS

Quality assurance activities occur during the execution phase of the project. It is the process of regular structured reviews to ensure the project will comply with the planned quality standards. This is usually done by means of a **Quality Audit.**

Quality audits are independent evaluations of quality performance to ensure that:
- Intended quality will be met
- Products are safe and fit for use
- Laws and regulations are followed
- Data systems are adequate
- Corrective action is taken, if needed
- Improvement opportunities are identified
- Quality standards, procedures and methods established during quality planning are reevaluated and are still relevant

A good quality assurance system will:
- Identify objectives and standards
- Be multifunctional and prevention oriented
- Collect and use data
- Establish performance measures
- Include a quality audit

Quality Theories

W. Edwards **Deming** is well known for his four-step cycle to improve quality: **Plan, Do, Check, Act (PDCA)**. He also developed 14 activities for implementing quality. For the PMP exam, know some major points of his works:
- Use participative approach to quality
- Adopt new philosophy of quality throughout the organization
- Cease the use of mass inspections
- End awards based on price
- Improve production and service
- Institute leadership
- Eliminate numerical quotas
- Emphasize education and training
- Encourage craftsmanship

Philip **Crosby** is also well known for his books on quality. Similar to Deming, he too developed 14 steps to improving quality. These steps emphasize management commitment, measurement, zero defect planning, goal setting, quality awareness and quality councils.

In addition, Crosby stressed four absolutes of quality:
- Quality is conformance to requirements
- The system of quality is prevention
- The performance standard is zero defects
- The measure of quality is the price of nonconformance

Joseph **Juran** developed the fitness-for-use concept of quality which emphasizes that the measure of high quality is achieved by ensuring that the product meets the expectations of the stakeholders and customers.

Juran's fitness-for-use concept looks at three components of quality. These components are known as the Juran trilogy:
- **Quality of Design**: design may have many grades
- **Quality of Conformance**: determined by choice of process, training, adherence to program and motivation
- **Quality Characteristics**: determine the characteristics important to the customer
  - Structural (length and frequency)
  - Sensory (taste and beauty)
  - Time oriented (reliability and maintainability)
  - Ethical (courtesy and honesty)

Juran also established the following trilogy as an approach to improving quality:
- **Plan**: attitude breakthrough, identify vital few new projects
- **Improve**: knowledge breakthrough, conduct analysis, institute change
- **Control**: overcome resistance, institute controls

Dr. Genichi **Taguchi** developed the concept of loss functions according to which, as variation for the target increases, losses will also increase. Taguchi's rule for manufacturing is based on the concept that the best opportunity to eliminate variation is during the design of a product and its manufacturing process. The Taguchi loss function can be used to measure financial loss to society resulting from the poor quality of a product.

PERFORM QUALITY CONTROL PROCESS

Quality control is performed as part of the monitoring and controlling process group. Quality control involves measurement of the process or performance using quality control tools. It also includes the technical processes that compare and report a project's actual progress with its standard. A good quality control system will:
- Select what to control
- Set standards
- Establish measurement methods

- Compare actuals to standards
- Act when standards are not met

Key outputs of the Perform Quality Control process are validated deliverables and defect repair recommendations. Based on these recommendations, corrective actions are performed as part of the Direct and Manage Project Execution process. Corrections are validated again within the Perform Quality Control process through defect repair reviews.

Quality Control versus Scope Verification

The Perform Quality Control process is usually performed before the Verify Scope process as it focuses on:
- The correctness of the deliverables
- Making sure the stated quality requirements have been met

Scope verification focuses on the acceptance of the deliverables by the customer.

Quality Control Tools

There are many exam questions on **Quality Control Tools.** You will need to know the uses and differences in the following tools and techniques. In general, to use these control tools effectively, an agreement must be made on what will be observed, the time frame for observation, the form of the presentation and how the data will be collected. These quality control tools are:

Cause and Effect Diagrams (also called fishbone or Ishikawa diagrams) show how various causes and subcauses relate to create problems or effects.

Control Charts give a graphical display of results of a process over time. Figure 8-1 on the following page shows a sample control chart. Control charts include a defined upper and lower control limit, a mean and a visual pattern indicating out-of-control conditions, such as **Outliers** (points outside upper [UCL] or lower [LCL] control limits). Control charts that produce particular patterns can provide visual information to the project manager.

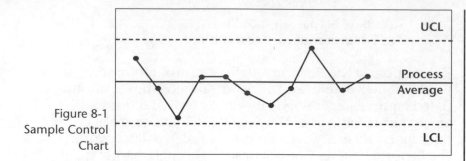

Figure 8-1
Sample Control
Chart

Some such patterns are:

- **Limit Huggers:** a run of points close to control limits
- **Run:** a series of consecutive points on the same side of the mean
- **Trend:** a series of consecutive points with an increasing or decreasing pattern
- **Cycle:** a repeating pattern of points
- **Rule of Seven:** a run of seven or more points above or below the mean indicating adjustment is needed

Flowcharts show how various elements of a system relate. System or process flowcharts are the most common types of flowcharts.

Histograms or vertical bar charts are commonly used in statistics as a graphical display of tabulated frequencies. The categories are usually denoted on the x-axis with the height of the bar displaying the proportion of cases that fall into each category.

Pareto Charts are histograms ordered by frequency of occurrence. Pareto charts are conceptually related to Pareto's law, which visually shows that 20% of causes produce 80% of defects. Figure 8-2 on the following page shows a sample Pareto chart.

Run Charts are line graphs showing data points plotted in the sequence of occurrence. It is used for analysis of trends. Run charts can be used for technical performance such as measuring errors or defects, or cost and schedule performance through the use of earned value

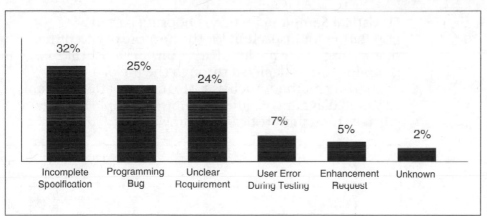

Figure 8-2
Sample Pareto Chart

management. A sample run chart showing trend analysis
is shown in Figure 8-3.

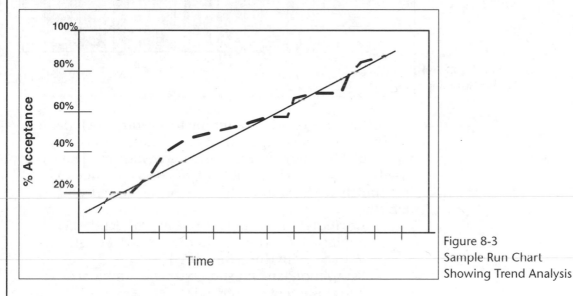

Figure 8-3
Sample Run Chart
Showing Trend Analysis

Scatter Diagrams are used to show the correlation
between two characteristics. If there is a strong
correlation, minor changes to one variable will change
the other variable. The relative correlation of one
characteristic to the other can be seen by the pattern
formed by the clusters of dots in the scatter diagram. If
the cluster approaches a line in appearance, then the
two characteristics are said to be linearly correlated.

Statistical Sampling involves choosing part of a population for inspection for the purpose of accepting or rejecting the entire lot. The results of statistical sampling can be depicted through the use of a variety of charting methods such as histograms, scatter diagrams or Pareto diagrams. Figure 8-4 shows a sample histogram created through statistical sampling.

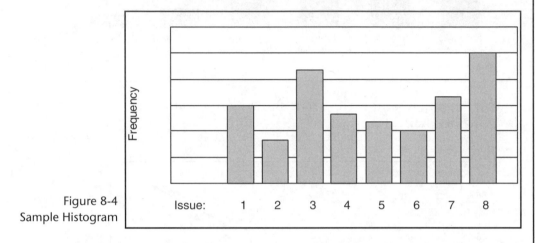

Figure 8-4
Sample Histogram

The advantages of using sampling techniques include less product damage, the ability to make decisions more quickly, fewer expenses and fewer sources. The disadvantage is the possibility of bad decisions due to incomplete information. Here are some sampling definitions:

- **Attribute**: characteristic of the product that is appraised in terms of whether or not it exists
- **Variable**: anything measured
- **Sampling Plan**: must include the sample size and the acceptance criteria
- **Producer's Risk**: the chance of rejecting a good lot prior to selling to the customer
- **Consumer's Risk**: the chance of accepting a bad lot after purchase

Inspections are used after the work is completed. **Checklists** or **Data Tables** may be used to assist in the measuring, examining and testing activities. Figure 8-5 on the facing page shows a sample inspections checklist.

Problem	Month 1	Month 2	Month 3	Total
A	II	II	I	5
B	I	I	I	3
C	IIII	II	IIII	12
Total	8	5	7	20

Figure 8-5
Sample Inspections
Checklist

Case Study Exercise

Exercise 8-1: Using the data in the table below for the Lawrence RV Garage Project, create a Pareto chart for the reasons each phase was completed later than planned. What do you think your results indicate?

Phase	Actual Start Variance	Actual End Variance	Actual Duration Variance	Actual Resources Variance	Actual Materials Costs Var	Notes
Site Prep	+4	+4	Per plan	Per plan	Per plan	Permit delay
Foundation	+6	+6	+1	Per plan	Per plan	Rain delay
Framing	+8	+9	+1	Per plan	Per plan	Materials delay
Rough-ins	+12	+12	Per plan	Per plan	Per plan	Materials delay
Roof	+13	+12	-1	Per plan	Per plan	Materials delay
Exterior						
Interior						
Grounds						
Completion						

8

SAMPLE PMP EXAM QUESTIONS ON QUALITY MANAGEMENT

Quality — Framework Question

1. PMI's basic approach to quality is intended to be compatible with all of the following EXCEPT:

   a) Deming
   b) Management by objectives
   c) The International Organization for Standardization (ISO)
   d) The cost of quality

Quality — Planning Questions

2. As a project manager on a new project, you are asked to put together a quality management plan. Since this project is very similar to your last successful project, although for a different customer and a different product grade, you decide to:

   a) Sit down with the customer and determine how the customer wants you to manage quality on this project from scratch
   b) Utilize the quality management plan from the last project, as is
   c) Ask the quality assurance manager to put a quality management plan together
   d) Review the existing quality management plan from the perspective of the new client keeping in the plan only those standards that are relevant to the new customer and modify or eliminate those that are not

Notes:

3. Your customer's organization has a reputation for providing the highest quality products and is paid well for maintaining that level of quality. You, as the project manager, should begin to develop a project management plan and schedule that:

    a) Models your project management plan after prior similar projects
    b) Ensures the appropriate amount of inspection and prevention are incorporated
    c) Performs analogous estimating to create the project budget
    d) Models your project schedule after prior similar projects

4. As a project manager on a new project, you are asked to put together a quality management plan. This project is similar to one you've worked on before, but the customer has agreed to provide ten resources to help test the new inventory system. You decide to:

    a) Sit down with the customer and determine how the customer wants you to manage quality on this project from scratch
    b) Utilize the quality management plan from the last project, as is
    c) Ask the quality assurance manager to put a quality management plan together
    d) Review the existing quality management plan from the perspective of the new client keeping in the plan only those standards that are relevant to the new customer and modify or eliminate those that are not

5. PMI is a strong supporter of the belief that quality is:

    a) Hard to deliver
    b) Planned, designed and built in to the project and product of the project
    c) Job one
    d) The pursuit of zero defects

Notes:

6. As a project manager, your customer wants you to develop a medical device product within six months. The requirements are complete and thorough. However, in your assessment after performing a work breakdown and scheduling exercise, you determine that the quality assurance and quality control activities of the project were underestimated, adding three months to the total project duration. One non-proprietary aspect of quality that you should quickly address with the customer is:

   a) Six Sigma
   b) Continuous improvement
   c) Cost of quality
   d) ISO 9000

7. A measurement is:

   a) an actual value
   b) an estimate
   c) a checklist
   d) a metric

Quality — Executing Questions

8. The tool and technique that examines problems experienced, constraints experienced and non-value-added activities is:

   a) Quality audits
   b) Other quality control tool and techniques
   c) Flowcharting
   d) Process analysis

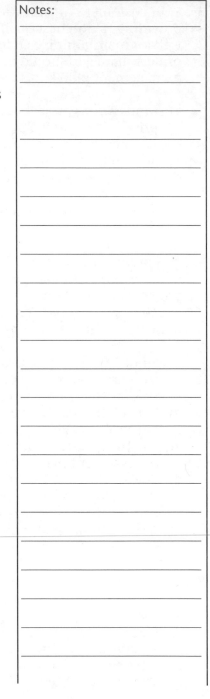

Notes:

9. You are the project manager for a business process improvement project for a strategic business process that is 50% complete. As a major milestone, a test was performed to determine if the new process being developed may actually make the production user less productive, if implemented. One way to analyze the results of this test is to perform:

   a) A root cause analysis in order to find out why the process is not meeting expectations
   b) Quality audits
   c) A defect repair review
   d) A Pareto chart

10. The tool and technique in which you order types of defects by frequency of occurrence is called:

   a) Quality audit
   b) Histogram
   c) Pareto chart
   d) Process analysis

Quality — Monitoring and Controlling Questions

11. As a project participant studying the processes within the *PMBOK® Guide*, you realize that the reason for the _____ process is to identify ways to eliminate causes of unsatisfactory performance.

   a) Perform Quality Control
   b) Plan Quality
   c) Quality Management
   d) Perform Quality Assurance

Notes:

8

12. You are the project manager for a business process improvement project for a strategic business process that is 50% complete. One component of the existing business process had been targeted for improvement because of the significant spikes in quality problems. The tool you can use to monitor success of the improvement project that measures compliance within acceptable limits is called:

    a) A root cause analysis in order to find out why the process is not meeting expectations
    b) A quality audit
    c) A control chart
    d) A Pareto chart

13. At a progress meeting, the quality assurance team shows that the number of negative findings per deliverable have increased in the past two weeks. This does not meet the project's expectations. As project manager the next step you may want to initiate in order to see why the problem is occurring is to:

    a) Develop a flowchart
    b) Call a meeting with the quality team to determine the cause of the problem
    c) Review the schedule variance on the project
    d) Review the vendor contracts to determine if they are at fault

14. As the project manager, you reviewed a scatter diagram in which a large majority of the points are collecting close to the diagonal line. This would communicate that the:

    a) Trend is moving upward which identifies a potential problem on the project
    b) Risk is increasing on your ability to meet the project schedule and cost
    c) Variables measured are closely related
    d) Variables are out of control

Notes:

15. Your project is nearing completion and you have scheduled a deliverable review meeting with your team for next week. The objective of the meeting will be to verify that each project deliverable has met the quality requirements set by the customer. This is an example of the _____ process.

a) Verify Scope
b) Perform Quality Control
c) Inspection
d) Perform Quality Assurance

8

ANSWERS AND REFERENCES FOR SAMPLE PMP EXAM QUESTIONS ON QUALITY MANAGEMENT
Section numbers refer to the *PMBOK® Guide*.

1. B Chapter 8

2. D Chapter 8
   PMI does not advocate that you start from scratch for every project, so choice A is out; for choice B, although PMI advocates re-use of management plans that are available, it does not expect that the project manager will use them exactly as is; for choice C, although the the quality management plan may be initiated by an existing internal quality process, it is the responsibility of the project manager to ensure that the quality management plan is completed.

3. B Chapter 8
   Although choices A, C and D are things that can be done, the focus must be on providing the highest level of quality for the project, based on the anticipated needs of a known client.

4. A Section 8.1
   Although PMI advocates re-use of management plans that are available, it does not expect that the project manager would use them exactly as is, so choice B is out; although the quality management plan may be initiated by an existing internal quality process, it is the responsibility of the project manager to ensure that the quality management plan is completed, so choice C is out; although choice D is an accurate recommendation, sitting down with a very involved customer as described in choice A would be better.

5. B Chapter 8

6. C Section 8.1.2.2
   Since this is a medical device, you must look to the customer to determine if the level of quality assurance and control is appropriate for the risk in selling this device to the marketplace.

7. A **Section 8.1.3.2**
For choice B, an estimate is a projection of what the actual value will be; for choice C, a checklist is a structured tool; for choice D, a metric is an operational definition that describes how something will be measured.

8. D **Section 8.2.2.3**
Quality audits are structured independent reviews to determine compliance to policies, processes or procedures, so choice A is out; for choice B, control tools such as histograms or cause and effect diagrams are used to measure performance; choice C is out because flowcharting helps analyze how problems occur.

9. A **Section 8.2.2.3**
Process analysis may include root cause analysis. Choice B is out because quality audits are used to audit the project policies, processes and procedures, NOT the results of the project; for choice C, a defect repair review is a verification that a defect has been repaired based on the defined deliverables of the project; choice D is out because a Pareto chart identifies defects that are more common than others.

10. C **Section 8.3.2.5**
Pareto charts are histograms that order defects by frequency of occurrence.

11. A **Section 8.3**
Quality management is the knowledge area. The Perform Quality Assurance process ensures that the project employs all necessary processes. The Plan Quality process is the process that identifies the quality standards that are relevant to the project. The Perform Quality Control process monitors specific project results and is the best answer.

8

12. C **Section 8.3.2.2**
Choice A is out because a root cause is a way to determine the cause, not monitor progress; for choice B, quality audits are used to audit the project policies, processes and procedures, NOT the results of the project; choice D is out because a Pareto chart identifies defects that are more common than others.

13. A **Section 8.3.2.3**
Flowcharts can help analyze how problems occur.

14. C **Section 8.3.2.7**
Scatter diagrams show relationships between two variables. The closer the points are together the stronger the relationship.

15. B **Section 8.3.3.3**
Choice A is out because Verify Scope is the process of obtaining the stakeholders' formal acceptance of the completed project scope and associated deliverables; choice C is out because inspection is the tool and technique used within the Perform Quality Control process; choice D is out because the Quality Assurance process makes sure quality processes are followed and not the quality of each deliverable.

CASE STUDY SUGGESTION SOLUTION

Exercise 8-1
Pareto Charts for the Lawrence RV Garage Project

5					
4					
3	▓				
2	▓				
1	▓	▓	▓		
Occurrences	Materials delay	Rain delay	Permit delay		

5					
4	▓				
3	▓	▓			
2	▓	▓		▓	
1	▓	▓	▓	▓	▓
Days delayed	Permit delay	Materials delay 2	Rain delay	Materials delay 1	Materials delay 3

Looking at the Pareto diagram for the reasons for delays, it appears that our materials suppliers cannot seem to get us what we need when we need it. We would need to investigate further to see if this is really a supplier problem or if our project manager is not giving our suppliers enough notice of when materials will be needed.

8

8

CHAPTER 9 | **HUMAN RESOURCES**

9

9

HUMAN RESOURCES MANAGEMENT

The human resources management section of the PMP exam focuses heavily on organizational structures, roles and responsibilities of the project manager, team building and conflict resolution. It has questions from the *PMBOK®* *Guide* as well as several of the publications listed in the bibliography to this study guide (Chapter 15, Appendix D).

This knowledge area stresses the importance of the project manager's ability to manage and develop a team of individuals in a project setting.

Many of the definitions used in this knowledge area, although not widely used in many organizations, have been seen in project management literature for many years. It is important to memorize the definitions from this chapter.

You must also understand the various organizational structures, the experience and educational requirements of the project manager, types of power exercised by the project manager and conflict management concepts.

Although both the administrative and behavioral aspects of human resources management are covered in the *PMBOK® Guide*, the exam seems to emphasize the behavioral aspect.

The project manager has the responsibility to ensure that the project team members follow ethical behavior as part of developing and managing the team.

Things to Know

1. The four processes of human resource management:
   • **Develop Human Resource Plan**
   • **Acquire Project Team**
   • **Develop Project Team**
   • **Manage Project Team**
2. Developing a **Responsibility Assignment Matrix**
3. The **Human Resource Plan**

9

> **EXAM TIP**
> The human resources knowledge area does not have any monitoring or controlling processes.

4. Understand **Project Manager Roles and Responsibilities**
5. The **Staffing Management Plan**
6. An approach to **Acquiring the Right Team**
7. The project manager and **Interpersonal Skills and Work Environment**
8. The four **Leadership Styles**
9. Types of **Power**
10. **Team Building Methods**
11. Five stages of **Team Development**
12. Characteristics of an **Effective Team**
13. The **Team Building Process** and **Barriers** to team building
14. **Sources of Conflict** and **Ways to Manage Conflict**
15. Six **Motivational Theories**
16. **Leadership** and **Influencing** skills
17. **Team Performance Assessment** and **Project Performance Appraisal**

Key Definitions

Authority: the right to make decisions necessary for the project or the right to expend resources.

Co-location: project team members are physically located close to one another in order to improve communication, working relations and productivity.

Leadership: the ability to get an individual or group to work towards achieving an organization's objectives while accomplishing personal and group objectives at the same time.

Organizational Breakdown Structure (OBS): different from a responsibility assignment matrix (RAM). The OBS is a type of organizational chart in which work package responsibility is related to the organizational unit responsible for performing that work. It may be viewed as a very detailed use of the RAM with work packages of the work breakdown structure (WBS) and organizational units as the two dimensions.

9

Power: the ability to influence people in order to achieve needed results.

Resource Calendar: a calendar that documents the time periods in which project team members can work on the project.

Responsibility Assignment Matrix (RAM): a structure that relates project roles and responsibilities to the project scope definition.

Team Building: the process of getting a diverse group of individuals to work together effectively. Its purpose is to keep team members focused on the project goals and objectives and to understand their roles in the big picture.

Virtual Teams: groups of people with shared objectives who fulfill their roles with little or no time spent meeting face to face.

DEVELOP HUMAN RESOURCE PLAN PROCESS

This process involves the identification, assignment and documentation of roles, responsibilities and reporting relationships. Therefore, it is closely linked with the Plan Communications process since the organizational structure influences communications requirements.

Although the various organizational structures are discussed in Chapter 2 on framework and in the equivalent chapter in the *PMBOK® Guide*, organizational structure does influence organizational planning and communications planning. Additional exam questions on functional, matrix and projectized organizational structures show up within this process. The organizational structure of the performing organization could be a constraint to the project team's options.

Enterprise Environmental Factors play a key role in the latitude a project manager has in acquiring and maintaining a competent project team.

Responsibility Assignment Matrix

This two-dimensional structure relates group or individual roles and responsibilities to project work. The **RAM** may be at a high level, showing group or unit responsibility, or it may be at an individual or schedule activity level. If used correctly, a RAM can establish functional responsibility, contracting strategy and manageable work packages for control and reporting.

Figure 9-1 shows a lower-level RAM in which roles and responsibilities for various phases are assigned to particular individuals using the following assignments:

- Specialized responsibility (R = Responsible)
- Identification of those who perform the work (P = Participant)
- Identification of those who may be consulted (I = Input Required)
- Identification of those who must be notified (RR = Review Required)
- Identification of those who must approve (A = Approval)

Figure 9-1
Sample RAM

Person / Phase	Mary	Ivan	Tim	Erica	Allan	Jannette	Jose
Business Requirements	RR	R	A	P	P	—	—
Functional Requirements	RR	P	A	P	R	P	—
Design	RR	P	I	I	R	P	P
Development	I	—	—	R	R	—	I
Testing	R	A	I	P	RR	RR	P
P - Participant A - Approval R - Responsible I - Input Required RR - Review Required							

Another commonly used RAM is an **RACI** format which differs from Figure 9-1 in that its criteria for responsibility are Responsible, Accountable, Consult and Inform. PMI advocates using the organizational process assets already existing in your organization.

Case Study Exercise

Exercise 9-1: Using the template below, create a RAM for the Lawrence RV Garage Project.

Responsibility Assignment Matrix					

P = Participant
R = Responsible
A = Approval
I = Input Required

Human Resource Plan

The human resource plan gives overall direction on project **Roles and Responsibilities**, project organization, staffing and how human resources will be managed, controlled and released.

Role and responsibility assignments (often in the form of a RAM), the staffing management plan (often in the form of a **Resource Histogram**) and the project organizational chart (sometimes including an organizational breakdown structure [OBS]) are included in the human resources plan, the only output of this process.

Project Manager's Roles: in the course of managing a project, the project manager will hold many roles. Some of the most important roles include being a/an (from PMI's *Principles of Project Management*, pages 178 to 180):
- Integrator, who produces product with available resources within time, cost and performance constraints
- Communicator, who interfaces with customers, stakeholders, upper management, project participants and functional managers
- Team leader, who is a team builder
- Decision maker, who makes or ratifies all required project decisions
- Climate creator or builder, who resolves conflicts

Project Manager's Responsibilities: the project manager's tasks and responsibilities include:
- Planning, scheduling and estimating
- Analyzing costs and trends
- Reporting progress and analyzing performance
- Maintaining client-vendor relationships
- Managing logistics
- Controlling costs
- Handling organizational and resource issues
- Handling procedural, contractual, material and administrative issues

EXAM TIP

A typical human resource plan will include:
- RAM
- Resource histogram
- Project OBS
- Resource acquisition approach

9

One of the most important outputs of the Develop Human Resource Plan process should be the documentation of the project manager's **Authority**. It should be published to delineate his or her role in regard to:

- Point of contact for project communication
- Resolving conflicts
- Influence to cut across functional and organizational levels
- Major management and technical decision making
- Collaborating in obtaining resources
- Control over allocation and expenditure of funds
- Selection of subcontractors

Staffing Management Plan

A staffing management plan, together with the project organization chart and the roles and responsibilities needed to complete the project, is an integral part of the Develop Human Resource Plan process. The staffing management plan:

- Describes how the project's human resource needs will be met and the timing of these resources
- Includes how and where staff will be acquired
- Describes the timetable and staff hours required of team members
- Defines the release criteria for team members
- Identifies team member training needs
- Provides clear criteria for recognition and rewards
- Could include strategies for compliance with various regulations, contracts or policies
- Contains safety policies and procedures

ACQUIRE PROJECT TEAM PROCESS

This process involves obtaining the people to work on the project. In many cases it is the project manager who must obtain the human resources for the project. Therefore, the key technique of this process is **Negotiation**. The people resources can be acquired from functional groups, other project teams or new hires. In addition, resources may be obtained from outside the performing organization, as discussed in Chapter 12 on project procurement management.

Acquiring the Right Team

There are five basic requirements for conducting a successful project. In order of importance, they are:
- Choosing the right people
- Finding people with a positive attitude
- Obtaining people with the appropriate skills
- Setting up the right organization
- Using the right methods

In order to acquire the people with the appropriate skills, project managers find it is becoming commonplace to work with **Virtual Teams**. The lower costs and improved technology of electronic communications such as email, electronic meetings and video conferencing make virtual teams feasible. However, **Team Building** becomes more challenging when team members spend little or no time meeting face-to-face. Frequent and regular communication becomes critically important for a virtual team to work. Ground rules for communication must be set with clear objectives, shared goals, protocols for conflict and issues resolution, involvement of the team in decision making and recognition of individual and team successes.

The ground rules for the method of team member interactions should be specified in the communications plan for the project. Therefore, communications planning is closely linked to the acquisition of team members for the project.

Acquiring the project team is truly an iterative process. As **Progressive Elaboration** is applied to the scope and schedule, new requirements for resources may be uncovered. It is important for the project manager to continually assess the human resource needs of the project.

DEVELOP PROJECT TEAM PROCESS

This process involves all aspects of improving the interactions and interpersonal relationships of the project team members to enhance project performance. As feelings of trust, cohesiveness and teamwork increase among team members, the project team improves its ability to achieve project objectives. Training and development of team members, setting ground rules, implementing team building activities and co-locating team members (where possible) are important techniques of this process.

Other critical techniques include using the general management skills of leadership, communication, negotiation, problem solving, influencing the organization and motivating the team by recognition and rewards. Project management skills, leadership styles, power, team building and the motivation of people are all concepts that fall into this process.

PMI recommends a concerted team building effort to be initiated at the start of every project. However, team building is a continuous process due to the arrival and departure of project participants and the alteration of **Roles and Responsibilities** over the **Project Life Cycle**.

Project Manager's Interpersonal Skills and Work Environment

Interpersonal Skills: in order to manage projects successfully, project managers require many skills. Some of the key skills for a project manager to know are:
- Communications skills, which are the ability to adapt to the audience being communicated to
- Leadership skills, which are the ability to see the big picture and use creativity and vision to help the team achieve its goals
- Decision-making skills, which are the ability to assess the current environment and develop ways for the team to reach consensus and make decisions

- Influencing skills, which are the ability to influence both the team and external parties when issues and conflict arise to solve problems
- Organizational skills, which are the ability to understand the resources available and to whom and when to delegate in order to best utilize those resources
- Team building skills, which are the ability to bring a group of individuals together to achieve a common goal and identify when skills of the team are lacking and develop plans to fill those gaps
- Integration skills, which are the ability to be flexible and adaptable in an ever-changing environment

Work Environment: time and stress are two factors that can enhance or diminish performance. The project manager faces greater time challenges than most functional or operational managers. A delay of one or more critical tasks could delay the entire project; therefore, the project manager must be able to influence groups and individuals to get things done. The difficulty associated with assigning priorities for work can place managers under continuous stress. Stress can be used as a driving factor in enhancing productivity but long-term stress often leads to poor performance and ill health.

The common characteristics of a project manager's work environment are:

- Extensive contact with people. The project manager is an integrator, which requires intense interaction with people.
- Fast pace. The project manager is under high pressure to deliver within the defined schedule and cost requirements, often leading to working longer hours.
- Risk identification and vigilance. The project manager must constantly look to the future for upcoming factors or triggers that could positively or negatively impact project deliverables.

Leadership Styles

There are four basic leadership styles that are typically found in organizations today (from Verma, *Managing the Project Team*, pages 146 to 147). These are:

- **Autocratic and Directing**, in which decisions are made solely by the project manager with little input from the team
- **Consultative Autocratic and Persuading**, in which decisions are still made solely by the project manager with large amounts of input solicited from the team
- **Consensus and Participating,** in which the team makes decisions after open discussion and information gathering
- **Shareholder and Delegating** (otherwise known as laissez-faire or hands off), often considered a poor leadership style in which the team has ultimate authority for final decisions but little or no information exchange takes place

A combination of styles may be necessary or appropriate in a given situation. A trend in organizations is a collaborative approach where team members take on a leadership role as needed.

Authority and power are related yet different. Project managers cannot be effective with authority alone. A certain level of power, or influence, over others is needed.

Types of Power: there are two types of power a project manager can use: legitimate (positional) power or personal power. These types of power are further broken down as follows (from Verma, *Human Resource Skills*, page 233):

- **Formal**: a legitimate form of power based on a person's position in the organization
- **Reward**: a legitimate form of power based on positive consequences or outcomes the person can offer; it can also result from personal influence

- **Coercive (Penalty):** a legitimate form of power based on negative consequences or outcomes the person can inflict; it can also result from personal influence
- **Referent:** a personal form of power based on a person's charisma or example as a role model (an earned power)
- **Expert:** a personal form of power based on the person's technical knowledge, skill or expertise on some subject (an earned power)

The project manager may experience **Power** and **Authority** problems for a variety of reasons, including:

- Power and authority not being perceived in the same way by everyone
- Poor documentation or lack of formal authority for the project manager
- Dual or multiple accountability of team members
- A culture that encourages individualism instead of teamwork
- Vertical or stove-pipe loyalties instead of cross-organizational structures
- The inability to influence or administer rewards and punishments

Team Building Methods

Team building activities are a technique in the Develop Project Team process. Team building is one of the many challenges faced by project managers. Teamwork improves overall performance, boosts team members' satisfaction and reduces stress. It must be practiced consistently and frequently throughout the life cycle of the project. Some ground rules for effective team building are:

- Start team building activities early
- Make sure all contributors to the project, whether full or part time, are included as part of the team
- Plan team building activities by phase or other major project or team change; team building must be reinitiated and repeated after

9

the occurrence of any serious risk events or change in project direction
- Recruit the best possible people
- Obtain team agreement on all major actions and decisions
- Communicate as frequently and openly as possible
- Recognize that team politics exist but do not take part or encourage them
- Be a role model
- Encourage and mentor team members
- Evaluate team effectiveness often
- Use proven and effective team building techniques
- Move ineffective team members to positions that match their skills quickly

EXAM TIP

Allowing the project manager to select key team members helps accelerate the time it takes the team to reach the "performing" state of team development.

Five Stages of Team Development are:
- **Forming:** the team members come together and learn about their roles and responsibilities
- **Storming:** the team members express their ideas and may be in disagreement about their approach to the project
- **Norming:** the team members settle in and accept their roles; they agree on the approach to the project and how to work together
- **Performing:** the team members accomplish their tasks and resolve conflict and issues effectively
- **Adjourning:** the team members complete their work and leave the project

Characteristics of an Effective Team are:
- Team members are interdependent
- Team members have reasons for working together
- Team members are committed to working together
- The team as a whole is accountable
- The level of competition and conflict is manageable

The Team Building Process: the project manager carries out the process of getting a group of individuals to work together effectively by utilizing the following methods:
- Planning for team building by clearly defining project roles and making sure project goals and members' personal goals coincide

- Negotiating for team members by obtaining the most promising members for technical knowledge and potential to be effective collaborators
- Organizing the team by matching assignments to skills, creating and circulating the project RAM
- Holding a kickoff meeting in which team members meet, technical and procedural guide lines are set and work relationships and communications plans are established
- Obtaining team member commitments
- Building open and frequent communications links
- Incorporating team building activities into project activities

Barriers to Team Building include:
- Differing outlooks, priorities and interests
- Unclear project objectives or outcomes
- Dynamic project environments
- Lack of team definition and structure
- Role conflicts
- Poor credibility of project leader
- Lack of team members' commitment
- Communication problems
- Lack of senior management's support

EXAM TIP

Whenever possible, plan team building activities early on in the project life cycle and continue such activities throughout the project to maintain morale and momentum.

MANAGE PROJECT TEAM PROCESS

This process involves observing and tracking team behaviors and performance, providing feedback, managing issues and conflict and providing input to organizational performance appraisals. Progressing toward project deliverables, resolving conflicts and issues and project performance appraising are the responsibility of the entire project team.

Team performance assessment from the Develop Project Team process, together with work performance information and performance reports, are some of the key inputs to this process. Observation and conversation, project performance appraisals, conflict management and the use of an issues log are techniques used to manage the project team.

Sources of Conflict

Conflicts are unavoidable on projects due to their temporary nature. These conflicts can arise from:
- Projects being carried out in high-stress environments
- Roles and responsibilities being unclear or ambiguous
- The multiple-boss syndrome in which the priority of work becomes an issue
- Technologies being new or complex
- Teams being brought together for the first time

The seven main sources of conflict have been demonstrated to vary significantly depending on the phase of the project, but during a project's life cycle, the seven sources of conflict can be ranked as follows (from Verma, *Human Resource Skills*, page 102):
- Schedule issues
- Priority of work issues
- People resource issues
- Technical options and performance trade-off issues
- Administrative procedures
- Interpersonal relationship issues
- Cost and budget issues

PMI considers schedule issues, priority of work issues, people resource issues, technical options and performance trade-off issues as being the most likely to cause tension in project environments.

Ways to Manage Conflict

The contemporary view of conflict management is that conflict can have a positive or negative impact on the project and the organization. It can and should be managed. Whether it is beneficial or detrimental to the project depends on the source of the conflict and the way it is handled by the project manager. Conflict is also a natural result of change and is inevitable among people.

> **EXAM TIP**
> PMI views the process of managing conflict within the project team as initially being the responsibility of the project team members.

Should a disruptive conflict continue or escalate, the project manager must become involved and help find a satisfactory solution to the conflict. Managing a conflict of work priorities for team members in a matrix organizational structure is generally the responsibility of the project manager. The project manager needs to apply various motivational techniques to overcome any such issues.

Conflict resolution is situational. While there are preferred forms, project managers may handicap themselves by using a single resolution method in all circumstances. The five ways to manage conflict are (from Verma, *Human Resource Skills*, page 139):

- **Problem Solving (Confrontation)**: the project manager directly addresses the disagreement and gets all parties to work together and want to solve the problem. The problem is defined, information is collected, alternatives are identified and the most appropriate solution is selected. This method is considered win-win and is recommended for long-term resolution.
- **Compromising**: various issues are considered and a solution that brings some degree of satisfaction to the conflicting parties is agreed on. Both parties give up something that is important to them. This method is considered lose-lose and is likely to be temporary.
- **Forcing**: one person's viewpoint is exerted at the expense of another party. This method is considered win-lose and it can build antagonism and cause additional conflicts. It may be appropriate in low-value situations.
- **Smoothing**: the opposing party's differences are deemphasized and commonalities are emphasized on the issue in question. This keeps the atmosphere friendly but this method does not resolve the conflict; it only delays it. Smoothing could be used with one of the above three methods.
- **Withdrawal**: retreating from the actual or potential issue or conflict situation. This method is appropriate only for situations in which a

cooling off period is needed. Withdrawal does not resolve the conflict; it only delays it.

Motivational Theories

There are six motivational theories that PMI emphasizes in the PMP exam (from Verma, *Human Resource Skills*, pages 70 to 75). These six theories were developed by Maslow, Herzberg, McGregor, Ouchi, Vroom and the team of Hersey and Blanchard.

Maslow's Hierarchy of Needs Theory. Maslow developed a model of needs in the form of a pyramid with five levels. He suggests that within every person there resides a hierarchy of needs that duplicates the levels of the pyramid. The needs of the lower level of the pyramid must be satisfied before higher level needs can be addressed. Motivation springs from needs that are not met, as the person strives to fulfill these needs. The levels of needs in this pyramid are, in order of the lowest to highest:
- **Physiological**, the need for food, shelter and items for survival
- **Safety**, the need to be safe from danger, threat and deprivation
- **Social**, the need for association with humans, friendship and acceptance
- **Self-Esteem**, the need for self-respect, status and respect from others
- **Self-Actualization**, the need for self-fulfillment through the development of powers, skills and one's own creativity

Herzberg's Theory of Motivation. Herzberg related Maslow's needs to the job. He suggested that motivation on the job is the result of two factors:
- **Hygiene,** such as the attitude of a supervisor or working conditions. Poor hygiene factors may destroy motivation but improving hygiene factors under normal circumstances is not likely to increase motivation. For example, a clean working environment does not motivate but a dirty work environment will demotivate.

- **Motivators,** such as interesting work, opportunities for personal growth, achievement and recognition. Such positive motivators offer opportunities to achieve and experience self-actualization. The worker must have a sense of personal growth and responsibility. Depending on the organizational culture, group success may be more important than individual achievement.

McGregor's Theory X and Theory Y

- **Theory X** assumes that workers need to be constantly watched and told what to do. Managers who subscribe to Theory X believe that the average worker dislikes work and avoids work whenever possible. This worker is only motivated by money, position and punishment. In addition, a worker avoids increased responsibility and seeks to be directed. Therefore, to induce adequate effort, the manager must threaten punishment and exercise careful supervision. The manager who practices Theory X normally exercises authoritarian-type control over workers and allows little participation by workers in decision making.
- **Theory Y** assumes the opposite set of characteristics about human nature. Managers who subscribe to Theory Y believe that workers are self-disciplined and will do the job themselves. The average worker wants to be active in a supportive work climate and finds the physical and mental effort on the job satisfying. The greatest results come from willing participation, which will tend to produce self-direction towards goals without coercion or control. The average worker seeks opportunity for personal improvement and self-respect. The manager practicing Theory Y normally advocates a participation management-employee relationship.

Ouchi's Theory Z. Theory Z is built off of McGregor's Theory X and Theory Y. Ouchi postulated that quality does not lie with technology but rather with a special way of handling people. His theory is based on the Japanese cultural values of lifetime employment, slow promotions, nonspecialized career paths and collective decision making.

- **Theory Z** postulates that high levels of trust, intimacy, confidence and commitment to workers by management results in high levels of motivation and productivity by workers

Vroom's Expectancy Theory. Vroom developed the Expectancy Theory.

- **Expectancy Theory** postulates that people think about the effort they should put into a task before they do it; if workers believe their efforts are going to be successful and rewarded, they will tend to be highly motivated and productive

Hersey and Blanchard's Life Cycle Theory.

- In the **Life Cycle Theory**, the leadership style must change with the maturity of individual employees; maturity is defined as the extent of job-related experience; in this theory, the situation drives the leadership style to be used to motivate each worker; generally, the project manager's style should move from directing, to coaching, to supporting, then to delegating as the project moves through its life cycle

Leadership and Influencing Skills

Many equate leadership with those who hold a senior-level title within the organization. Leadership requires creating a vision for your team and planning for and executing that plan to reach those goals. Included in the responsibility of leaders is providing support to ensure that the team has every opportunity to succeed.

Project mangers ARE leaders and must use a variety of skills, including influence, to break down barriers and gain support even without a senior-level title.

Team Performance Assessment and Project Performance Appraisal

As part of the Manage Project Team process, the project manager should be involved in project performance appraisals. The focus here is on evaluating how individuals are performing within the context of the project, providing feedback and identifying ways to enhance their performance through training.

Team performance assessments, a tool and technique of the Develop Project Team process, differ from project performance appraisal in that they are focused on the evaluation of the team's effectiveness in meeting the objectives of the project. By design, these are not individual assessments. The results of a team performance assessment may be recommendations for improvement for individuals, but these assessments are focused on the overall team's performance and on assessing how the team can improve its ability to perform as a group.

Motivating people to perform work to the best of their ability is a challenge faced by every project manager. Compensation in terms of money is not enough; other methods must be considered, some of which are:
- **Fringe Benefits** in education, profit sharing, medical benefits, etc.
- **Perquisites** or **Perks** such as a parking space, window office or company car
- **Arbitration** or dispute resolution using a third party to resolve conflict
- **Career Planning** outlining possibilities for growth
- **Training** in new skills
- **Productivity Incentives**
- **Team Camaraderie**

EXAM TIP

Project managers who are involved in team performance assessments increase the reward and penalty power over team members.

SAMPLE PMP EXAM QUESTIONS ON HUMAN RESOURCES MANAGEMENT

Human Resources — Planning Questions

1. As the project manager on a new technology project, you determined the cost of the project to be $1 million. However, you created the estimate in the first month before the full project resources had been identified. This past week, two senior contractors were added to the team on tasks that you had anticipated to be filled with college graduates with some training. As the project manager you should:

   a) Do nothing; the project cost baseline has been approved, so you will need to save cost on another activity to stay on plan
   b) Initiate an additional planning session to adjust the project cost baseline to account for the new resource changes
   c) Submit a change request for the additional resources
   d) Swap out two lesser costing resources on other schedule activities to make up the difference

2. As a project manager you have found that by involving project team members in the planning process:

   a) The planning process will inevitably take longer
   b) They will be more willing to put in overtime on the project
   c) Additional expertise can be leveraged and commitment to the project is strengthened
   d) They will know exactly what to do and when without any intervention from the project manager

3. It has been found that organizations with a high percentage of successful projects make sure project team members:

    a) Have assigned roles and responsibilities for completing the project
    b) Have the skills necessary to perform their function without additional training
    c) Have strong application area knowledge
    d) Perform work only when it is scheduled

4. All of the following are functions of the project sponsor EXCEPT:

    a) Clarifying scope
    b) Influencing others
    c) Assisting with project funding
    d) Creating the WBS

5. Training needs, recognition, rewards and _____ are considerations for the staff management plan.

    a) Organizational Theory
    b) Safety
    c) Networking
    d) Position Descriptions

6. You are the project manager on a medical device upgrade project. The project is having issues with product quality and it has been identified that the product designs are significantly flawed, causing the engineering manager to get involved and to assign an engineer to totally rework the designs. The original engineer was a new employee to the organization and didn't really have past experience in this type of technology. This would be an example of not considering resource _____ early on in the planning phase.

    a) Responsibility
    b) Role
    c) Authority
    d) Competency

Notes:

9

Human Resources — Executing Questions

7. The process mainly concerned with obtaining human resources for the project is the:

   a) Develop Project Team process
   b) Acquire Project Team process
   c) Acquire Resources process
   d) Plan Procurements process

8. You are the project manager on a government energy contract. When selecting resources to participate in your project, you will need to consider the following:

   a) RACI
   b) Product grade
   c) Continuous improvement process
   d) Availability

9. As the project manager for a business process improvement project, it was decided that Bob and Jane would work at a different facility than the rest of the project team. Bob and Jane are experts on the critical business process being re-designed. This poses additional challenges to the project manager and requires the use of tools and techniques for:

   a) Virtual teams
   b) Time management
   c) Quality management
   d) Integration

10. Virtual teams where team members work in different locations and time zones add complexity to managing the team members. All of the following are examples of challenges that could exist EXCEPT:

    a) Confronting conflict
    b) Having satisfied employees
    c) Team building and sharing in project successes
    d) Ensuring understanding of expectations

9

11. As the project manager of a software development project where 90% of your team works remotely, one challenge you will face is the lack of co-location. One way you can overcome this obstacle is:

    a) Call more regular teleconference meetings
    b) Plan for a face-to-face kick-off meeting early in the project
    c) Fly everyone into the corporate office once a week
    d) Get everyone access to a chat system

12. As the project manager of a software development project, your lead technical architect and lead programmer typically do not see eye-to-eye on technical approaches. In the weekly status meeting, their "discussions" escalated to where one of the team members approached you and questioned whether or not the meeting was productive. You should:

    a) Discuss the concerns with the team as a group and come to a consensus as to how to address them
    b) Discuss the concerns with the technical architect and programmer either together or separately but away from the rest of the project team
    c) Tell the entire team at the next meeting that those kinds of discussions will not be allowed
    d) Dis-invite the technical architect as he is the most stubborn of the two

13. Obstacles that can hinder the team's ability to achieve stated objectives are called:

    a) Issues
    b) Risks
    c) Assumptions
    d) Milestones

Notes:

9

14. You are handed a project that is in trouble and upon your initial evaluation of the current situation, you realize that morale on the project is terrible. Part of the reason is that the project team members don't really understand the project objectives and the prior project manager really didn't take the time to explain them, letting the project team members to figure it out on their own. In order to show strong leadership to your new team, you:

a) Ask senior management for an extension, since obviously the project team members are not able to deliver in the timeline specifics
b) Review the project objectives with the team members and help them to set a plan in place so that they can actually see results and have a sense of accomplishment
c) Let the project team members continue down their current path since you are new to the project
d) Replace several members of the project team with those that are more committed to the project deliverables

15. As the project manager of a major aerospace vendor, you regularly attend and present project performance reviews with senior management. Topics typically discussed include all of the following EXCEPT:

a) Forecast of project estimates at completion
b) Team performance achievements
c) Individual team member improvement plans
d) Risks affecting team performance

Notes:

9

ANSWERS AND REFERENCES FOR SAMPLE PMP EXAM QUESTIONS ON HUMAN RESOURCES MANAGEMENT

Section numbers refer to the *PMBOK® Guide.*

1. B   **Section 9**
       In most best practice cases, doing nothing is usually not the correct answer, so choice A is wrong; change requests are usually initiated for scope changes, but choice C is a change in the assumptions on specific tasks, so only the assumptions need to change; choice D is similar to choice A and is not necessarily the best practice option.

2. C   **Section 9**
       Although likely, there are no studies to prove choice A; willingness to work overtime and increased commitment to the project are not necessarily related, so choice B is out; remember that your team members are not experts in scheduling or managing a project, so choice D is out.

3. A   **Section 9**
       For choices B and C, if skills or knowledge of the application area are lacking, training should be planned and carried out within the timeframe of the project; choice D is wrong because performing work exactly according to the schedule is not always appropriate as many tasks will have float and can be shifted without impacting the critical path.

4. D   **Section 9**
       The creation of the WBS should be done by the project manager with input from any of the stakeholders.

5. B   **Section 9.1.3.1**
       Choices A, C and D are all tools and techniques of the Develop Human Resource process.

6. D **Section 9.1.3.1**
Not possessing the appropriate skill and capacity can significantly impact the product quality of the project.

7. B **Section 9.2**
Choice A is wrong because the Develop Project Team process strives to improve the competencies and interaction of team members to enhance project performance; acquire resources is not a *PMBOK® Guide* process, so choice C is out; for choice D, Plan Procurements is a process under procurement management, although this process may be executed if any team members are contract resources.

8. D **Section 9.2**
Choice A is wrong because RACI refers to the roles documented in a Responsibility Assignment Matrix (RAM); for choice B, product grade reflects the technical characteristics of a product, not its functionality; for choice C, CIP does not specifically affect how you select resources.

9. A **Section 9.2.2.4**
Although having remote workers can impact how you manage time, quality and integration, having remote workers REQUIRES that you leverage tools and techniques for virtual teams.

10. B **Section 9.2.2.4**
Choice B is correct because the assumption here is that team members have a choice to work remotely.

11. B **Section 9.3.2.5**
Meetings without a purpose are not always productive, so choice A is out; although choice C is a good idea, it may not be financially or logistically possible; chat is not the best way to build rapport, so choice D is out; getting people to meet each other face-to-face becomes extremely valuable especially when a large remote team is being utilized.

12. B   Section 9.4.2.3

This is an example of managing conflict. Choices A and C are not the best answers as they may put the technical architect and lead programmer in a defensive position; for choice D, dis-inviting contributors to your team does not instill confidence and team work.

13. A   Section 9.4.2.4

A risk is an event that has a probability of occurring, while obstacles have already occurred, so choice B is out; choice C is a restriction but it doesn't necessarily mean that it will hinder the team's ability; choice D is a significant point or event in the project.

14. B   Section 9.4.2.5

Leadership is not about ignoring or shifting the problem. It is about determining, along with the team members, how to solve problems and work together to achieve goals.

15. C   Section 9.4.2

Project performance appraisals address individual team member needs for improving performance and will most likely not be part of a formal project review with senior management. It may, however, be addressed indirectly within the risks presented.

CASE STUDY SUGGESTED SOLUTION

Exercise 9-1:
RAM for the Lawrence RV Garage Project

Responsibility Assignment Matrix										
	Project Management	Site Work	Foundation/Slab	Framing	Dry-in	Exterior	Rough Utilities	Interior	Grounds	Acceptance
Concrete crew			P						P	
Finish carpentry crew								P		
Lath & Plaster contractor						P				
General contractor	A	R	R	R	R	R	R	R	R	R
Architect	A	I	I	I	I	I	I	I	I	I
Owner	A	I	I	I	I	I	I	I	I	A
Inspector		A	A	A	A	A	A	A	A	A
Electric company		P					P			
Site excavation crew		P							P	
Electric contractor		P					P	P		
Plumbing contractor							P	P		
Framing crew				P	P	P	P			
Roofing contractor					P					
Heating and AC contractor							P	P		
Insulation contractor								P		
Drywall crew								P		
Painting crew								P		

P = Participant
R = Responsible
A = Approval
I = Input Required

9

COMMUNICATIONS

10

COMMUNICATIONS MANAGEMENT

One of the primary and most important roles of the project manager is communication — communication of project objectives, management strategies and the project plan. A project manager's responsibility is to facilitate understanding, thereby enhancing the team's effectiveness.

Inadequate communication, one-way communication, incomplete messages and unclear messages are common problems in many projects. Communications skills fall under both general management and project management skills and are necessary for effective exchange of information. The project manager has a responsibility to:
- Know what kind of message to send
- Know how to translate the message
- Build consensus and confidence, not compromise

Many of the questions in the communications management section of the PMP exam are taken from the *PMBOK® Guide*. There will be questions on specific PMI terms and concepts; however, there will also be many general questions that require you to choose the best answer. Common sense and your own experience will play a large role in your ability to answer the questions on this topic.

EXAM TIP
90% of the project manager's time is spent communicating (from Kerzner, page 232).

10

You will most likely have questions related to formal and informal communication, verbal versus written communication and push versus pull communication. You are also likely to have questions related to analyzing stakeholders so that you can manage them.

Things to Know

1. The five processes of communications management:
   - **Identify Stakeholders**
   - **Plan Communications**
   - **Distribute Information**
   - **Manage Stakeholder Expectations**
   - **Report Performance**

2. **Stakeholder Analysis** and **Stakeholder Register**
3. **Communications Requirements Analysis**
4. **Communications Channels**
5. Use of **Communications Technology**
6. The **Communications Model**
7. **Barriers to Communication**
8. **Communications Methods**
9. **Communications Management Plan**
10. Purpose of **Performance Reports**
11. **Communicating** to **Manage Expectations**
12. Communicating with **Issues Logs** and **Action Logs**
13. **Variance Analysis** and **Forecasting for Performance Reporting**

Key Definitions

Active Listening: the receiver confirms listening by nodding, eye contact and asking questions for clarification.

Effective Listening: the receiver attentively watches the sender to observe physical gestures and facial expressions. In addition, the receiver contemplates responses, asks pertinent questions, repeats or summarizes what the sender has sent and provides feedback.

Feedback: affirming understanding and providing information.

Noise: anything that compromises the original meaning of the message.

Nonverbal Communication: about 55% of all communication, based on what is commonly called body language.

Paralingual Communication: optional vocal effects, the tone of voice that may help communicate meaning.

IDENTIFY STAKEHOLDERS PROCESS

Because project managers spend a large portion of their time communicating, they must ensure they have identified all the project stakeholders who should receive information. Stakeholders may be actively involved, they may be affected by the project, or they may have influence over the project.

Along with identifying stakeholders, the project team should perform an analysis of stakeholders' power, interest, influence, involvement and expectations so they can develop an appropriate strategy for communicating with them.

> **EXAM TIP**
> Stakeholders can have varied and also conflicting needs for communication.

Inputs into this process include the project charter, which defines internal and external stakeholders, procurement documents, organization structure, templates for assessing stakeholders and lessons learned.

Stakeholder Analysis

Once stakeholders have been identified, the project team will conduct an analysis of their interests, influence, involvement and expectations. The team will:

- Identify potential stakeholders and include as much demographic information as feasible
- Assess and prioritize attributes that influence a stakeholder's significance and importance to the project, such as:
  - **Power:** legitimate authority or other types of power over the project, control of resources and sources of control over the project
  - **Interest:** the beneficial or detrimental stake that a stakeholder has in the project, support or opposition to the project and indifference to the project
  - **Influence:** level of participation, contribution and connection to the project
  - **Impact:** effect of a stakeholder's influence

- Use models to combine effects of the attributes evaluated, such as a power/interest grid; an example of a power/interest grid is shown in Figure 10-1
- Assess their responses to potential project situations

High	High Power	High Power	
	Low Interest	High Interest	
Power	Low Power	Low Power	
Low	Low Interest	High Interest	
	Low	**Interest**	High

Figure 10-1
Power/Interest Grid

One output of this process is a **Stakeholder Register**, where the identification and analysis of stakeholders is documented. Another output is a stakeholder management strategy that summarizes key stakeholders, their level of participation and the functional organizations represented.

PLAN COMMUNICATIONS PROCESS

During the Plan Communications process, the communications requirements of the stakeholders are determined. These stakeholders' informational needs are documented in the communications management plan and contain communication requirements such as:
- Who needs what information?
- When will they need it?
- How will it be given to them?
- Who will give it to them?

Communications Requirements Analysis

This tool is intended to focus on the project stakeholders' needs for information and should include the type and value of information and how it will be presented.

The project manager must take into consideration and analyze all of the information provided to stakeholders across the organization, as well as information external to the organization.

Understanding the logistics of the project team is important. If teams are virtual, it is even more critical to ensure that communication between team members is covered within this analysis.

The Communications Channels

There are many communication channels utilized by a project manager; these include:
- Upward communication to management
- Lateral communication to peers, other functional groups and customers
- Downward communication to subordinates

Communication channels are the number of one-to-one communications that exist for the team. The more channels, the more complex the communications analysis. Figure 10-2 on the next page shows communications channels.

There is a simple formula to determine the number of communication channels that exist on a project:

(n[n - 1])/2 where n indicates the number of people

For example, if 5 people work on a project, n = 5, communication channels = 5(4)/2 = 10.

With 7 people, n = 7, channels = 7(6)/2 = 21. The number of channels has more than doubled with just two additional team members.

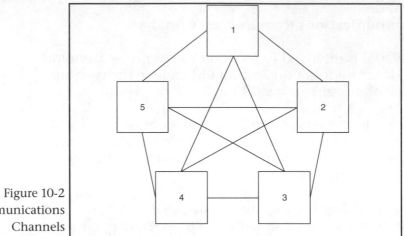

Figure 10-2
Communications
Channels

Case Study Exercise

Exercise 10-1: How many channels are there on a project with 50 people?

Communications Technology

In analyzing communications, you must also address the types of technologies available to facilitate communications and make their transfer more effective. Some considerations include the urgency of information receipt, the types of technology available, the amount of training required, the length of the project, and the number of **Virtual Team** members and stakeholders.

The Communications Model

PMI emphasizes the basic communication model that consists of the following components: a sender, a receiver, a medium through which messages are sent and received, noise and feedback. Figure 10-3 on the following page shows a communications model.

The sender encodes the message, chooses the medium in which to send the message and attaches symbols, gestures or expressions to confirm that the message is understood. As the message passes through the medium, it encounters "noise" that interferes with transmission and meaning. The receiver decodes the message based

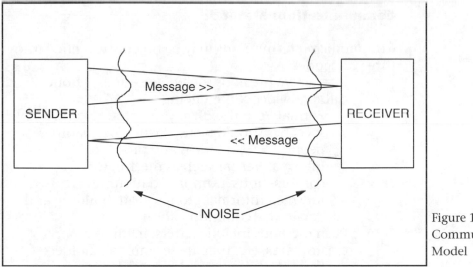

Figure 10-3
Communications
Model

on background, experience, language and culture. The receiver sends a feedback message through the medium to the sender that may be an acknowledgement of receipt or a response indicating understanding.

Barriers to Communication

In addition to the large number of communication links required as the resources increase, other barriers also exist to deter effective communication. Some of these barriers are:

- Ineffective listening
- Improper encoding of messages
- Improper decoding of messages
- Naysayers
- Hostility
- Language
- Culture

Language and **Culture** are also sources of problems in communication. Additional material on this topic is found in Chapter 13 on professional responsibility.

Communications Methods

Communications methods may be broadly classified into three categories:
- **Interactive** methods include meetings, phone calls and videoconferencing
  - **Formal Verbal** such as presentations and speeches should be used when persuading people to accept ideas and products
  - **Informal Verbal** such as meetings, conversations, humor and inquiries are used for small informal groups, team building and day-to-day communication
- **Push** methods include letters, memos, reports, emails, faxes, etc. that are sent to stakeholders
  - **Formal Written** should be used for key documents such as project plans, the project charter, communicating over long distances, complex problems, legal documents and long or technical situations for a wide and varied audience
  - **Informal Written** should be used for status updates, information updates and day-to-day communication
- **Pull** methods include intranet sites and knowledge repositories and are more likely to use formal written methods

EXAM TIP
Email is an informal communication method according to PMI.

Communications Management Plan

The communications management plan is the only output of the Communications Planning process. It should be created by the project manager and becomes part of the project management plan. The communications management plan must also include the:
- Stakeholder communication requirements
- Information required
- Method used to convey information
- Reporting responsibilities
- Distribution schedule
- Performance reporting process

The use of a communications matrix can help identify and organize this information. Note that the **Organizational Structure** (functional, matrix or projectized) will influence the information and distribution channels of the project. There are many formats for communications matrices. No matter what the format, the objective is to identify who is being communicated to, when communication is needed, how communications will be distributed and who is responsible for their delivery.

Case Study Exercise

Exercise 10-2: Use the table on the following page to develop a sample communications matrix for the Lawrence RV Garage Project. Identify the different kinds of communication vehicles, their frequency, who is responsible for creating each one and who receives each one.

DISTRIBUTE INFORMATION PROCESS

The Distribute Information process involves the execution of the communications management plan by making the identified needed information available to stakeholders. It also involves responding to various ad hoc requests for information from stakeholders.

Although it is performed during all phases of the **Project Life Cycle**, the focus here is in the executing process group.

Performance Reports

Performance reports are the main vehicle to distribute information. They can be used to determine progress and work completed, status, issues and action items and forecasts. Forecasts may be prepared using earned value analysis, discussed in Chapter 7, or by developing new estimates, reviewing past projects, conducting an audit, etc.

> **EXAM TIP**
> Performance reports must be aligned with the stakeholder register.

10

Communications Matrix							

R = Report progress
P = Prepare Report
A = Attend meeting (* = when appropriate)
RR = Review Report

MANAGE STAKEHOLDER EXPECTATIONS PROCESS

Managing stakeholders' communications, expectations and requirements is addressed in this process. The project manager is responsible for helping stakeholders understand the risks and benefits of the project.

Communicating to Manage Stakeholder Expectations

Project managers should:
- Influence expectations to increase the likelihood of project acceptance
- Address concerns and anticipate future problems
- Resolve issues or risks that have occurred, which may result in project changes

The project manager uses various methods to communicate effectively, such as frequent and regular meetings, developing and tracking issues via an issues log and resolving conflict.

Face-to-face meetings should be used as much as possible in the Manage Stakeholder Expectations process. When stakeholders' presence is virtual, other means such as phone calls, mail, teleconferencing, web meetings and other electronic tools must be used extensively to ensure effective communications.

Issues Logs are a key tool in communicating about and monitoring a project. An issues log should contain the owner assigned to resolve the issue and the target date for the resolution of the issue. An **Action Item Log** is the same as an issues log when it is used as a control document of issue owner's resolution. The log of resolved issues together with the solution to the issue become primary outputs of this process. Any approved change requests, corrective actions, updates to the project management plan and the organizational process assets (including the lessons learned) are also outputs of this process.

REPORT PERFORMANCE PROCESS

The Report Performance process involves collecting and disseminating project information, communicating **Progress**, utilization of resources and **Forecasting** future progress and status. The work results of other processes are analyzed and combined into performance reports. These performance reports may include:

- Performance and status reports
- Trend and forecasting reports
- Approved change requests
- Process updates
- Risk monitoring and control outcomes

Variance Analysis

Earned Value techniques are very helpful in providing answers to common time and cost performance questions such as:

- Where are we in the project schedule?
- What is the percentage of completion?
- What is the estimated time to complete the project?
- Are we ahead or behind schedule?
- What are actual expenditures to date?
- What are the committed expenditures?
- What are the estimated remaining costs?
- Are we under budget or over budget?

Forecasting Methods

As part of reporting project performance, project managers must understand and provide estimates of future performance of the project in terms of a forecast.

General categories of forecasting methods include:

- **Time Series:** the use of historical data as the basis of the forecast; an example of a time series method is the use of CPI in earned value analysis
- **Economic Method:** identification of a causal effect on the outcome of the project; for example, the volatility of the price of oil may have a significant

impact on the project team's ability to control material costs

- **Judgmental Method:** the use of expert judgment as a basis for cost

There are other methods that can be used. The project manager must determine the appropriate method and apply it to the performance reporting. Forecasting techniques are described in more detail in Chapter 7 (Cost).

SAMPLE PMP EXAM QUESTIONS ON COMMUNICATIONS MANAGEMENT

Communications — Initiating Questions

1. The project charter includes information about those who may be _____ the project.
   a) Disinterested in
   b) Affected by
   c) Financially invested in
   d) Working on

2. You are a project manager on a hotel construction project. The CEO and sponsor of the project retired from the business and a new CEO has been named. One of the first things you should do as the project manager is:

   a) Introduce yourself to the new CEO and tell him/her how wonderful your team is
   b) Schedule a meeting with the CEO to review the detail project schedule and earned value analysis that you finished last Friday
   c) Determine the communication needs of the stakeholder and modify the communications management plan
   d) Keep your head down and continue to perform your job

3. An example of an assumption as it relates to communications planning can be:

   a) The physical location of team members
   b) That the entire team has access to the centralized document repository
   c) That there are enough resources available to support the project
   d) That there are enough funds to ensure successful completion of the project

Notes:

Communications — Planning Questions

4. You are a project manager on a hotel construction project. The CEO and sponsor of the project retired from the business and a new CEO has been named. The new CEO wants the team to provide a monthly formal presentation to the senior management team. You will need to:

   a) Throw out all prior status reports and create this new one from scratch
   b) Add the monthly deliverable to the project schedule and budget
   c) Hire an administrative assistant since you don't know how to use PowerPoint
   d) Bring the team together and assign team members to each of the agenda items for this review

5. Noise can impact communication because:

   a) It interferes with understanding the message
   b) It is too loud for stakeholders to hear well
   c) It distracts the sender
   d) It is usually deliberate

6. For effective communication, a message is encoded in the appropriate language, sent and then the receiver decodes the message. The message may not be decoded correctly due to _____.

   a) Feedback message
   b) Noise
   c) Sender
   d) Encoding

10

7. Many factors go into the planning of communications needs for a project. All of the following should be considerations EXCEPT:

   a) Expected project staffing
   b) Information urgency
   c) Project duration
   d) Past experience with a similar project

Communications — Executing Questions

8. All of the following communication skills are used in both project management and general management EXCEPT:

   a) Active listening
   b) Probing
   c) Body language
   d) Persuading

9. You are assigned as a new project manager of a project that is 40% complete. You are assigned due to the sudden departure of the prior project manager. You review the current issues logs and meeting minutes. You determine that there has been insufficient communication to the stakeholders and you immediately put in place:

   a) Administrative closure procedures
   b) A formal project review
   c) A weekly face-to-face status meeting
   d) A quality audit

10. When a customer requests additional work not covered under the contract, what kind of correspondence with the customer is recommended?

   a) Formal written communication
   b) Formal verbal communication
   c) Informal written communication
   d) Email communication

Notes:

11. As the project manager on a software development project, you schedule phase end lessons learned reviews with the entire project team. The results of the session will be:

   a) Distributed to all stakeholders regardless of the results that are gathered
   b) Kept by the project manager for future projects
   c) Shared only with the team members as a learning experience
   d) Used to identify who on the team was not performing up to standard

12. You are assigned as a new project manager of a project that is 40% complete. You review the current issues logs and meeting minutes. You determine that there are three critical issues that have not yet been resolved and these issues appear to be the reason for the stakeholders' frustration. One of the first actions you must take is to:

   a) Review the outstanding issues with the stakeholders and discuss options for corrective action
   b) Update the communications management plan
   c) Increase the frequency of communication to stakeholders
   d) Perform a contingency reserve analysis to determine the amount of cost reserves available

Notes:

10

13. As the project manager of a very complex business process change project you have several groups of stakeholders that will be negatively impacted by the project delivery. It is your responsibility to engage the management of these groups and ensure a successful implementation. You employ many different methods to overcome the expected resistance to change and are able to gain the trust and confidence of these impacted groups. This is an example of using _____ skills.

   a) Negotiating
   b) Public speaking
   c) Management
   d) Interpersonal

Communications — Monitoring and Controlling Questions

14. The purpose of the Report Performance process is to provide all of the following EXCEPT:

   a) Forecasting of the outcome of the project
   b) Analysis to develop recommended corrective action as required
   c) Generation of requested changes as required
   d) Development of an integrated cost and schedule baseline

Notes:

15. You are the project manager on a large construction project that is 50% complete and about 10% over budget to date. You are asked to put together a forecast of the budget at completion. Your organization doesn't have any formal forecasting methods so you employ a method that looks at past similar projects to determine the likelihood of the project finishing on time and no more than the 10% over budget state. This is an example of a _____ method of forecasting.

a) Judgmental
b) Econometric
c) Time series
d) Estimate at completion

Notes:

10

ANSWERS AND REFERENCES FOR SAMPLE PMP EXAM QUESTIONS ON COMMUNICATIONS MANAGEMENT
Section numbers refer to the *PMBOK® Guide.*

1. B   **Section 10.1.1.1**
Although both choices B and D could be correct answers, the project charter may not be detailed enough to identify those who would be working on the project; however, the charter should always include those stakeholders who will be affected by the project.

2. C   **Section 10.1.2.1**
Although some of these answers appear to be correct, before embarking on a campaign to demonstrate your team's effectiveness, the best thing you can do is to LISTEN to what the new stakeholder will want from you. Engage in active listening and review the stakeholder analysis.

3. B   **Chapter 10**
Choice A is a constraint to communication planning; choices C and D are assumptions with human resources and cost management, not communications.

4. B   **Section 10.2**
Choices A and C are not necessarily the case in all projects; choice D is not a bad answer, but the question doesn't necessarily define the size and agenda items of the presentation. Choice B is the most correct answer because the development of the presentation is added work that will need to be performed on the project to support the stakeholder's needs.

5. A   **Section 10.2.2.3**
Noise in this context does not mean the loudness of the sound. It can be a distraction the receiver is experiencing and is usually not deliberate.

6. **B** **Section 10.2.2.3**
   Although choices A, C and D all interfere with the transmission or understanding of the message (noise), choice B is the most general answer. Effective communication only occurs if the receiver has decoded and understands the message.

7. **D** **Section 10.2.2.2**
   Although past experience with similar projects may be considered, unless that past project was with the same stakeholders, the other three answers are more appropriate as factors to consider.

8. **C** **Chapter 10**
   Body language is a dimension of communication and not a skill.

9. **C** **Chapter 10**
   Administrative closure procedures establish the methodology to transfer the project products or services to production and/or operations, so choice A is out; for choice B, a formal project review is not necessary; the best answer is to start increasing communication with the stakeholders; choice D is out because a quality audit addresses the project policies and procedures.

10. **A** **Chapter 10**
    This question is an example of a question where all the answers are correct. The reader has to choose the "best" answer, based on experience and common sense. When working with a customer and when you don't want to have any misinterpretation, formal written communication is best in managing the stakeholder relationship.

11. A   Section 10.3.3.1
Lessons learned are outputs of the Distribute Information process and should be shared with all stakeholders. Hopefully the project manager will not keep the lessons learned to him or herself, so choice B is out; in addition, just sharing the results with the team is not optimal either, so choice C is out; for choice D, lessons learned reviews should not be perceived as negative events; you must take great care in making these reviews a learning experience so that people will openly participate in future reviews.

12. A   Section 10.4
It is always best to take the time to understand the issues before acting. For choice B, there is no need to update the communications management plan if there is no need to change; for choice C, there is no need to increase the frequency of communication unless the cause of missing the issues was due to the lack of communication, but that doesn't appear to be the case in this example; choice D does not apply because a reserve analysis compares the amount of the contingency reserves remaining to the amount of risk remaining.

13. D   Section 10.4.2.2
Overcoming resistance to change is an interpersonal skill that is critical in this kind of situation.

14. D   Section 10.5
The cost and schedule baseline was developed in the cost management and time management processes.

15. A   Section 10.5.2.2
Forecasting by analogy is a form of judgmental method.

10

CASE STUDY SUGGESTED SOLUTIONS

Exercise 10-1

$[50 (50 - 1)]/2 = 2450/2 = 1225$

Exercise 10-2
Communications Matrix for the Lawrence RV Garage Project

Communications Matrix								
	Report Progress Weekly	Weekly Status Meeting	Weekly Earned Value Reports	Phase Review Meeting	Phase-end Earned Value Reports	Final Project EV Reports	Final Project Acceptance	Lessons Learned Report
Owner		A	RR	A	RR	RR	A	RR
Architect		A	RR	A	RR	RR	A	RR
General contractor	R	A	P	A	P	P	A	P
Site excavation crew	R	A*						
Concrete crew	R	A*						
Framing crew	R	A*						
Drywall crew	R	A*						
Painting crew	R	A*						
Finish carpentry crew	R	A*						
Electric contractor	R	A*	RR	A*	RR	RR		RR
Plumbing contractor	R	A*	RR	A*	RR	RR		RR
Roofing contractor	R	A*	RR	A*	RR	RR		RR
Insulation contractor	R	A*	RR	A*	RR	RR		RR
Heating and AC contractor	R	A*	RR	A*	RR	RR		RR
Lath & Plaster contractor	R	A*	RR	A*	RR	RR		RR
Inspector							A*	
Electric company							A*	

R = Report progress
P = Prepare Report
A = Attend meeting (* = when appropriate)
RR = Review Report

10

RISK

CHAPTER 11 | RISK

RISK MANAGEMENT

Project risk management is considered by some to be the most difficult section of the PMP certification exam. Exam takers consider it demanding because it addresses many concepts that project managers have not been exposed to in their work or education. Questions, however, do correspond closely to *PMBOK® Guide* material so you should not have much difficulty if you study the terminology found in this guide.

The mathematical questions are not very difficult; however, they do require you to know certain theories, such as expected monetary value and decision tree analysis. You should also expect questions related to levels of risk faced by both buyer and seller based on various types of contracts.

Project managers have an ethical responsibility to communicate potential risks and their impact on the project's success.

Things to Know

1. The six processes of risk management:
   * **Plan Risk Management**
   * **Identify Risks**
   * **Perform Qualitative Risk Analysis**
   * **Perform Quantitative Risk Analysis**
   * **Plan Risk Responses**
   * **Monitor and Control Risks**
2. Understand the **Utility Theory**
3. **Risk Categories** and their use
4. The tools and techniques of **Identifying Risk**
   * **Brainstorming**
   * **Delphi Technique**
   * **Interviewing**
   * **SWOT Analysis**
   * The **Risk Register**
5. **Risk Probability and Impact**
6. Quantitative analysis tools of
   * **Interviewing**
   * **Probability Distribution**
   * **Sensitivity Analysis**

> **EXAM TIP**
> PMI places heavy emphasis on the concept that project risk can be decreased significantly by actively planning, identifying, assessing and developing responses to potential risk events and managing their impact on the project.

- Expected Monetary Value Analysis
- Decision Tree
- Monte Carlo Simulation

7. Strategies for **Risk Responses**

Key Definitions

Contingency Plan: a response to a risk event that will be implemented only if the risk event occurs.

Contingency Reserve: a dollar or time value that is added to the project schedule or budget that reflects and accounts for risk that is anticipated for the project.

Decision Theory: a technique for assisting in reaching decisions under uncertainty and risk. It points to the best possible course whether or not the forecasts are accurate.

Fallback Plan: a response plan that will be implemented if the primary response plan is ineffective.

Heuristics: rules of thumb for accomplishing tasks. Heuristics are easy and intuitive ways to deal with uncertain situations; however, they tend to result in probability assessments that are biased.

Issue: a risk event that has occurred.

Opportunities: risk events or conditions that are favorable to the project.

Residual Risk: in implementing a risk response plan, the risk that cannot be eliminated.

Risk: an uncertain event or condition that could have a positive or negative impact on the project objectives. Therefore, the primary elements of risk that must be determined are:

- Probability of the risk event or condition occurring
- Impact of the occurrence, if it does occur
- Expected time the risk event may occur
- Anticipated frequency of the risk event occurring

11

Secondary Risk: in implementing a risk response, a new risk that is introduced as a result of the response.

Stakeholder Risk Tolerance: the stakeholders' attitude toward risk is an enterprise environmental factor that must be considered in the risk management plan. Risk responses should balance stakeholders' risk attitudes.

Threat: risk events or conditions that are unfavorable to the project.

Workarounds: unplanned responses to risks that were previously unidentified or accepted.

PLAN RISK MANAGEMENT PROCESS

The Plan Risk Management process plans for risks that may occur during the project. It is the process of deciding how to approach and plan for activities to handle project risks and documenting these decisions in a risk management plan, which is the primary output of the risk management planning process. This important document is a subsidiary component of the project management plan.

Key inputs to this process are the project scope statement, the schedule, cost and communications management plans and the **Enterprise Environmental Factors**. The organizational **Culture** and attitudes towards risk are factors that must be considered as part of the project environment. Organizational and individual tolerances for risk are not often considered an aspect of project management but they will make a difference to the approach taken toward project risks. Since different organizations and individuals have varying levels of tolerance for risk, decisions should be made based on the tolerances of the project team. An appropriate method for describing **Risk Tolerance** is the **Utility Theory**.

> **EXAM TIP**
> The risk management plan contains:
> 1. Risk approach and methodology
> 2. Roles and responsibilities of the risk management team
> 3. Risk management budget
> 4. Timing of the risk management process
> 5. Risk categories
> 6. Definitions of probability and impact
> 7. Probability and impact matrix
> 8. Revised stakeholder risk tolerances
> 9. Risk planning report formats
> 10. Methods of tracking risks

11

Utility Theory

The project manager is called on to make decisions dealing with project risk. These decisions will be based on the various stakeholders' tolerances for risk as described using the utility theory.

Figure 11-1 depicts the three structures of the utility theory. The x-axis denotes the money at stake and the y-axis denotes utility, or the amount of satisfaction the person obtains from the payoff.

- **Risk Averse:** when there is more money at stake, the risk averter's satisfaction diminishes; he or she prefers a more certain outcome and demands a premium to accept projects of high risk
- **Risk Neutral:** tolerance for risk remains the same as the money at stake increases
- **Risk Seeker:** for the risk seeker, the higher the stakes, the better; as risk increases, the risk seeker's satisfaction increases; he or she is even willing to pay a penalty to take on projects of high risk

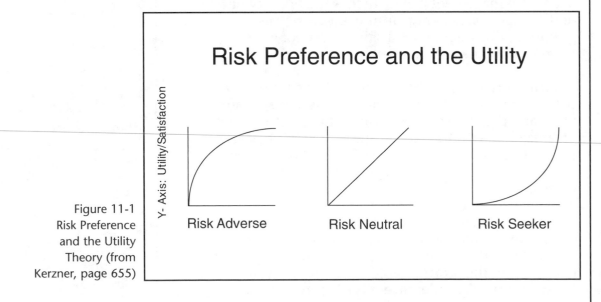

Figure 11-1
Risk Preference and the Utility Theory (from Kerzner, page 655)

Risk Categories

Risk categories are commonly included in the **Risk Management Plan**. An organization may have a standard set of risk sources that should be considered in advance of the **Identify Risks** process. These sources of risk are defined in the **Risk Breakdown Structure** (RBS). There may be many categories of risk, including:

- **External Risks** such as from vendors, regulations, customers and market conditions. For example, you know that snow storms will occur in the northwest but you do not know when and how many snow storms will occur (Note that *force majeure* risks, such as earthquakes, floods, acts of terrorism, etc., should be covered under disaster recovery procedures instead of risk management.)
- Project management risks, such as poor estimates of time and resources or the lack of skills and knowledge in project management concepts and discipline by the project manager and/or team members
- Organizational risks, such as resource conflicts, a delay in the availability of resources or a lack of funds
- Technical risk, such as complex or new software technology, quality or performance issues or unrealistic project goals

> **EXAM TIP**
>
> A risk breakdown structure (RBS) can provide a structure that can ensure a systematic evaluation and identification of all project risk. Do not confuse it with the resource breakdown structure discussed in the *PMBOK® Guide* Chapter 9.

IDENTIFY RISKS PROCESS

The Identify Risks process involves identifying and documenting the types of risks that may occur during the project. It is important to think of each risk event as having a three-part anatomy:

- The uncertain event or condition that poses the risk
- The impact of that event or situation
- The source of the risk

The identification of risks is an iterative process that occurs with the help of the project team, stakeholders and even people outside the organization. Information gathering is a tool or technique of this process.

10

Information can be gathered by many means, including brainstorming, the Delphi Technique, interviewing and Strength, Weaknesses, Opportunities and Threats (SWOT) analysis.

Brainstorming

Information gathered through brainstorming is:
- Used extensively in project planning
- Possibly used to postulate risk scenarios for a particular project
- Improved by including participants with a variety of backgrounds
- Helpful in project team building
- Effective in finding solutions to potential problems

The Delphi Technique

The Delphi Technique:
- Derives a consensus using a panel of experts to arrive at a convergent solution to a specific problem
- Is useful in arriving at probability assessments relating to risk events in which the risk impacts are large and critical

Interviewing

Experienced project managers or subject matter experts are interviewed to identify project risks based on their knowledge of technical or external issues.

SWOT Analysis

SWOT analysis is a technique that:
- Examines potential risks from the perspectives of strengths, weaknesses, opportunities and threats, i.e., SWOT, to look for internally generated risk events

Risk Register

The only output of the Risk Identification process is the **Risk Register** that contains a list of the identified

EXAM TIP

The risk register is a critical deliverable in any project. Every process within the risk management knowledge area includes updates to the risk register as part of the process outputs, reinforcing the concept of an iterative approach to risk planning.

11

risks and potential responses. This risk register is used to document risk planning and assessment activities and to track the status, triggers, and responses to project risks. The identification, tracking and reviewing of project risks is ongoing throughout the **Project Life Cycle**. The risk register is a component of the risk management plan and the project management plan. It is updated in each of the risk management processes. An example of a risk register is shown in Figure 11-2 .

Risk Events	Category	Probability	Impact	Score/ Priority	Risk Response Strategy	Risk Trigger
Poor Estimate of Testing	Project Management	2	4	8	Mitigate	Missed Milestone
Part Failure	Technical	2	2	4	Transfer	Test Failure
PM Promoted	Organization	3	4	12	Accept	Reorgani-zation
Shipping Delay	External	4	5	20	Mitigate	Labor Dispute

Figure 11-2
Sample Risk Register

PERFORM QUALITATIVE RISK ANALYSIS PROCESS

Once risks have been identified, they must be analyzed to determine the likelihood of the risk occurring (risk probability) and the consequences it could have on the project (risk impact) if and when it occurs. This process has an advantage of being a rapid and cost effective way to assess risks.

Qualitative risk analysis involves the activities of:
- Assessing the probability and impact of identified risks
- Determining timing and urgency
- Prioritizing risks
- Ranking risk events in order of importance
- Evaluating the quality of data related to risk
- Determining which risks require additional analysis

Risk Probability and Impact

The risk management plan should define the probability and impact scale to be used in assessing and determining the relative importance of each risk for the project. By calculating the risk score, which is the product of the probability times the impact, the project team will determine if the risk is low, moderate or high priority.

Probability & Impact Score for a Risk						
Probability	Risk Score = P X I					
5	5	10	15	20	25	HIGH
4	4	8	12	16	20	
3	3	6	9	12	15	MED
2	2	4	6	8	10	
1	1	2	3	4	5	LOW
	1	2	3	4	5	
	Impact (Ratio Scale)					

Figure 11-3
Prioritizing Risks

11

EXAM TIP

The probability impact matrix tool is an easy and effective way for the project manager to access the priority of issues on the project.

Example of a Risk Event: We have a year-long project in northern Maine and need to calculate the risk of snow impacting our schedule. The likelihood that a snowstorm will occur in Maine this winter is high. But since our workforce works virtually, the impact of a large storm on workforce productivity is low. This risk event would have a score of 5(high probability)X1(low impact) for a score of 5. It would be reflected in the upper left hand corner of the grid in Figure 11-3 and considered a medium risk.

PERFORM QUANTITATIVE RISK ANALYSIS PROCESS

Quantitative risk analysis involves further analyzing identified risk events for their effect on **Project Objectives**. This analysis may include:

- Numerically analyzing the effects, often stating the effects in monetary terms
- Evaluating the range of impacts of risks on project objectives of cost, schedule, scope and quality
- Determining the extent of overall project risk
- Using probabilistic models to determine trends, ranges of acceptable risk and probability of success for a given value

Interviewing

Just as interviews with subject-matter experts and other stakeholders are useful in identifying risks, they are also important in quantifying risks and defining ranges of values. These values typically take the form of three-point estimates for cost or duration, which are used in revising budget or time estimates.

Probability Distributions

Various types of probability distributions are used to represent the uncertainty that risks represent. Discrete distributions may be used in developing **Decision Tree** values. Continuous distributions, such as the beta or triangular distributions shown in Chapter 1, are used in modeling and simulations.

Sensitivity Analysis

Sensitivity analysis is a modeling technique used to compare the relative importance of variables. It may be applied to different risk events and the most sensitive variable is the one that has the greatest influence on the project. The implication is that the project team should focus on the risks with the greatest sensitivity.

Expected Monetary Value Analysis

A risk event may be quantified by combining probability and impact, which is the expected monetary value (EMV).
- For opportunities, the EMV will be a positive value
- For threats, the EMV will be a negative value
- EMV is the basis for most simulation programs
- EMV provides a predictor of the outcome that has the least bias
- EMV is used with the discrete risk events depicted in a decision tree

Figure 11-4
A Decision Tree

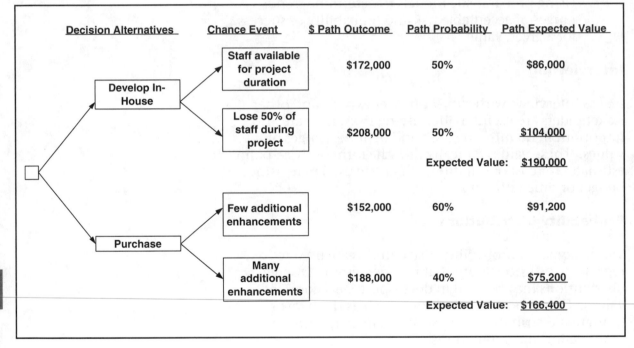

Decision Alternatives	Chance Event	$ Path Outcome	Path Probability	Path Expected Value
Develop In-House	Staff available for project duration	$172,000	50%	$86,000
	Lose 50% of staff during project	$208,000	50%	$104,000
			Expected Value:	$190,000
Purchase	Few additional enhancements	$152,000	60%	$91,200
	Many additional enhancements	$188,000	40%	$75,200
			Expected Value:	$166,400

Decision Tree

A decision tree is used when a choice will be made among several options and those choices are affected by several key variables.
- The decision tree diagram depicts key interactions among risk events
- The outcomes are typically described in monetary terms

- The risk events may relate to time, cost, scope or quality considerations
- Each branch of the decision tree is defined by probability and impact
- Each individual path has a value described by EMV

Figure 11-4 on the previous page shows a decision tree analysis for the choice of developing software in-house versus purchasing software. The risk if they develop software in-house is that they will lose 50% of the staff during the project. This will cause the cost of the project to increase to $208,000 from $172,000.

The risk for purchased software is the uncertain number of enhancements that will be necessary for implementation. If there are few enhancements, the cost will be $152,000. If there are many enhancements, the cost will be $188,000.

Based on the identified risks, the expected cost for developing in-house is $190,000 and for purchase is $166,400. Purchasing software is the better choice.

Monte Carlo Simulation

With the advent of specialized software add-ins to most project management software packages, a Monte Carlo simulation is an accessible and powerful technique to model the project and its associated risks. The model includes the following:
- A range of outcomes for each variable
- A specified probability distribution
- A random number generation of the results of the project activities based on the specified range and probability distribution
- A large number of iterations of the project activities

The results of the simulation provide a cumulative probability distribution that shows the likelihood of achieving a particular value of cost or time. It helps the project team determine the amount of contingency that would be appropriate for the project.

PLAN RISK RESPONSES PROCESS

During the Plan Risk Responses process, the action plans for how risks should be handled are determined. This process includes the activities of:
- Developing options
- Determining actions
- Enhancing opportunities
- Reducing threats
- Assigning responsibility for risks
- Adding resources or activities in the project management plan
- Determining appropriate responses based on the priority of risks

The primary outputs of this process are the updates to the risk register, updates to the project management plan and any risk-related contractual agreements.

Risk Response Strategies

The tools and techniques for risk response planning have been divided into strategies for threats, opportunities, and contingent response strategies.

The strategy for both threats and opportunities is:
- **Accept:** acceptance means accepting the consequences of the risk; it can be active, such as developing a contingency plan should the risk occur, or it can be passive, such as accepting a lower profit if some activities overrun

The strategies for **Negative Threats** or **Risks** are:
- **Avoid:** avoidance eliminates a specific threat, usually by eliminating the cause; examples of avoidance include not doing the project or doing the project in a different way so that the risk no longer exists
- **Transfer:** transference reduces the direct risk by shifting it to a third party, such as insurance companies, clients or vendors; transferring does not eliminate the overall risk

11

- **Mitigate:** mitigation reduces the EMV of a risk event by reducing the probability of its occurrence or reducing the impact of the risk; an example of mitigation would be using proven technology to lessen the probability that a product will not work

The strategies for **Positive Opportunities** or **Risks** are:
- **Exploit:** exploitation increases chances of making the opportunity happen and it helps eliminate the uncertainty
- **Share:** sharing an opportunity is done with a third party, and so leverages that party's ability to capitalize on the opportunity
- **Enhance:** enhancing increases the probability of an opportunity's occurrence or its positive impact

The strategies for contingent response are:
- **Contingency Plans:** action plans for specific risk events whose expected value has not been reduced to an acceptable level
- **Financial Reserves:** allocations of funds or signature authority to the project manager's contingency reserve
- **Staffing Reallocation Reserve:** reassigning, in an emergency, previously identified individuals with critical knowledge, skill and location availability

> **EXAM TIP**
> Contingency can be planned for any project constraints, such as in time, resources or financial reserves.

Case Study Exercise

Exercise 11-1: Identify at least three potential risk events for the Lawrence RV Garage Project. Perform qualitative analysis on risk events and develop a response plan for each of the three events. Create a risk register summarizing your risk response planning.

MONITOR AND CONTROL RISK PROCESS

The Monitor and Control Risks process involves the tracking of identified risks that have or have not yet occurred, identifying new risks and recalculating risk scores for increased or decreased priority. Thus, the iterative steps of this process are to determine if:

- Risk responses have been implemented as planned
- Risk responses are effective
- Project assumptions are still valid
- Risk exposure has changed
- Risk triggers have occurred
- Policies and procedures have been followed
- New risks are identified
- Risk events have occurred that were previously not defined

Variance and trend analysis are techniques of the monitor and control risk process. **Earned Value Management** and other techniques may be used to monitor project performance. If they show a significant deviation from cost and schedule baselines, project risk may be increasing. Earned value management is discussed in Chapters 6 (Time) and 7 (Cost). Some tips in performing risk monitoring and control are:

- Work the top priority risk events
- Appoint a risk response owner for top risks
- Review performance weekly, as earned value analysis may indicate deviations to investigate
- Work all top risks concurrently
- Reprioritize the top risks as time passes and as new risks are identified and added
- Take corrective actions or use contingency plans as necessary
- Continue tracking and adjusting at regular intervals throughout the project's life cycle
- Use workarounds for unplanned events to minimize loss, repair damage and prevent recurrence of a risk event

SAMPLE PMP EXAM QUESTIONS ON RISK MANAGEMENT

Risk — Planning Questions

1. Why use risk management?

   a) Some businesses have minimal risk
   b) Planning only focuses on the past
   c) Uncertainty is often explicit and formal
   d) Uncertainty is present in all projects

2. Which of the following statements is true regarding project risk?

   a) Risks are primarily related to negative impacts on at least one project objective
   b) Project risk is something that has already happened
   c) Risks may have positive or negative outcomes
   d) Project risk should include the chance of a unique event such as a tsunami

3. Aspects of the organization's environment that contribute to project risk are called risk _____.

   a) Conditions
   b) Probability
   c) Events
   d) Impacts

4. The Identify Risks process identifies which risks _____ affect the project.

   a) Might
   b) Will always
   c) Have a high probability to
   d) Significantly

5. As the project manager on a construction project, you know your company generally prefers aggressive schedule estimates. Your CEO feels strongly that employees need to be challenged and provided a "stretch" goal which increases the chance of exceeding customer expectations. In some cases, extenuating circumstances have caused the organization to miss project schedules, but over 90% of the projects are completed on time to the satisfaction of the customer. Your CEO is an example of a:

   a) Risk accepter
   b) Risk seeker
   c) Risk averter
   d) Risk deflector

6. In performing a probability and impact analysis with your team, the use of _____ is typically required, since there may be little information from past projects.

   a) Current project files
   b) Diagramming techniques
   c) Risk register
   d) Expert judgment

7. As a project manager on a construction project, your team has identified that 20% of all risk events identified are associated with the risk category of human resources. Knowing this information will allow you to:

   a) Hire more people on your project
   b) Develop a risk response plan for human resource risk
   c) Track variances to the plan when risk events occur
   d) Justify the cost of highly qualified team members

Notes:

11

8. The output of a decision tree analysis is:

   a) Expected monetary value for each alternative
   b) A trend for each alternative
   c) Estimate to completion
   d) A probability distribution

9. An input to the Plan Risk Responses process is:

   a) A risk management plan
   b) Risk register updates
   c) Strategies for negative and positive risks
   d) Expert judgment

10. The only strategy that is applicable to both opportunities and threats is:

   a) Exploit
   b) Mitigate
   c) Transfer
   d) Acceptance

11. You are assigned as a new project manager of a project that is 40% complete. You are assigned due to the departure of the prior project manager. You review the current issues logs and meeting minutes. You talk to the project sponsor and other key stakeholders and are told that the business environment that you are working in is in a critical state and that it is imperative that this project be completed on time to help the organization weather a volatile market shift. You:

   a) Update the work breakdown structure for additional work
   b) Document the lessons learned knowledge base
   c) Add schedule activities to the project schedule
   d) Review the risk register for risk events that will cause a delay

Notes:

11

Risk — Monitoring and Controlling Questions

12. The _____ process includes identifying new risks and monitoring residual risks.

    a) Identify Risks
    b) Monitoring and Controlling Project Work
    c) Monitor and Control Risks
    d) Plan Risk Management

13. All of the following are objectives of the Monitor and Control Risks process EXCEPT:

    a) Analyzing new risks
    b) Developing a risk breakdown structure
    c) Monitoring triggers
    d) Evaluating the effectiveness of risk responses

14. A tool and technique for the Monitor and Control Risks process is:

    a) Additional risk identification
    b) Additional risk planning
    c) Corrective action
    d) Risk reassessment

15. Reserve analysis compares:

    a) The effectiveness of the risk management process to the project objectives
    b) Current project cost estimates with similar past project costs
    c) Project performance to the planned schedule
    d) The amount of contingency reserves remaining to the amount of risk remaining

Notes:

11

ANSWERS AND REFERENCES FOR SAMPLE PMP EXAM QUESTIONS ON RISK MANAGEMENT

Section numbers refer to the *PMBOK® Guide*.

1. **D** **Chapter 11**
   The inherent temporary nature of projects invites uncertain events or conditions to occur. If these events do occur they could have a positive or negative effect on the project objectives.

2. **B** **Section 11**
   Positive risk events are opportunities; negative risk events are threats.

3. **A** **Section 11**
   Risk events are described by their cause and impact; risk impacts are the effects on the project if the risk should occur.

4. **A** **Section 11.2**
   For choices C and D, the extent is unknown and could be 0% to 100%.

5. **B** **Section 11.3**
   Stakeholder risk tolerances are considered in the Plan Risk Management and the Qualitative Risk Analysis processes. A risk seeker is more willing to request "stretch" goals.

6. **D** **Section 11.3.2.6**
   Past project files may be useful, so choice A is out; choice B gives a technique of the Identify Risks process; for choice C, the risk register will house the results of the probability and impact analysis.

7. **B** **Section 11.3.3**

8. **A** **Section 11.4.2.2**
   EMV is the expected monetary value of each alternative within the decision tree.

9. A   **Section 11.5.1**
Expert judgement and strategies are tools and techniques, while risk register updates is an output of the plan risk responses process.

10. D   **Section 11.5.2**

11. D   **Section 11.2.1.1**
A project manager must be aware of the objectives of the project and must respond appropriately when environmental situations change.

12. C   **Section 11.6**
Risk management is an iterative process.

13. B   **Section 11.6**
A risk breakdown structure is developed during the Plan Risk Management process.

14. D   **Section 11.6.2.1**

15. D   **Section 11.6.2.5**

11

CASE STUDY SUGGESTED SOLUTION

Exercise 11-1
Risk Management Plan for the Lawrence RV
Garage Project

Some possible risk events:

> Permit delays
> Permit(s) not granted
> Subcontractor bids over (or under) expectations
> Schedule overruns
> Weather delays
> Materials delays
> Labor delays
> Schedule delays other than weather, materials or labor
> Budget overruns due to materials, labor or
>   subcontractor invoices
> Owner or architect change requests
> Inspection denials
> Quality problems

Response plan:

As a mitigator, review permit application to determine that it is completed properly with all the necessary attachments. As a contingency plan, if a permit is delayed, meet with the permitting agency to determine the cause of the delay and the steps to extradite it.

Risk Event	Category	Probability	Impact	Score/ Priority	Risk Response Strategy	Risk Trigger
Permit Delayed	External	3	2	6	Accept	Permit not Received

Risk register:
The qualitative estimates will vary greatly depending on personal experiences. The key is to get the project manager to think about risks BEFORE they happen and to have a plan for dealing with risk events. Although we have indicated a possible response plan and risk register for only one of the many possible risk events, a project manager would have to devise a response plan and risk register for all valid risks to a project.

PROCUREMENT

CHAPTER 12 | **PROCUREMENT**

12

PROCUREMENT MANAGEMENT

Project procurement management questions on the exam tend to be more process oriented than legally focused. You do not need to know any country's specific legal code; however, the nature of many of the questions requires an understanding of United States contract law. In the United States, a contract is a formal agreement, all changes must be in writing and formally controlled and a court system is used for handling disputes. You must have a firm understanding of the procurement process in order to answer these questions accurately.

You must know the basic differences between the primary categories of contracts (cost reimbursable, fixed price and time and material) and the risks inherent in each category for both the buyer and the seller. Several questions will also test your knowledge of various contract types within each category. **International Contracting** is also within the limits of exam questions; the timing of foreign currency exchange and duty on goods delivered to foreign countries may also come up.

Things to Know

1. The four processes of project procurement management:
   - **Plan Procurements**
   - **Conduct Procurements**
   - **Administer Procurements**
   - **Close Procurements**
2. **Teaming agreements**
3. The purpose of the **Make-or-Buy Analysis**
4. Three contract types:
   - **Fixed Price**
   - **Cost Reimbursable**
   - **Time and Material**
5. Calculating total fees and total contract costs
6. The **Procurement Management Plan**
7. The procurement **Statements of Work (SOW)**
8. Procurement documents: **IFB**, **RFB** and **RFQ**
9. Evaluating sellers with **Source Selection Criteria**
10. Procurement **Negotiation**

EXAM TIP
PMI discusses procurement management from the perspective of the buyer in the buyer-seller relationship, and from the perspective that the seller is external to the buyer's organization. The type, terms and conditions of the contract become key inputs in the contract administration process. Memorize the key contract types — **Cost Reimbursable, Fixed Price** and **Time and Material** — and who bears the burden of risk in each type of contract.

EXAM TIP

Many procurement questions are process oriented so it is important to know the steps of procurement management outlined in the *PMBOK® Guide*.

Key Definitions

Bidder Conference: the buyer and potential sellers meet prior to the contract award to answer questions and clarify requirements; the intent is for all sellers to have equal access to the same information.

Buyer: the performing organization, client, customer, contractor, purchaser or requester seeking to acquire goods and services from an external entity (the seller). The buyer becomes the customer and key stakeholder.

Commercial-Off-The-Shelf (COTS): a product or service that is readily available from many sources; selection of a seller is primarily driven by price.

Contract: the binding agreement between the buyer and the seller.

Letter Contract: a written preliminary contract authorizing the seller to begin work immediately; it is often used for small value contracts.

Letter of Intent: this is NOT a contract but simply a letter, without legal binding, that says the buyer intends to hire the seller.

Point of Total Assumption: in a fixed price contract, the point above which the seller will assume responsibility for all costs; it generally occurs when the contract ceiling price has been exceeded.

Privity: the contractual relationship between the two parties of a contract. If party A contracts with party B and party B subcontracts to party C. There is no privity between party A and party C.

12

Seller: the bidder, contractor, source, subcontractor, vendor or supplier who will provide the goods and services to the buyer. The seller generally manages the work as a project, utilizing all processes and knowledge areas of project management.

Single Source: selecting a seller without competition. This may be appropriate if there is an emergency or prior business relationship.

Sole Source: selecting a seller because it is the only provider of the needed product or service.

PLAN PROCUREMENTS PROCESS

The Plan Procurements process is the first step in the Project Procurement process. In this process, the project team identifies which project requirements can be met by purchasing products or services from sellers outside the organization. It will include documenting decisions to buy and the process to procure products or services. The team, along with the procurement department, will also identify sellers and special circumstances that may influence the sellers who may bid. The Plan Procurements process should take place during the Define Scope process and will rely on the scope statement, WBS, documentation of requirements, the risk register and other planning outputs related to the schedule, resource requirements, quality and cost. Most organizations have some level of formal purchasing procedures that must be followed.

Teaming Agreements

Teaming agreements are established between two or more parties to provide the products or services required. They are contractual agreements, such as a partnership or joint venture, which define the buyer-seller responsibilities. They are used when both parties bring something of value to the project. Understanding any teaming agreements is important input in planning procurements.

> **EXAM TIP**
> All procurement processes except the Plan Procurements process are the only *PMBOK® Guide* processes that are truly optional. These processes are only used if procurement is determined to be necessary to the project.

12

Make-or-Buy Analysis

Make-or-buy analysis is a technique to determine if a particular work product should be purchased externally or produced internally within the performing organization.

Cost is usually a major factor in the make-or-buy decision. PMI advocates that the actual or direct out-of-pocket costs to purchase the product as well as the indirect costs of managing the procurement must be considered in any make-or-buy decision. Many other factors may be considered in the make-or-buy decision: in one situation they may require a "make" decision;" in other situations they will require a "buy" decision. Some of these are:

- Availability of human resources and skills
- Direct control/customization required
- Design secrecy and proprietary information
- Availability of product
- Reliability of suppliers
- Small volume requirements
- Limited capacity/time
- Production capacity
- Competition
- Degree of standardization
- Maintenance, support, and service required

Contract Types

The primary objective of contract type selection is to have risk distributed between the buyer and seller so that both parties have motivation and incentives for meeting the contract goal. If the product or service is not well defined, both the buyer and seller are at risk.

The following factors may influence the type of contract selected:

- Overall degree of cost and schedule risk
- Type/complexity of requirement
- Extent of price competition
- Cost/price analysis
- Urgency of requirement/performance period
- The level of detail in the statement of work

- Frequency of expected changes
- Industry standards for types of contracts used

There are three general types of contracts:

- **Fixed Price** (FP) or lump sum contracts involve a predetermined fixed price for the product; it is the preferred type of contract in many situations and used when the product is well defined
- **Cost Reimbursable** (CR) or **Cost Plus** contracts involve payment based on the seller's actual costs, a fee, and a potential incentive for meeting or exceeding project objectives; it may be easier to initiate but requires more oversight by the buyer
- **Time and Material** (T&M) contracts (sometimes called **Unit Price** contracts) contain characteristics of both FP and CR contracts and are generally used for small dollar amounts; these contracts may be priced on a per-hour or per-item basis (fixed price) but the total number of hours or items is not determined (open-ended cost type arrangements like CR contracts)

Fixed Price Contracts

In fixed price contracts, the seller is paid an agreed upon price for the work to be performed which must include the seller's profit and any necessary contingencies. Therefore, the seller bears a higher burden of the cost risk than the buyer. Typical types of fixed price contracts are:

- **Firm-Fixed Price** (FFP): also called a lump sum contract. The seller bears the greatest degree of risk; this is a common type of contract where the seller agrees to perform a service or furnish supplies at an established contract price

12

Example 1 of FFP:

Contract price	$100,000	
Seller's actual cost		$70,000
Buyer's total payments	$100,000	

The seller's actual cost is usually not disclosed in this type of contract. The seller's profit is $30,000 in this example.

Example 2 of FFP:

Contract price	$100,000
Seller's actual cost	$130,000
Buyer's total payment	$100,000

The seller loses $30,000 on this contract.

- **Fixed Price Incentive Fee** (FPIF): This is a complex type of contract in which the seller bears a higher burden of risk but the purpose of the incentive is to shift some of the risk back to the buyer. Typically, for every dollar the seller reduces cost below the target, the cost savings are split between the buyer and seller based on the share ratio. A ceiling price is established so the buyer does not pay more than the ceiling price; therefore if costs exceed the ceiling, the seller receives no additional payments

Example 1 of FPIF:

Target cost		$100,000
Target profit	$10,000	
Contract price value	$110,000	
Ceiling price	$120,000	
Share ratio (buyer/seller)	80/20	
Seller's actual cost		$80,000
Difference		$20,000

Profit calculation:

Seller's share of difference (20%)	$4,000
Target profit	$10,000
Total profit	$14,000

Total calculation:

Actual cost	$80,000
Total profit	$14,000
Buyer's total payment	$94,000

Example 2 of FPIF: Same targets and ceiling as above. If the project's actual cost increases to $130,000, the buyer pays seller $120,000 (the ceiling amount), the seller receives no additional payments and may have no profit on the product or service sold.

- **Fixed Price with Economic Price Adjustment (FP-EPA):** this contract may be used when the term of the contract spans multiple years; it provides for adjustment to the contract prices when specified economic events occur and is intended to reduce the seller's risk of price changes of their purchased items

  Example of FP-EPA: Contract price is $100,000 for each of three years. If a commodity used in the production of the product or service increases due to inflation, the contract price will be increased.

Cost Reimbursable Contracts

In this type of contract the buyer and seller agree to the costs to be reimbursed and an agreed to amount for profit. Therefore, the buyer bears the highest cost risk. Common forms of cost reimbursable contracts include:

- **Cost Plus Fixed Fee (CPFF):** this is a common form of cost reimbursable contract. The buyer bears the burden of the cost risk in a CPFF contract because the buyer pays all costs. The seller's fee, or profit, is fixed at a specific dollar amount. This fee may be a percent of the original estimated cost. This type of contract is often used in research projects and projects where the scope of work lacks clear definition.

EXAM TIP

Buyers' risk from the various contract types (from highest to lowest):

CPFF→ CPIF→ FPIF → FFP

12

Example 1 of CPFF:

Estimated cost	$100,000
Fixed fee	$10,000
Contract value	$110,000

Seller's actual cost	$150,000
Fixed fee	$10,000
Buyer's total payment	$160,000

Example 2 of CPFF: The fee in a CPFF contract may be renegotiated when the buyer approves change orders that increase or decrease the scope of the project. If the original estimated cost is $100,000, and the fixed fee is $10,000, the estimated total cost is $110,000. If project scope increases as approved by the buyer, and cost increases to $120,000, the fixed fee may be renegotiated to $12,000. The total actual cost the buyer pays is $132,000.

- **Cost Plus Incentive Fee (CPIF):** in this type of contract, risk is shared by both buyer and seller. The seller is paid for agreed to, allowable costs plus an agreed upon fee, plus an incentive that is both specific and measurable. If the final costs are less than the expected costs, both the buyer and seller benefit by splitting the cost savings on a prenegotiated sharing formula. This type of contract is used in long performance period types of contracts.

The difference between FPIF and CPIF contracts is that FPIF contracts include a ceiling, above which the seller will not recover any cost. CPIF contracts do not have a ceiling on cost, but they often have maximum and minimum fees.

Example of CPIF:

Target cost		$100,000
Target fee	$10,000	
Maximum fee	$15,000	
Minimum fee	$7,000	
Share ratio (buyer/seller)	80/20	

Seller's actual cost	$120,000
Difference (over target cost)	($20,000)

Profit calculation:

Target profit	$10,000
Seller's share of overage (20%)	$4,000
Calculated profit	$6,000

Minimum profit	$7,000

Total calculation:

Actual cost	$120,000
Total profit	$7,000
Buyer's total payment	$127,000

- **Cost Plus Award Fee (CPAF):** an award pool is created and managed by an award committee. Subjective judgments are used to determine the award, giving the buyer more flexibility than in a CPIF contract. Administrative costs are high.

Time and Material Contracts

Time and material (T&M) contracts (sometimes called **Unit Price Contracts**) contain characteristics of both FP and CR contracts and are generally used for small dollar amounts. These contracts may be priced on a per-hour or per-item basis (fixed price) but the total number of hours or items is not determined (open-ended cost type arrangements like CR contracts). A **Purchase Order** is a simple form of unit price contract that is often used for buying commodities. It is a unilateral contract and only signed by one party instead of bilateral contracts that are signed by both parties.

- **Example of T&M:** in anticipation of a hurricane forecast for the site of a construction job, the buyer's project manager asks the contractor to prepare for high winds on a time and materials basis to be invoiced after the work is completed. The seller buys 20 8X4-ft. plywood panels for a total of $1,000 and hires local labor for 15 hours at $10 per hour for a total of $150. The seller submits an invoice for $1,150.

Procurement Management Plan

The procurement management plan gives overall guidance for how procurements will be conducted, including types of contracts, risk response plans, standard documents to be used, how to work with the procurement department, defining schedule and lead time criteria, identifying pre-qualified sellers, etc.

Procurement Statement of Work

The procurement statement of work (SOW) is written to describe the procurement item in sufficient detail to allow prospective sellers to determine if they are capable of providing the item. Key details to know about an SOW are:
- The SOW describes the portion of the product to be purchased
- If the seller is producing the entire product then the procurement SOW = product description; otherwise the product description is a broader definition of the project
- In government terms, the SOW describes a procurement item that is a clearly specified product or service and a **Statement of Objective (SOO)** is used for procuring an item that is presented as a problem to be solved
- Each procurement item needs its own SOW
- Multiple products and services may be grouped as one procurement item

Types of specifications:
- **Performance:** the final product or objective to be accomplished, leaving it up to the seller to decide how the item should be built or what its design characteristics should be; this type of specification is usually used in new technology, research or complex developmental contracts

- **Design:** this type of specification describes in close detail how the work is to be done; it is often used in construction equipment purchasing contracts or where the specifications are well defined

Procurement Documents

Procurement documents are another output of the Plan Procurement process. These documents are prepared by the **Buyer** to help **Sellers** understand the project's needs and to solicit proposals. Procurement documents provide information for prospective sellers that generally include:

- The procurement statement of work
- Background information for the product
- Procedures for replying
- Guidelines for preparation of the proposal
- Pricing forms
- A target budget or maximum
- Proposed terms and conditions of the contract
- Evaluation criteria for how proposals will be rated or scored

Procurement documents need to provide enough detail to ensure consistent, comparable responses from the sellers, yet allow potential sellers the flexibility to provide creative, viable solutions. Well-designed procurement documents enable:

- More complete proposal responses
- Facilitated comparisons of the sellers' responses
- Pricing that is close to objectives
- Increased understanding of the buyer's need and scope of work
- Decreased number of changes to project work

Procurement documents vary from industry to industry. The choice of which type of procurement document to use depends on the form of the procurement statement of work and contract type selected. Common procurement documents include:

- **Invitation for Bid (IFB)** or **Request for Bid (RFB):** buyer requests a single price for the entire package of work; items of service are typically high dollar value and are standardized

- **Request for Quotation (RFQ)**: buyer requests a price quote per item, hour, etc.; items are relatively low dollar value; this may be used to develop information that may be used in an RFP

Source Selection Criteria

Evaluation Criteria for how sellers will be selected are another output of the Plan Procurement process. Additional weight may be given to one or more criteria depending on the needs of the project. Evaluation criteria may include:

- Seller's price or cost criteria, life cycle cost
- Seller's understanding of the project need and requirements, their technical abilities, warranty, proprietary technology and intellectual property rights
- Seller's past performance, management approach, ability to manage risk, and current working relationships
- Seller's financial capacity and reputation, capacity to produce the product, size and type of business, including certification as a small, disadvantaged or minority-owned enterprise

CONDUCT PROCUREMENTS PROCESS

After the procurement documents are sent out to prospective sellers, the Conduct Procurements process involves obtaining responses from these sellers. The key outputs of this process are selected sellers and the contract.

The organization may conduct several types of competition among sellers:

- **Full, Open Competition**: all sellers are invited to bid; this may create more work for the department handling the bid process; it may also lead to unqualified sellers being selected when there is a requirement to select the lowest bid
- **Pre-Qualification of Sellers**: sellers must qualify to bid by submitting information; a limited number of sellers will be selected to bid

- **Single Source**: a seller is selected with no competitive bidding; this may be appropriate when there is an emergency, a specialized service is required, or the seller has entered into a long term agreement with the buyer's organization; in government contracts, reasons for selecting a single source must be documented and approved
- **Sole Source**: a seller is selected because that seller is the only provider of the product or service

Case Study Exercise

Exercise 12-1: There are four building supply vendors that can provide our materials, two local roof truss manufacturing companies and several potential stucco sub-contractors we can choose from. List the various vendors and determine 1) how we should solicit each vendor, and 2) which type of contract would be best to use in each situation.

Procurement Negotiations

Negotiation is a general management skill that comes up frequently in project management. Although the primary objective of negotiation is to reach agreement on a fair and reasonable price, product and delivery, PMI advocates the importance of a **Win-Win** situation in which a good relationship is developed with the seller. A **Win-Lose** situation may result in contract issues and problems for both the buyer and the seller.

Some of the key items to be considered in negotiation are:
- Responsibilities and roles
- Technical and business management approaches and methodologies
- Who has final authority
- The applicable law that may apply
- Price
- Contract financing and payment terms

Negotiation Tactics

There are several negotiation tactics (Adapted from *Principles of Project Management*, PMI):

- **Imposing a Deadline**: a powerful tactic since it emphasizes the schedule constraints of the project and implies a possible loss to both parties
- **Surprises**: one party springs a surprise on the other, such as a change in dollar amount
- **Stalling**: one party claims it does not have the authority, that the person with authority is not available or that it needs more information
- **Fair and Reasonable**: one party claims the price is equitable because another organization is paying it
- **Delays**: necessary when arguments are going nowhere, tempers are short or one party is off on a tangent
- **Deliberate Confusion**: either distorting facts and figures or piling on unnecessary details to cloud the issues
- **Withdrawal**: either the negotiator is so frustrated he or she does not continue or one side makes an attack and then retreats
- **Arbitration**: a third party is brought in to make decisions, including a decision on the final outcome
- **Fait Accompli**: one party claims "What is done is done" and cannot be changed

> **EXAM TIP**
>
> A contract, offer or acceptance may be oral or written, though written is preferred.

Contracts

A contract is the major output of the Conduct Procurements process. A contract represents a formal agreement and requirements must be stated in as much detail as possible. To manage contracts effectively, changes should be in writing and formally controlled by both the buyer and seller. A valid enforceable contract allows disputes to be resolved in the court system or through alternative methods. In the United States, commercial contracts are regulated by the Uniform Commercial Code (UCC); government contracts are regulated by the Federal Acquisition Regulation (FAR).

Black's Law Dictionary describes the following ten tests for a contract:
- Agreement between two or more parties
- Promise to do or not to do something
- An offer
- Unconditional acceptance
- Mutual assent: both parties agree to the terms
- No contract if there are modifications or partial acceptance
- Consideration: something of value
- Legal capacity: of proper age and, within an organization, having the proper authority
- Legal purpose: and does not violate public policy
- Form required by law: real estate contracts are required to be in writing in most jurisdictions

Organizations frequently have standard contracts that are preprinted. If signed as is, these are legally sufficient and will form a valid contract. Contracts are likely to include:
- A description of the procurement statement of work
- Term for inspection, warranty and support
- The schedule, where the work will be performed and where delivered
- The price, payment terms, fees, incentives, penalties, and any other modifications
- How disputes will be resolved

> **EXAM TIP**
> The contract administrator is typically a specialist in managing projects and is ideally is not the project manager.

When necessary, standard contracts may be modified to fit the requirements of a project. These are called **Special Provisions** and can be arranged by the project manager together with the **Contract Administrator** and legal counsel if necessary.

ADMINISTER PROCUREMENTS PROCESS

The Administer Procurements process involves making sure that the seller is performing the work according to contractual requirements and that both buyer and seller are meeting their contractual obligations. Key project management processes that must be integrated with administer procurements include:

- **Direct and Manage Project Execution**: performing the work of the project plan
- **Report Performance**: monitor costs, schedule, and seller's performance; scheduled payments or seller's compensation should be linked to seller's performance
- **Perform Quality Control**: inspect and verify results for compliance; non-conformance may lead to breach of contract
- **Perform Integrated Change Control**: ensure changes are properly managed and communicated; contested changes are called claims, disputes, or appeals
- **Monitor and Control Risks**: review performance of the contracted work to make sure negative risks are reduced or that positive risks are enhanced

Contract Change Control System

Since project managers are often faced with multiple or ambiguous interpretations of the contract in deciding on the scope of work involved, there is high potential for conflict between the **Buyer** and **Seller**. Some buyer organizations may utilize a centralized group whose specific function is to handle contract administration. This group may contain one or more contracting officers or **Contract Administrators** who are assigned to various projects. In such cases, this person is the only one with authority to change the contract. A **Contract Change Control System** is a key tool and technique of the Administer Procurements process. It defines the process by which the contract may be modified.

Contract change modifications fall into three categories:
- **Administrative Change:** often a unilateral contract change, in writing, that does not affect the substantive rights of the parties
- **Change Order:** a written order, signed by the contracting officer, directing the seller to make a change
- **Legal**: mutual agreement to modify with supporting consideration

Changes may be contested when the **Buyer** and **Seller** cannot agree on how much should be paid for the change. These may be called **Claims**, **Disputes**, or **Appeals**. If changes are contested, they may be resolved in a court of law or through alternative **Dispute Resolution** procedures such as **Mediation** or **Arbitration**.

CLOSE PROCUREMENTS PROCESS

Each procurement item will be closed during the Close Procurement process. This may occur at various times during the project and will be part of the overall Close Project process. The major objective of the Close Procurement process is to verify that work was completed correctly and satisfactorily. It also involves the administrative work of documenting the records and lessons learned, resolving claims and disputes, and completing any unique terms and conditions specified in the contract.

Challenges in Closing Procurements

Some issues that could impact the Close Procurements process are:

- **Waiver:** relinquishing rights under the contract; the **Waiver Pitfall** occurs when the project manager for the buyer knowingly accepts incomplete, defective, or late performance without objection; in doing so, the project manager waives his or her right to specific performance
- **Contract Breach:** failure to perform a contractual obligation
- **Material Breach of Contract:** a significant failure to perform that may result in the non-faulted party being discharged from any further obligations under the contract
- **Time is of the Essence:** when explicitly stated in the contract, the seller's failure to perform within the allotted time will constitute a material breach of the contract

> **EXAM TIP**
> Typically the closure process is the trigger that releases final payment to subcontractors.

12

- **Subcontract Management:** if the seller subcontracts to a third party, the buyer has no direct control over the performance of the third party; the seller must manage the third party and pay them

Effects of default for non-performance by the **Seller** are:
- Seller is not entitled to compensation for work in process not yet accepted by the buyer
- Buyer is entitled to repayment from seller of any advance or progress payments applicable to such work
- Buyer may order delivery of completed or partially completed work
- Seller must preserve and protect property buyer has interest in
- Seller is liable for excess procurement costs

Early termination of a contract is a special case of closing procurements. It may result from:
- Mutual agreement of both parties
- Default of one party
- Convenience of the buyer

Closure Outputs

As organizational process assets are updated, the Close Procurement process will provide:
- A **Procurement File**
  - A complete set of indexed records to be included with the final project archives when closing the phase or project
  - Contract documents for documenting work and work performance
- **Deliverable Acceptance**
  - Formal written notice to seller as defined in the contract
- **Lessons Learned** documentation
  - Documentation from **Procurement Audits** or lessons learned as well as an evaluation of the seller for future reference
  - Recommendations for improving the process

SAMPLE PMP EXAM QUESTIONS ON PROCUREMENT MANAGEMENT

Procurement — Planning Questions

1. Who has responsibility for making sure that items procured meet the needs of the project and follow the organization's policies?

   a) The procurement department
   b) The project sponsor
   c) The project management team
   d) The project buyer

2. As a project team member you notice that your project manager is in the process of identifying which project deliverables could be met by procuring products and services from prospective sellers. This project manager was in the midst of which planning process?

   a) Plan Procurements
   b) Collect Requirements
   c) Resource Planning
   d) Sequence Activities

3. In the Plan Procurements process, it is a good practice to:

   a) Use only approved sellers
   b) Select only sellers that you have personally worked with
   c) Seek out leaders in the industry
   d) Review the risks involved in each make-or-buy decision

4. All of the following are outputs of the Plan Procurements process EXCEPT:

   a) The statement of work
   b) The procurement management plan
   c) Make-or-buy decisions
   d) Make-or-buy analysis

Notes:

5. The procurement management plan is a plan to:

   a) Describe how the procurement processes will be managed
   b) Provide guidance on how project scope will be defined, documented and verified
   c) Define the roles and responsibilities to support risk on the project
   d) Define how contracts should be developed and is separate from the project management plan

Procurement — Executing Questions

6. You are the project manager looking to hire a construction company to build an apartment complex. Your company is looking for a reputable firm that has experience in building apartment complexes within budget. Before distributing proposals, you've asked the procurement department to come up with a list of firms that are locally-based and have a reputation for delivering within budget. This is an example of:

   a) Contract negotiation
   b) Qualified sellers list
   c) Proposal evaluation technique
   d) Seller rating systems

7. You are the project manager on a large contract. Because of a lack of expertise within your existing project team, you will need to procure a major component of the project. From a short list of qualified sellers, you ask for detailed proposals and apply specific weighting criteria. This will be accomplished during which process?

   a) Define Scope
   b) Plan Procurements
   c) Conduct Procurements
   d) Administer Procurements

Notes:

12

8. The bidder's conference is a part of which process?

   a) Plan Procurements
   b) Conduct Procurements
   c) Administer Procurements
   d) Select Procurements

9. It is good practice to have a contract include all of the following EXCEPT:

   a) Terms and conditions
   b) A detailed work breakdown structure
   c) Periods of performance
   d) Roles and responsibilities

Procurement — Monitoring and Controlling Questions

10. Which of the following is not part of the Administer Procurements process?

    a) Answering questions of potential sellers
    b) Evaluating seller performance
    c) Confirming progress payments have been sent
    d) Confirming that changes to the contract are made

11. The Administer Procurements process is responsible for:

    a) Clarifying the structure and requirements of the contract
    b) Integrating the inputs of conducting procurements into the overall management of the project
    c) Defining the roles and responsibilities to support risk on the project
    d) Applying the appropriate project management processes to the contractual relationship

Notes:

12. A critical tool and technique used within the Administer Procurements process is:

   a) Contract negotiation
   b) Proposals
   c) A contract change control system
   d) A payment schedule

Procurement — Closing Questions

13. A contract that is terminated early is a special case of:

   a) Disputes
   b) Closing the project or phase
   c) Closing procurements
   d) Administering procurements

14. A procurement audit is a tool and technique for which closing process?

   a) Monitor and Control Project Work
   b) Close Procurements
   c) Direct and Manage Project execution
   d) Close Project or Phase

15. The requirements for the Close Procurements process are usually defined in the:

   a) Terms within the contract
   b) Enterprise environmental factors
   c) Procurement specification
   d) Integrated project plan

Notes:

12

ANSWERS AND REFERENCES FOR SAMPLE PMP EXAM QUESTIONS ON PROCUREMENT MANAGEMENT

Section numbers refer to the *PMBOK® Guide*.

1. C   Section 12

2. A   Section 12.1
   The purpose of the Plan Procurements process is to identify which project needs can be best met by purchasing products, services or results.

3. D   Section 12.1

4. D   Section 12.1.3
   Make-or-buy analysis is a tool and technique of the plan procurements process.

5. A   Section 12.1.3.1

6. B   Section 12.2.1.4

7. C   Section 12.2.1

8. B   Section 12.2.2.1
   The bidders conference is a tool and technique of this process.

9. B   Section 12.2.3.2
   Not all contracts will have a detailed WBS.

10. A   Section 12.3

11. D   Section 12.3

12. C   Section 12.3.2.1

13. C   Section 12.4

14. B   Section 12.4.2.1

15. A   Section 12.4.3.1

CASE STUDY SUGGESTED SOLUTION

Exercise 12-1:
Purchase Plan for the Lawrence RV Garage Project

General Building Materials Vendors

These are commonly available commodities and should be solicited via an invitation for bid (IFB). We will supply the bill of material (BOM) from the architect. Selection will be based solely on price. Once selected, we will send the winner a purchase order (PO) for the materials listed in the BOM and set up a delivery schedule based on our plan.

Truss Manufacturers

Trusses are essentially custom made for each building, so we should solicit via a request for proposal (RFP). Because the proposed solutions may be significantly different, we will have to evaluate each for its impact on our budget and schedule. Once we decide, a firm fixed price (FFP) contract should be issued since we will know exactly how many trusses are needed.

Stucco Contractors

We expect the stucco subs to supply all their own materials including tarpaper, rigid foam insulation, chicken wire and the ingredients that make up the stucco. We should solicit via a request for proposal (RFP) for all work and materials. Because the prices of some of the materials used are going up rapidly, the contract should be a combination of cost reimbursable for the materials and a firm fixed price for the balance.

12

RESPONSIBILITY

R

13

13

PROFESSIONAL RESPONSIBILITY

A major portion of professional responsibility questions on the PMP exam is based on ethics. Common sense, ethical values and your own experience will play a large role in your ability to answer the questions on this topic. The PMI Project Management Professional Code of Professional Conduct (available at www.pmi.org) is a key component of this part of the exam. In addition, you should have an understanding of cultural and global values necessary to manage projects in today's multinational environment.

Things to Know

1. What is **Professional Responsibility**
2. The **Code of Conduct**
3. The importance of **Culture** in the project environment
4. **Driving Forces in Global Businesses**
5. How to apply professional responsibility concepts to **Working on Multicultural Teams**
6. **Professional Responsibility and** *PMBOK® Guide* **Knowledge Areas**

Key Definitions

Communication Context: languages generally fall on a sliding scale of high to low context. Recipients of high-context language messages need to know the situation and environment of the message in order to understand it. An example of a high-context message is poetry, in which rhyme, meter, allegory and similar poetic devices enhance one's experience of the poet's intent. Recipients of low-context language messages understand the message as received. An example of a low-context message is a statement of fact, such as "you have a dozen eggs."

Culture: everything that people have, think and do as members of their society and that is shared by at least one other person.

Knowledge Area: a collection of processes, inputs, tools, techniques and outputs associated with a topical area. Knowledge areas are a subset of the overall project management body of knowledge that recognizes "good practices."

Performance Domains: a broad category of duties and responsibilities that define a role. A performance domain expresses the actual actions of the project manager in a particular domain.

Process Groups: a set of project management processes that are required for any project; they are typically performed in sequence but have interdependencies within and across process groups.

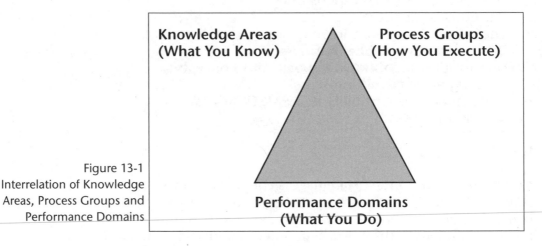

Figure 13-1
Interrelation of Knowledge Areas, Process Groups and Performance Domains

PROFESSIONAL RESPONSIBILITY

Knowledge areas, process groups and performance domains are equally important in the field of project management, as depicted in Figure 13-1. In 1999 PMI assembled a group of thirteen experts, together with representatives from Columbia Assessment Services (CAS), with a charter to delineate the field of project management. They analyzed how each of these three aspects of project management defined the job of a project manager.

13

In general, PMI advocates that the project manager always carry himself or herself with professionalism, which includes:

- Ensuring individual integrity and professionalism
- Contribute by sharing lessons learned, best practices, research, etc.
- Enhancing individual competence
- Balancing stakeholders' interests
- Interacting with team members and stakcholders in a professional and cooperative manner

CODE OF CONDUCT

The Code of Ethics and Professional Conduct describes the expectations that we, as project managers, have of ourselves and of our fellow practitioners. It articulates the ideals to which we aspire as well as the behaviors that are mandatory in our professional and volunteer roles.

The Code of Ethics and Professional Conduct is broken into four sections: responsibility, respect, fairness and honesty. Below is a summary of each of the four sections. See www.pmi.org for a downloadable version of the Code of Ethics and Professional Conduct.

Responsibility

As practitioners in the global project management community we aspire to:

- Make decisions and take actions based on the best interests of society, public safety, and the environment
- Accept only those assignments that are consistent with our background, experience, skills, and qualifications
- Fulfill the commitments that we undertake
- Take ownership and make corrections promptly when we make errors or omissions
- When we discover errors or omissions caused by others, communicate them to the appropriate body as soon they are discovered
- Protect proprietary or confidential information that has been entrusted to us

- Uphold this Code and hold each other accountable to it

And we require the following of ourselves and our fellow practitioners:
- Uphold the policies, rules, regulations and laws that govern our work, professional and volunteer activities
- Report unethical or illegal conduct to appropriate management
- Bring violations of this Code to the attention of the appropriate body for resolution
- Only file ethics complaints when they are substantiated by facts
- Pursue disciplinary action against an individual who retaliates against a person raising ethics concerns

Respect

As practitioners in the global project management community we aspire to:
- Inform ourselves about the norms and customs of others and avoid engaging in behaviors they might consider disrespectful
- Listen to others' points of view
- Approach directly those persons with whom we have a conflict or disagreement
- Conduct ourselves in a professional manner

And we require the following of ourselves and our fellow practitioners:
- Negotiate in good faith
- Do not exercise the power of our expertise or position to influence the decisions or actions of others in order to benefit personally at their expense
- Do not act in an abusive manner toward others
- Respect the property rights of others

Fairness

As practitioners in the global project management community we aspire to:
- Demonstrate transparency in our decision-making process
- Constantly reexamine our impartiality and objectivity, taking corrective action as appropriate
- Provide equal access to information to those who are authorized to have that information
- Make opportunities equally available to qualified candidates

And we require the following of ourselves and our fellow practitioners:
- Proactively and fully disclose any real or potential conflicts of interest to the appropriate stakeholders
- Refrain from engaging in the decision-making process or otherwise attempting to influence outcomes, where a conflict of interest may be present
- Do not hire or fire, reward or punish, or award or deny contracts based on personal considerations
- Do not discriminate against others based on, but not limited to, gender, race or age
- Apply the rules of the organization without favoritism or prejudice

Honesty

As practitioners in the global project management community we aspire to:
- Earnestly seek to understand the truth
- Be truthful in our communications and in our conduct
- Provide accurate information in a timely manner
- Make commitments and promises in good faith
- Strive to create an environment in which others feel safe to tell the truth

And we require the following of ourselves and our fellow practitioners:

- Do not engage in or condone behavior that is designed to deceive others
- Do not engage in dishonest behavior with the intention of personal gain or at the expense of another

CULTURE

Culture is an important concept in the professional responsibility domain. In today's society where the global economy is influencing more and more organizations, it is important for the project manager to understand how culture can impact the project and what can be done to ensure success in a multicultural project environment.

Culture is everything that people have, think and do as members of their society and is shared by at least one other person. It is important to understand that culture is learned and it is not bred into a particular ethnicity. Culture is a cluster of related values that individuals have in common and believe in. Can people's beliefs be influenced? Of course they can. What an individual believes in his or her childhood is influenced by experiences and encounters throughout his or her life, which will shape his or her value system.

Culture is very complex yet dynamically stable. By this we mean that culture evolves over time. Cultural changes do not happen overnight; they are adaptations to human learning, environmental conditions and the interactions between them.

Cultures are integrated from the perspective that a particular value may be related to other values within the culture; cultures are not random assortments of values.

Cultural differences require different management approaches by the project manager. Knowing what values each project participant has will greatly improve the overall effectiveness of the project manager. Cultural differences should also be considered a value-add to the project. Diversity provides an opportunity for new solutions to old problems. Do not shy away from a culturally diverse project. You may learn a lot!

DRIVING FORCES IN GLOBAL BUSINESSES

The basic assumptions driving business changed during the 1990s. Before, we heard things like continuity, planning, diversification, scale, security, uninformed customers and national borders as driving business factors. Now we hear about change, coping with the unexpected, focus, segmentation, flexibility, responsiveness, speed, demanding customers and freedom of movement as the most prevalent factors driving business.

> **EXAM TIP**
>
> All cultures experience continual cultural change.

WORKING ON MULTICULTURAL PROJECT TEAMS

All cultures of the world face a number of common problems and share a number of common features. Project managers must understand the:
- Economic systems and how they meet the basic physiological human needs of their people
- Family systems that develop over time
- Educational systems that determine how children are taught the way of life of the society
- Social control systems and how social order is preserved
- Supernatural belief systems that explain the unexplainable

In addition, a project manager must consider the variations in thinking styles between countries.
- Inductive thinking is based on analysis
- Deductive thinking is based on logically deriving principles from theoretical constructs rather than raw data

13

Cultural differences set the stage for conflict and misunderstanding. As a project manager, the ability to identify these barriers and overcome them is critical in a successful project execution. Some such barriers are:

- Ethnocentrism, or the belief that our own beliefs are inherently superior
- Incorrectly attributing a cause when witnessing a behavior that is different from one's own
- Generalizations such as stereotypes and other negative preconceived ideas
- Misunderstanding the meanings associated with particular gestures, facial expressions and body positions
- Misunderstanding the appropriate time and place for talking business
- Inappropriately having conversations on topics such as politics, sex, religion and age
- Not recognizing status and power differences
- Not knowing the communication styles of the culture
- Inability to understand native languages

To overcome these barriers, a project manager should:

- Pay attention to feedback
- Actively communicate
- Be aware of conflict escalation and not let misunderstandings or ignorance get out of control
- Apply damage control before things get out of hand
- Maximize his or her influence to facilitate the flow of communication

WORKING ON VIRTUAL TEAMS

Managing virtual teams adds additional risks and challenges to the project manager, which affects how project managers function within a project environment. As discussed in earlier chapters, virtual teams require an added level of communication to ensure virtual team members stay informed and can be effectively managed.

The professional responsibility domain requires that project managers utilize all appropriate tools within their reach to treat all team members fairly and ethically. Managing virtual teams is a reality in many organizations and must be treated as such.

PROFESSIONAL RESPONSIBILITY AND *PMBOK®* *GUIDE* KNOWLEDGE AREAS

The professional responsibility domain touches both knowledge areas and process groups detailed within the *PMBOK® Guide*. The next few pages address each of these knowledge areas and how professional responsibility may be applied to each one.

Integration Knowledge Area

The development of and execution of the project plan is directly impacted by the diverse nature of the project team. Often it is only the project manager who has the responsibility to maintain a vision of the whole project and its outcome, while project participants work on small project work packages and sponsors deal with larger, enterprise perspectives.

Scope Knowledge Area

Defining the scope of the project requires that the project manager and sponsor look historically and use expert judgment to detail the work for the project accurately. Understanding where the project is or potentially will be performed is critical in defining the scope of the project. The project manager's responsibility is to ensure that only what is agreed to by the sponsors is produced and that no one promises more than he or she can deliver.

Time Knowledge Area

Understanding the various countries involved and their orientation toward time is important in accurately estimating effort and duration. Professional responsibility extends to ensuring common understanding of the precision and accuracy of time objectives and performance among potentially different cultural expectations.

Cost Knowledge Area

In evaluating costs, the project manager must address and review the different political and business issues facing organizational costs such as taxes, resource availability and salaries. In enterprise reporting, a project manager has an obligation to differentiate how costs are reported in a project management system, paying particular attention to the interface with the accrual expectations underpinning commonly accepted financial accounting practices.

Quality Knowledge Area

Different cultures may approach quality in much different ways. It is important to define clearly the expected quality level. Professional responsibility involves working with and identifying variances in such a way that individuals are not discouraged from reporting because of a fear of being individually blamed.

Human Resources Knowledge Area

Globalization adds new challenges to human resource management. Some of these challenges are:
- Identifying and retaining highly qualified people
- Improving the quality and quantity of management
- Sustaining and improving performance at all levels
- Increasing the talent within the organization
- Providing competitive and technically competent management
- Emphasizing total quality management
- Establishing training as part of the management culture
- Ensuring top management's commitment to global human resources initiatives
- Making human resources management part of the strategic business objectives

Project managers are responsible for anticipating potential conflicts in cultural and business practices and for gaining acceptance of the project's objectives.

Communications Knowledge Area

Communicating across cultures has many challenges for organizations as well as team members.
- High-context language messages require the reader or listener to know the situation — the context — that the message is discussing; low-context language messages do not require this knowledge; they contain all the information needed to understand them in the message itself
- Low-context communication is the more explicit and straightforward communication pattern

Figure 13-2 shows how some languages fall on a scale of low- to high-context languages.

Swiss German	English	Italian	Arabic	Japanese
Low Context				High Context

Figure 13-2
Low- to High-
Context Languages

Factors complicating effective communication across cultures include:
- Slang
- Euphemisms
- Proverbs, or wise sayings
- Humor
- Nonverbal communication
- Personal space
- Personal contact
- Individualism versus group cohesion

In addition, the project manager has a responsibility to ensure that no illegal, offensive, inaccurate or incomplete communication is conducted.

13

Risk Knowledge Area

Understanding cultural differences is critical in effectively assessing and managing risk in an organization. It is essential to gain the sponsor's informed consent for the relative importance of risk events and the actions to be taken to avoid, transfer, mitigate or accept them.

Procurement Knowledge Area

Negotiating across cultures requires strategies to deal effectively with unique issues. When thinking cross-culturally, the project manager should:
- Concentrate on long-term relationships
- Determine what each party has at stake
- Know that timing can make a difference
- Try to make the experience a win-win; be flexible
- Do his or her homework and prepare
- Learn to listen

In such a diverse environment, the project manager's responsibility and exposure to liability is significant. He or she must ensure legal, ethical and fair financial dealings.

SAMPLE PMP EXAM QUESTIONS ON PROFESSIONAL RESPONSIBILITY

1. Cultures are thought of as:

   a) Illogical ethnic practices
   b) Integrated wholes
   c) Unrelated hobbies and customs
   d) A set of related belief practices

2. Effective verbal communication is expected to be:

   a) Always high context
   b) Implicit and direct
   c) Direct, low context and explicit
   d) Explicit, direct and unambiguous

3. As part of your project, you hold a focus group to determine the perceived benefits of the product of your project. You wish to publish these results to your customer, so you post the results and the participants on your team's website. Before doing this, you should do all of the following EXCEPT:

   a) Make sure there are appropriate firewalls to protect the participants of the focus group
   b) Make sure all participants of the focus group have signed an authorization to post the results
   c) If any participants decline posting the information, remove any reference of the participant
   d) If only one participant declines posting the information, post the results as is

4. Performance domains include:

   a) Plan-do-check-act cycles, control charts and histograms
   b) Communications, schedule development, risk management and performance improvements
   c) Initiating, planning, scheduling, tracking, implementing, closing and professional responsibility
   d) Planning, executing, controlling and professional responsibility

Notes:

5. Professional responsibility is a domain that covers aspects such as:

   a) Knowledge, skills, tools and techniques
   b) Planning, organizing, staffing, executing and controlling ongoing operations
   c) Legal, ethical and professional behavior
   d) Impacts of bad weather, global business and professional behavior

6. The PMI Code of Ethics and Professional Conduct is divided into four sections. They are:

   a) Ethics, responsibility, respect and truth
   b) Responsibility, honesty, respect and fairness
   c) Honesty, truth, fairness and professional responsibility
   d) Responsibility, respect, fairness and ethics

7. All of the following tasks are in the performance domain of professional responsibility EXCEPT:

   a) Measure project performance continually by comparing results to the baseline
   b) Enhance individual competence by increasing and applying professional knowledge to improve services
   c) Balance stakeholders' interests by recommending approaches that strive for fair resolution in order to satisfy competing needs and objectives
   d) Interact with a team in a professional manner by respecting personal, ethnic and cultural differences

Notes:

13

8. You are the project manager in a construction project. The framing subcontractor stated earlier this week that he will be able to meet the delivery schedule. You find out from the laborers on site that the framing subcontractor has laid off half of its staff, several of whom were working on this project. When reporting the status of the project to senior management you should:

   a) Report no slip in schedule
   b) Contact the subcontractor to obtain a revised status
   c) Report that schedule risk was increased and why
   d) Add a buffer task to the training task

9. The PMI Code of Ethics and Professional Conduct advocates project management practitioners to aspire to all of the following EXCEPT:

   a) Respecting the property rights of others
   b) Taking responsibility for all decisions
   c) Fulfilling the commitments we undertake
   d) Being truthful in our communications and our conduct

10. Of the six performance domains, which are considered to be important?

   a) None of them; only process groups and knowledge areas are important
   b) All of them
   c) Planning, executing and controlling are important; the other three are of little importance
   d) Professional responsibility is the most important; the other five domains are handled by the process groups

Notes:

13

11. In selecting resources for your project, you must share the resource pool with other project teams. Your project requires a critical technical skill that only one resource possesses — Jack! In planning you:

    a) Request Jack for 100% of the time for the full project duration
    b) Request Jack 100% for the design and execution phases even though you only have half-time work for him
    c) Talk to each of the other project managers and determine which project needs Jack the most, and then adjust schedules accordingly
    d) Take Jack out to dinner and explain how critical this project is and how working on the project will be good for his career

12. When submitting your application for the PMP exam, you should do all of the following EXCEPT:

    a) Document all experiences truthfully
    b) Ask a friend to be your reference as a supervisor since you are not sure where your previous supervisor works
    c) Keep records of all project management training attended
    d) Do your best to obtain appropriate contacts who can verify your background

13. Two project team members are arguing over the solution to a specific problem. You, as the project manager, intervene. The best course of action should be:

    a) Listening to both solutions and deciding for the team members
    b) Pulling together other interested parties and facilitating a decision in an appropriate fashion
    c) Listening to both solutions and taking the options to stakeholders for a decision
    d) Asking each of the team members to perform an independent assessment and presenting their recommendations at next week's team meeting

Notes:

14. You are the project manager for a medical device company. You find out that one of the quality assurance analysts falsified some of the test results based on encouragement from the director of marketing. You are fairly certain the report is true. You should:

    a) Confront the quality assurance analyst privately to confirm the allegations
    b) Confront the quality assurance analyst in the next team meeting
    c) Contact the director of marketing and ask if he or she has instructed the quality assurance analyst to falsify records
    d) Talk to your sponsor and determine a best course of action to validate the accusations

15. You have just been invited to present your product to a Japanese company's senior executives in Japan for two days. On initial meeting, the first thing you should do is:

    a) Introduce yourself and discuss the agenda for the meetings
    b) Hug each participant in the meeting
    c) Be passive in your presentation
    d) Spend time with participants and get to know them personally

Notes:

13

ANSWERS AND REFERENCES FOR SAMPLE PMP EXAM QUESTIONS ON PROFESSIONAL RESPONSIBILITY

Section numbers refer to the *PMBOK® Guide.*

1. **B Ferraro**
   Cultures are coherent and logical systems, the parts of which to a degree are interrelated.

2. **D Trompenaars and Hampden-Turner**
   Speech patterns in some cultures are considerably more ambiguous, inexact and implicit than in others. Restricted codes use shortened words, phrases and sentences and rely heavily on hidden, implicit, contextual cues. However, the project manager should always be as explicit, direct and unambiguous as possible given the cultural conditions.

3. **D PMP Code of Ethics and Professional Conduct: II.A.1**

4. **D Introduction: PMP Exam Specification**

5. **C Introduction: PMP Exam Specification**

6. **B PMP Code of Ethics and Professional Conduct**

7. **A Page 28: PMP Exam Specification**

8. **B PMP Code of Ethics and Professional Conduct**
   The Code of Ethics and Professional Conduct advocates honesty of the project manager and responsibility to seek to understand the truth.

9. **B PMP Code of Ethics and Professional Conduct**
   The Code of Ethics and Professional Conduct advocates transparency in decision making, but it is not necessary for the project manager to take responsibility for all decisions.

10. **B Introduction: PMP Exam Specification**

11. C   **PMP Code of Ethics and Professional Conduct**
PMI does not condone deceit or competition without considering the needs of the organization

12. B   **PMP Code of Professional Conduct**

13. B   **PMP Code of Ethics and Professional Conduct**
It is not good practice to decide without engaging in a constructive decision-making process and without any understanding of time sensitivity; you are not sure if waiting until next week is appropriate.

14. D   **PMP Code of Ethics and Professional Conduct**
As the project manager, you have an obligation to report any unethical behavior. You may need to strategize with your sponsor before confronting anyone.

15. D   **Brake, Walker and Walker page 97**
In a Japanese cultural context, project managers would do best to focus on personal contact and relationship building before getting down to business.

CHAPTER 14 | **FINAL EXAM**

SAMPLE FINAL EXAM

If you take this sample final exam, you should spend 80 minutes answering these 60 sample questions. This timing is similar to the average time per question used by PMI in the actual PMP exam.

1. Once initiated, a project should be halted if:

   a) The project manager leaves
   b) The statement of work by the buyer is incomplete or ambiguous
   c) The project is found to be supportive of the organization's strategic goals
   d) The business need no longer exists

2. _____ coordinate(s) people and other resources to carry out the plan.

   a) Resource planning
   b) Resource leveling
   c) Controlling processes
   d) Executing processes

3. Configuration management is NOT:

   a) The cause of variances and the reasoning behind the corrective action taken
   b) Any documented procedure used to identify the functional characteristics of an item
   c) A documented procedure used to record and report change
   d) A subset of the overall project management system

Notes:

14

4. As a project is carried out and slack time is consumed on individual tasks, the slack left over for the remaining tasks is:

   a) Insignificant
   b) Reduced
   c) Unchanged
   d) Increased

5. The communication method in which two or more parties perform a multidirectional exchange of information is called:

   a) Push communication
   b) Interactive communication
   c) Communication model
   d) Pull communication

6. Culture is:

   a) Taught
   b) Learned
   c) Hereditary
   d) Genetic

7. Project risk includes:

   a) Threats to the project's objectives and opportunities to improve on those objectives
   b) Threats to the project's objectives and contingency plans to manage those risks
   c) Known risks that can be quantified
   d) All known risks to the project's objectives

8. All of the following are information gathering techniques EXCEPT:

   a) Interviewing
   b) Sampling
   c) Expert panels
   d) Root cause analysis

Notes:

14

9. An input to human resource planning includes:

   a) Staff management plan
   b) Individuals or groups who are external to the project
   c) Performance improvements
   d) Collective bargaining agreements

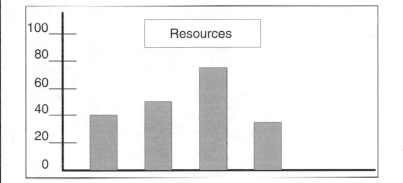

10. The above chart is an example of a (an):

   a) Resource histogram
   b) Work assignment chart
   c) RAM
   d) Organization chart

11. In crashing a task, you would focus on:

   a) As many tasks as possible
   b) Noncritical tasks
   c) Accelerating performance of tasks on critical path
   d) Accelerating performance by minimizing cost

Notes:

14

12. The difference between grade and quality is that:

    a) Grade is looking at the attributes of the product, whereas quality is concerned with how well the product meets requirements
    b) Grade is fitness-for-use, while quality is concerned with how well the product meets requirements
    c) Grade is the cost to confirm to specific requirements
    d) Grade and quality are actually synonymous

13. Successful projects are defined by all of the following EXCEPT:

    a) Meeting stakeholders' needs, wants and expectations
    b) Meeting project objectives
    c) Producing a quality product
    d) Managing teams effectively

14. Which of the following is an output of the Verify Scope process?

    a) Work result
    b) Formal acceptance of deliverables
    c) Inspection results
    d) Work breakdown structure

15. Generalizations become destructive when they:

    a) Degenerate into stereotypes
    b) Are used for estimating
    c) Are true
    d) Are believed by people

Notes:

14

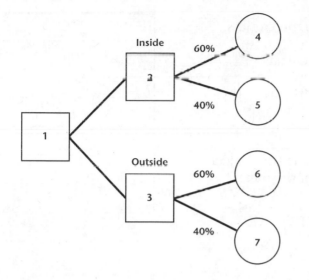

Notes:

A party is to be held.
- If the party is held inside, 100 people can attend at $10 each
- If the party is outside, 200 people can attend at $10 each
- There is a 40% chance of rain on the date of the party
- If it rains and the party is held inside, only 80 people will attend
- If it rains and the party is held outside, only 100 people will attend

16. In the example above, if the goal of the project is to maximize revenue, which of the two options maximizes revenue and why:

a) Held inside because expected monetary value is $1,800
b) Held inside because expected monetary value is $920
c) Held outside because the expected monetary value is $3,000
d) Held outside because the expected monetary value is $1,600

17. A contract is legally binding once signed unless:

    a) It is declared null and void by one party
    b) It is in violation of applicable law
    c) One party is unable to finance its part of the work
    d) One party is unwilling to perform the work

18. What is the probability of completing the project within ± two standard deviations of the mean?

    a) 96.3%
    b) 68%
    c) 99.9%
    d) 95.45%

19. A modification of a logical relationship that allows an acceleration of the successor task is called:

    a) Free float
    b) Early start time
    c) Lead time or negative lag time
    d) Lag time

20. As the project manager of a small technology project, you see that your customer has submitted a request for a change to ensure project quality, but that change will cause a significant delay in the delivery date. At the change control meeting where the change is being discussed, your response to the request should NOT be:

    a) "Changes cannot be requested until the project is complete."
    b) "Let's understand why this change request is important to the project."
    c) "Has there been any change in the business environment that warrants this change?"
    d) "Would you (the customer) be willing to push out the schedule three weeks in order to deliver this change with the initial project deliverables?"

Notes:

14

21. During the negotiation process, once an agreement is reached, you should do all of the following EXCEPT:

    a) Stay positive and respectful
    b) Define the agreement as specifically as possible
    c) Continue negotiating
    d) Express your desire for a long and prosperous relationship

22. Which of the following project scope management processes involves subdividing the major project deliverables into smaller, more manageable components?

    a) Create WBS
    b) Define Scope
    c) Verify Scope
    d) Decomposition

23. Which of the following statements concerning planning procurements is correct?

    a) Well-designed procurement documents can facilitate accurate and complete responses from prospective sellers
    b) Procurement documents must be rigorous with no flexibility to allow consideration of sellers' suggestions
    c) Procurement documents should be standardized
    d) Creation of procurement documents is performed in the Conduct Procurements process

24. The primary objective of incentive clauses in a contract is to:

    a) Reduce risk for the seller by shifting risk to the buyer
    b) Help bring the seller's objectives in line with those of the buyer
    c) Help the seller control costs
    d) Reduce costs for the buyer

Notes:

14

25. The bidders' conference is a part of which process?

    a) Plan Procurements
    b) Conduct Procurements
    c) Close Procurements
    d) Administer Procurements

26. Outputs from the Plan Communications process include:

    a) Stakeholder register
    b) Communications management plan
    c) Performance reports
    d) Formal acceptances

27. As project manager you know that in order to determine how to satisfy the quality standards that are relevant to the project, you need to perform the _____ process.

    a) Plan Quality
    b) Quality Management
    c) Perform Quality Assurance
    d) Perform Quality Control

28. A project has a 60% chance of finishing on time and a 30% chance of finishing over budget. What is the probability that the project will finish on time and within budget?

    a) 12%
    b) 18%
    c) 42%
    d) 48%

Notes:

29. The critical path in a schedule network is the path that:

    a) Takes the longest time to complete
    b) Must be done before any other tasks
    c) Allows some flexibility in scheduling a start time
    d) Is not affected by schedule slippage

Excavation Budget (in person days)

Task	Planned Value	Actual Cost	Earned Value
Survey	500	2,000	400
Remove Debris	2,000	3,500	2,000
Dig Hole	3,000	2,000	2,800
Emplace Forms	1,200	1,000	1,100
Pour Concrete	5,000	3,000	2,500

30. In the above table, which task has been completed?

    a) Survey
    b) Remove debris
    c) Dig hole
    d) Emplace forms

31. All of the following are techniques that can be used to measure the total income of a project compared to the total money expended at any period of time EXCEPT:

    a) IRR
    b) NPV
    c) PV
    d) EVM

14

32. An example of a contingency response is:

   a) Provide allowances to account for price changes that can occur over the life of the project due to inflation
   b) Provide incentive fees paid to managers for good performance
   c) Allocate funds to offset poor cost or schedule estimates
   d) Hire contract labor if it is determined that our current team is not sufficient to support the work defined

33. Which of the following describes a role of the project manager during the contract negotiation process?

   a) He or she should try to be involved
   b) He or she is not involved
   c) He or she supplies an understanding of the requirements of the project
   d) He or she tells the contracts manager how the contracting process should be handled

34. Risk _____ will help guide risk _____.

   a) Score, responses
   b) Rank, updates
   c) Plan, reporting
   d) Plan, identification

Notes:

35. During your status review meetings with the project team, a request was made to add some more resources on a critical task in order to keep the project on schedule. As the project manager, you make the formal request to your sponsor to add more resources in order to stay on schedule. The sponsor agrees, which allows you to:

a) Pull funds from management contingency reserves
b) Slip the schedule
c) Report the resource issue and potential solution on the issues log
d) Go over budget on the specific tasks that need the resources

36. Forcing as a means of managing conflict is one in which:

a) The person retreats from the conflict situation
b) A viewpoint is exerted at the potential expense of the other party
c) Both parties give up something to get to an acceptable form of resolution
d) The disagreement is directly addressed

37. In which type of organization is project team building generally most difficult?

a) Functional
b) Matrix
c) Projectized
d) Project expediter

38. A contractor completes work as clearly specified within the SOW but the buyer is not pleased with the results. In this case, the contract is considered to be:

a) Complete because the contractor met the terms and conditions of the contract
b) Incomplete because formal acceptance has not been provided by the buyer
c) Incomplete because the specs are incorrect
d) Complete because the contractor is satisfied and work results follow the SOW

Notes:

39. Extensive use of _____ communication is likely to assist in solving complex problems.

   a) Chat
   b) Written
   c) Formal
   d) Verbal

40. What is the sender responsible for?

   a) Confirming that the message is understood
   b) Ensuring the receiver agrees with the message
   c) Scheduling communications exchange
   d) Presenting the message in the most agreeable manner

41. You are a project manager on an international project with team members from five different continents. You are frustrated with the performance of the team from France in meeting its scheduled deliveries. The team is regularly late by at least one week. You have not yet confronted the team on the issue and you plan to discuss this with your executive sponsor and to suggest that an action plan be implemented. Your best approach would be:

   a) Request to shift the activities from France to the Brazilian team since that team has been meeting its delivery dates consistently with minimal quality concerns
   b) Identify the reasons for the delays and work with the team in France to develop a schedule that can be agreed to by all parties, even if this means that you travel to the site to assess the environment and work directly with the team
   c) Implement a time tracking system within the French facility so that you can more accurately assess how these workers are performing their work and whether or not they are working the appropriate number of hours to meet the defined schedule

Notes:

d) Hold a conference call with the team in France and demand that all team members work overtime for the next two weeks to catch up on the work that has been delayed

42. Legitimate power is:

a) Derived from a person's formal position in the organization
b) Bestowed due to a person's personal qualities and abilities
c) Based on a person's charisma
d) Acquired based on technical knowledge, skill or expertise on some topic or issue

43. A tool or technique for the Monitoring and Controlling Risk process is:

a) Risk identification
b) Probability and impact analysis
c) Probability
d) Reserve analysis

44. A procurement audit is:

a) A complete set of indexed records to be included in the final project files
b) A structured review of the compliance with organizational policies and procedures
c) A structured review of the procurement process from the Plan Procurements through the Close Procurements processes
d) A process to assess the magnitude of any variations that occurred on any procurement contract

Notes:

14

Task	PV	AC	EV	SPI	CPI
1	95	100	95	1.00	0.95
2	150	130	110	0.73	0.84
3	130	130	130	1.00	1.00
4	80	80	90	1.10	1.10

Notes:

45. In the chart above, which task is ahead of schedule and under cost?

a) Task 1
b) Task 2
c) Task 3
d) Task 4

46. All of the following statements are generally true about the Control Scope process EXCEPT:

a) Control Scope is concerned with influencing the factors that create scope changes to ensure the changes are beneficial
b) Part of Control Scope is determining that a scope change has occurred
c) Control Scope must be integrated with other control processes
d) Control Scope describes how project scope will be managed

47. All of the following are common characteristics of project life cycle descriptions EXCEPT:

a) Cost and staffing levels are low at the start, higher towards the end and drop rapidly as the project ends
b) Risk and uncertainty are highest at the end of the project
c) The probability of successfully completing the project is low at the start and gets progressively higher as the project continues
d) The ability of stakeholders to influence the final characteristics of the project product is highest at the start of the project

14

48. The Delphi Technique is:

   a) A numbering system to identify each element of the work breakdown structure uniquely
   b) A forecasting technique that relies on gathering expert opinions
   c) An analytical technique similar to the design of experiments
   d) A variation of Monte Carlo analysis

49. A project manager incorporates a Pareto diagram because it helps to _____.

   a) Determine if a process is out of control
   b) Focus on stimulating thinking
   c) Explore a desired future outcome
   d) Focus on the most critical issues to improve quality

50. Close Project or Phase is a process within which knowledge area?

   a) Define Scope
   b) Communications
   c) Procurement
   d) Integration

51. An example of cost of conformance to quality is:

   a) Quality training
   b) Scrap
   c) Warranty costs
   d) Rework

52. During the execution phase of a project, company ABC begins to make use of control charts on all its projects. What does a control chart help with?

   a) Exploring a desired future outcome
   b) Determining if a process is out of control
   c) Focusing on stimulating thinking
   d) Focusing on the most critical issues to improve quality

Notes:

14

Case	PV	AC	EV
1	10,000	10,000	10,000
2	10,000	8,000	10,000
3	10,000	8,000	8,000
4	9,000	12,000	10,000
5	10,000	12,000	12,000
6	10,000	10,000	12,000
7	12,000	12,000	10,000
8	10,000	8,000	9,000
9	12,000	10,000	11,000

53. Based on the chart above, what is the CPI of Case 9?

a) 1.10
b) 1.91
c) 0.83
d) 1.20

54. Based on the chart above, what is the SV for Case 8?

a) 1,000
b) 2,000
c) -1,000
d) -2,000

55. The normal risk of doing business that involves the chance of both a profit and a loss is called:

a) Business risk
b) Pure risk
c) Chance
d) Opportunity risk

Notes:

56. Professional responsibility is a domain that covers aspects such as:

    a) Knowledge, skills, tools and techniques
    b) Planning, organizing, staffing, executing and controlling ongoing operations
    c) Legal, ethical and professional behavior
    d) Impacts of bad weather, global business and professional behavior

57. The procurement management plan describes how the procurement processes will be managed. It includes all of the following EXCEPT:

    a) Constraints
    b) Metrics for evaluating sellers
    c) Types of contracts to be used
    d) Terms and conditions

58. As the project manager, you are scheduling some activities in which there is a delay between the finish of the activity and the start of the successor activity. These dependencies would be reflected in the schedule with a _____.

    a) Finish-to-start relationship
    b) Lag
    c) Start-to-finish relationship
    d) Lead

59. After the 5th month on her project, a project manager found that the cumulative actual expenditures totaled $120,000. The planned expenditures for this length of time were $100,000. How is the project doing?

    a) It is ahead of schedule
    b) It is in trouble because of a cost overrun
    c) It will finish within the original budget
    d) The information is insufficient to make an assessment

Notes:

14

60. A project manager practices cost control for his projects by calculating an EAC. Calculating the EAC by adding the remaining project budget (modified by a performance factor) to the actual cost to date is used most often when the:

    a) Current variances are viewed as atypical ones
    b) Original estimating assumptions are no longer reliable because conditions are changing
    c) Current variances are viewed as typical of future variances
    d) Original estimating assumptions are considered to be fundamentally flawed

SAMPLE FINAL EXAM ANSWERS with explanations and references can be found in Chapter 15, Appendix B.

Notes:

14

a

CHAPTER 15 | APPENDICES

APPENDIX A

SAMPLE ASSESSMENT EXAM ANSWERS AND REFERENCES

Section numbers refer to the *PMBOK® Guide*.

1. **D** **Section 4.2.3 Integration Management**
   Know the purpose and contents of the project management plan.

2. **A** **Section 4.1 Integration Management**
   A project should not be initiated for personal gain. Projects are formally initiated after some sort of needs assessment or feasibility analysis has been completed.

3. **A** **Section 6.5 Time Management**
   The forward pass yields early start and early finish dates and the backward pass yields late start and late finish dates. Float or slack is calculated from late finish minus early finish. The path with zero float is the critical path.

4. **C** **Section 1 Introduction**
   In general, project management is supposed to increase the quality of the products of projects, so costs for rework and warranties should be reduced.

5. **B** **Section 4.4 Integration Management**
   The monitoring and controlling project work process is concerned with comparing actual project performance against the project management plan.

6. **D** **Section 7.3.2.1 Cost Management**
   Earned value performance compares the baseline plan to actual schedule and cost performance and is part of the performance review tool and technique.

15

7. A   Section 3.2 Introduction
Subprojects are typically referred to as projects and managed as such. They can utilize a less-experienced project manager.

8. A   Section 2.4.2 Introduction
Unlike functional organizations in which each employee has a clear supervisor, employees in matrix organizations have two bosses. This is often a source of conflict.

9. D   Section 9.4.2.3

10. A   Section 6.2.2.1 Time Management
The critical path consists of activities with zero float that cannot be delayed without impacting the project schedule.

11. D   Section 12.3 Procurement Management
Claims administration is a tool and technique under procurement management Administer Procurements process and will only be performed on projects in which items are being procured.

12. A   Section 2.1.1 Project Life Cycle and Organization
Know the common characteristics of project life cycles. Cost of changes and error correction generally increase as the project continues.

13. B   Section 11 Risk Management
Although risk management is the process of identifying, analyzing and responding to project risk, it includes minimizing the probability and consequences of adverse events to project objectives and increasing the probability and impact of positive events.

14. B   Section 8.3.2.4 Quality Management
Choice A is a specific type of histogram ordered by frequency of occurrence; choice C is a fishbone or cause-and-effect diagram; choice D is a graphical representation of a process.

15. D   Section 11 Risk Management
The inherently temporary nature of projects
invites uncertain events or conditions to occur;
if these events do occur, they could have a
positive or negative effect on the project
objectives.

16. B   Section 4.5 Integration Management
The project manager needs to coordinate change
requests across the knowledge areas; e.g., a scope
change request can impact project cost, risk,
quality and staffing requirements.

17. B   Section 1.2 Introduction
A project has a definite beginning and a definite
end to create a unique product, service or result.

**18. C   Section 4.6 Integration Management and
Professional Responsibility**
The best choice is to give the customer some
value for the money already spent and close out
the project.

19. B   Section 4.1 Integration Management
Although choices A, C and D can be considered
correct, they are only a subset of the project. A
project should be initiated to address a specific
need of the organization.

**20. C   Section 3 Project Management Processes
for a Project**
See Figure 3-7 of the *PMBOK® Guide*. Acceptance
criteria are part of the scope statement. The
WBS feeds activity definition, communications
planning and cost budgeting, which all feed
schedule development.

21. A   Section 2.4.2 Project Life Cycle and Organization
A project-based organization derives its revenue
from performing projects.

22. A   Section 12.1.2.3 Procurement Management
Although the *PMBOK® Guide* does not go into the burdens of risk, it is important to know that the seller bears the heaviest burden of risk in fixed price contracts and the buyer bears the heaviest burden of risk in cost reimbursable contracts.

23. C   Section 5.3.3.1 Scope Management
Project objectives should already have been defined as part of the scope statement, an output of the Plan Scope process. Defining the scope precedes the Create WBS process, where the WBS is created.

24. C   Section 9.4.2.3 Human Resources Management
Both parties give up something; therefore, it is a compromise.

25. D   Section 9.3 Human Resources Management
The project manager's responsibilities include obtaining project-specific training for the development of team members.

26. B   Section 1.3 Introduction
Strong project management can assist an organization in profitability, competitive advantage, etc., but its main purpose is to meet project requirements and deliver per the project objectives.

27. D   Section 4.1 Integration Management
The project management process does not assume that projects are fiscally sound. Projects are initiated to support organizational strategies. Projects should not be initiated for personal interests or gains.

28. D   Section 7.1.1 Cost Management
Parametric estimating is a tool or technique used in calculating cost estimates.

29. C **Section 4.1.3.1 Integration Management**
Objectives should be SMART (specific, measurable, attainable or assignable, realistic and time based).

30. B **Section 4.6.3 Integration Management**
An important output of the close project process is the confirmation that the project's product has met customer requirements and there is formal acceptance by the customer.

31. B **Section 10 Communications Management**
Communication skills are an important part of general management as well as project management. Effective communication only occurs if the receiver has decoded and understands the message.

32. A **Section 6.5.2 Time Management**
Critical path method requires calculating slack or float to determine the path with least scheduling flexibility.

33. A **Section 5.3 Scope Management**
A work package can be scheduled, monitored and controlled.

34. B **Section 11 Risk Management**
Not all projects are capital projects or require procurement processes to be executed.

35. B **Section 6.5.2 Time Management**
Precedence diagramming method is an example of a schedule networking technique.

36. A **Section 6.5.2.4 Time Management**
Resource leveling smoothes out resource requirements from period to period, often resulting in an extension of the schedule.

37. C   Section 6.5.2.7 Time Management
Since the critical path is the longest amount of time to complete a project, only the tasks on the critical path should be crashed in order to shorten the project schedule. Crashing usually results in higher cost.

38. D   Section 8.3.3.3 Quality Management
In addition to validated deliverables, an output of the Perform Quality Control process is validated change requests.

39. A   Section 5.5 Scope Management
The project manager must first determine if the requested changes impact the business need the project was undertaken to address. If the project justification, product, deliverables or objectives are impacted, the request is valid and the project sponsor must be notified.

40. A   Section 10.4 Communications Management
As part of the Report Performance process, the project manager should know how resources are being utilized in order to complete work that is scheduled.

15

APPENDIX B

SAMPLE FINAL EXAM ANSWERS AND REFERENCES

Section numbers refer to the *PMBOK® Guide*.

1. **D Section 4.4 Integration Management**
   The Monitor and Control Project Work process includes the assessment of whether or not the project will meet the objectives it was initiated for.

2. **D Section 3.5 Project Management Processes for a Project**

3. **A Section 4.5 Integration Management**
   Choice A is lessons learned. Pay special attention to negatives.

4. **B Section 6.6.2.2 Time Management**
   As slack is consumed, there is less slack available for the remaining noncritical tasks.

5. **B Section 10.2.2.4 Communications Management**
   Meetings, phone calls and video conferences are all forms of interactive communication.

6. **B Professional Responsibility**
   Culture is transmitted through the process of learning and interacting with one's environment, rather than being something inherent.

7. **A Section 11 Risk Management**
   Risks can be both positive and negative.

8. **B Section 11.2.2.2 Risk Management**
   Sampling is a quality technique.

9. **D Section 9.1.1.2 Human Resource Management**
   Collective bargaining agreements are an enterprise environmental factor that must be considered in human resource planning.

10. **A Section 9.1.3 Human Resource Management**

11. C   Section 6.5.2.7 Time Management
Only by accelerating the performance of the
critical path tasks can project duration be
shortened. Accelerating performance of
noncritical tasks does not affect project duration.

12. A   Chapter 8 Quality Management
During the planning of a project, it is important to
understand the expected levels of grade and quality
that are needed. This will help in determining the
level of quality control that will be required on the
project.

**13. D   Section 3 Project Management Processes
for a Project**

14. B   Section 5.4.3 Scope Management
The primary focus of the scope verification
process is acceptance of completed deliverables.

15. A   Professional Responsibility

16. D   Section 11.4 Risk Management
Held outside because the expected monetary
value if the party is held outside is $1,600 which is
greater than $920 if it is held inside. Of course,

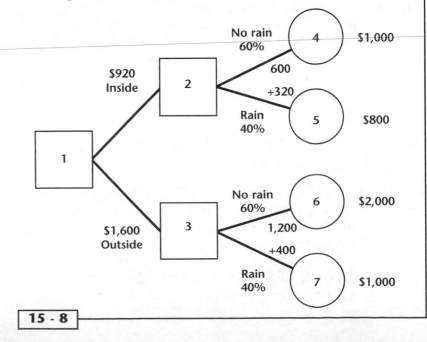

you can only choose whether to hold the party inside or outside; you cannot choose whether it rains or not.

17. B Section 12.5 Procurement Management
Both the buyer and seller must understand the legal implications of action taken when administering the contract.

18. D Time Management, see Lewis, page 181
Memorize the percentages for 1, 2 and 3 standard deviations from the mean and know what the bell-shaped curve looks like.

19. C Section 6.2.2.3 Time Management
See lead and lag definitions in the glossary.

20. A Chapter 5 Scope Management
It is a best practice to always review and understand the customer's perspective before communicating any negative feedback.

21. C Section 12.2.2.7 Procurement Management
You should stop negotiating when an agreement has been reached. Over negotiating may lead to agreement failure.

22. A Section 5.3 Scope Management
Decomposition is a tool and technique of the create WBS process

23. A Section 12.1 Procurement Management
The objective of procurement documents is to seek proposals from prospective sellers.

24. B Section 12.1.2 Procurement Management
The different types of contracts bear various risks to the buyer and the seller. An incentive clause helps share the risk.

25. B Section 12.2.2.1 Procurement Management

26. B   Section 10.2.3 Communications Management
The stakeholder register is an input to the Plan Communications process.

27. A   Section 8.1 Quality Management
Quality management is the knowledge area. The Perform Quality Assurance process ensures that the project employs all necessary processes. The Plan Quality process identifies the quality standards that are relevant to the project. The Perform Quality Control process monitors specific project results.

28. C   Section 11.4.2.1 Risk Management
60% x 70% = 42% probability to finish on time and within budget.

29. A   Section 6.5 Time Management
The critical path is defined as the path that takes the longest to complete or the path with no slack or float. It has no room for schedule flexibility because any slippage along the critical path will cause project delay.

30. B   Section 7.3 Cost Management
For "remove debris," schedule variance = earned value - planned value = 2,000 – 2,000 = 0. Zero schedule variance means that a task is complete.

31. D   Section 7 Cost Management
Earned value management does not include any income data.

32. D   Section 11.5.2.3 Risk Management
One of the more commonly used risk response techniques is a contingent response strategy, which is designed for use only if certain predefined conditions occur.

33. C   Section 12.2.2.7 Procurement Management
While A is true, C is more descriptive of the project manager's role in negotiating.

34. A **Section 11.3.2.2 Risk Management**
The results of the qualitative risk analysis are shown in the probability and impact matrix as risk scores, which help guide the risk responses.

35. C **Section 10.4.1.3 Communications Management**
For choice A, it is much more difficult to actually obtain management contingency reserves; for choice B, by definition, you are asking for more resources to keep the schedule on track ; choice D is not always the case because you may be able to re-baseline these schedule activities.

36. B **Section 9.4.2.3 Human Resource Management**
Choice A is withdrawal (nothing solved), choice C is compromising (lose-lose) and choice D is problem solving (confrontational) and considered win-win. Forcing is win-lose.

37. B **Section 2.4.2 Introduction**
Team building is easiest in choice A and is next easiest in choice C. The organizational structure of the performing organization is a constraint in organizational planning that crosses over to team building.

38. B **Section 12.4 Procurement Management**
Although the contract work is complete, the contract is not closed. The buyer must provide written notice to the contractor that the contract has been completed. Without this formal acceptance and closure, the contract cannot be closed. However, the contractor can demand that the buyer close out the project as work was done to the agreed-on specifications of the SOW.

39. B **Section 10 Communications Management**
Chat is a form of written communication, so choice B is a more generic answer.

40. A **Section 10.2 Communications Management**

41. B   **Code of Ethics and Professional Conduct**
Although you may be frustrated, there was a reason the French team was assigned the work it was assigned. In fairness, you must assess the situation before making any rash decisions.

42. A   **see Verma,** *Human Resource Skills*, **page 233**
The team's influencing skills play an important role in negotiating staff assignments as do the politics of the organizations involved. Other legitimate forms of power are reward and coercive (penalty). Choice C is referent power (a form of personal power) and choice D is expert power (also a form of personal power).

43. D   **Section 11.6.2.5 Risk Management**

44. C   **Section 12.4.2.1 Procurement Management**
Choice A defines a contract file; choice B defines a quality audit and choice D defines a performance measurement.

45. D   **Section 7.3.2 Cost Management**
Both SPI (1.1) and CPI (1.1) are greater than 1 for task 3.

46. D   **Section 5.5 Scope Management**
The scope management plan defines how scope will be managed.

47. B   **Section 2.1.1 Project Life Cycle and Organization**
Understand Figure 2-1 and Figure 2-2 in the *PMBOK® Guide*.

48. B   **See the *PMBOK® Guide* Glossary**

49. D   **Section 8.3.2.5 Quality Management**

50. D   **Section 4.6 Integration Management**

51. A   **Section 8.1.2.2 Quality Management**
Choices B, C and D are costs of nonconformance.

52. B   **Section 8.3.2.2 Quality Management**
Control charts illustrate how a process behaves over time.

53. A   **Section 7.3.2.1 Cost Management**
Cost Performance Index (CPI) = Earned Value/
                                    Actual Cost

CPI = \$11,000/\$10,000
CPI = 1.10

54. C   **Section 6.6.2.2 Time Management**
Schedule Variance (SV) = Earned Value -
                                  Planned Value

SV = \$9,000 - \$10,000
SV = -\$1,000

55. A   **Risk Management, see Wideman,** *Project and Program Risk Management*
Know the types of risk (pure, business, known and unknown).

56. C   **PMI Role Delineation Study of October 2005, page 29**

57. D   **Section 12.1.3.1 Procurement Management**
Terms and conditions are part of the contract.

58. B   **Section 6.2.2.3 Time Management**
Although the activities described have a finish-to start relationship, the delay in the start of the successor is a lag.

59. D   **Section 7.3.2.2 Cost Management**
The earned value or the value of the work physically accomplished needs to be known.

60. C   **Section 7.3.2 Cost Management**
Since the project manager is using a remaining budget modified by a performance factor, he or she is assuming that current variance is expected to reflect in future work.

15

APPENDIX C

GLOSSARY

This is a supplement to the *PMBOK® Guide*. Some of these terms are not in the *PMBOK® Guide*'s glossary but may be used in test questions.

Active Listening: the receiver confirms listening by nodding, eye contact and asking questions for clarification.

Activity Attributes: similar to a WBS dictionary because they describe the detailed characteristics of each activity. Examples of these attributes are description, predecessor and successor activities and the person responsible.

Application Area: a category of projects that have unique components that may not be present in other categories of projects. For example, IT projects approaches are different from residential development projects.

Authority: the right to make decisions necessary for the project or the right to expend resources.

Backward Pass: used to determine the late start and late finish dates of the activities.

Bidder Conference: the buyer and potential sellers meet prior to the contract award to answer questions and clarify requirements; the intent is for all sellers to have equal access to the same information.

Buyer: the performing organization, client, customer, contractor, purchaser or requester seeking to acquire goods and services from an external entity (the seller). The buyer becomes the customer and key stakeholder.

Capability Maturity Model Integration (CMMI): defines the essential elements of effective processes. It is a model that can be used to set process improvement goals and provide guidance for quality processes.

Change Control: the procedures used to identify, document, approve (or reject) and control changes to the project baselines.

Change Management: the process for managing change in the project. A change management plan should be incorporated into the project management plan.

Chart of Accounts: the financial numbering system used to monitor project costs by category. It is usually related to an organization's general ledger.

Code of Accounts: the numbering system for providing unique identifiers for all items in the WBS. It is hierarchical and can go to multiple levels, each lower level containing a more detailed description of a project deliverable. The WBS contains clusters of elements that are child items related to a single parent element; for example, parent item 1.1 contains child items 1.1.1, 1.1.2 and 1.1.3.

Co-location: project team members are physically located close to one another in order to improve communication, working relations and productivity.

Commercial-Off-The-Shelf (COTS): a product or service that is readily available from many sources; selection of a seller is primarily driven by price.

Communication Context: languages generally fall on a sliding scale of high to low context. Recipients of high-context language messages need to know the situation and environment of the message in order to understand it. An example of a high-context message is poetry, in which rhyme, meter, allegory and similar poetic devices enhance one's experience of the poet's intent. Recipients of low-context language messages understand the message as received. An example of a low-context message is a statement of fact, such as "you have a dozen eggs."

Constraints: a restriction or limitation that may force a certain course of action or inaction.

Contingency Plan: a response to a risk event that will be implemented only if the risk event occurs.

Contingency Reserve: a dollar or time value that is added to the project schedule or budget that reflects and accounts for risk that is anticipated for the project.

Contract: the binding agreement between the buyer and the seller.

Control Account: the management control point at which integration of scope, budget and schedule takes place and at which performance is measured.

Crashing: using alternative strategies for completing project activities (such as using outside resources) for the least additional cost. Crashing should be performed on tasks on the critical path. Crashing the critical path may result in additional or new critical paths.

Crashing Costs: costs incurred as additional expenses above the normal estimates to speed up an activity.

Critical Path: the path with the longest duration within the project. It is sometimes defined as the path with the least float (usually zero float). The delay of a task on the critical path will delay the completion of the project.

Culture: everything that people have, think and do as members of their society and that is shared by at least one other person.

Decision Theory: a technique for assisting in reaching decisions under uncertainty and risk. It points to the best possible course whether or not the forecasts are accurate.

Decomposition: the process of breaking down a project deliverable into smaller, more manageable components. In the Create WBS process, the results of decomposition are deliverables, whereas in the define activities process project deliverables are further broken down into schedule activities.

Direct Costs: costs incurred directly by a project.

Effective Listening: the receiver attentively watches the sender to observe physical gestures and facial expressions. In addition, the receiver contemplates responses, asks pertinent questions, repeats or summarizes what the sender has sent and provides feedback.

Enterprise Environmental Factors: external or internal factors that can influence a project's success. These factors include controllable factors such as the tools used in managing projects within the organization or uncontrollable factors that have to be considered by the project manager such as market conditions or corporate culture.

Expert Judgment: judgment based upon expertise appropriate to the activity. It may be provided by any group or person, either within the organization or external to it.

Fallback Plan: a response plan that will be implemented if the primary response plan is ineffective.

Fast Tracking: overlapping or performing in parallel project activities that would normally be done sequentially. Fast tracking may increase rework and project risk.

Feedback: affirming understanding and providing information.

Finish-to-Finish: a logical relationship in which the predecessor must finish before the successor can finish.

Finish-to-Start: a logical relationship in which the predecessor must finish before the successor can start. This is the most common relationship and the default for most software packages.

Fixed Costs: nonrecurring costs that do not change if the number of units is increased.

Float: the amount of time that a schedule activity can be delayed without delaying the end of the project; calculated as the difference between late finish date and early finish date.

Forward Pass: used to determine the early start and early finish dates of activities.

Gantt Charts: bar charts that show activities against time; although the traditional early charts did not show task dependencies and relationships, modern charts often show dependencies and precedence relationships; these popular charts are useful for understanding project schedules and for determining the critical path, time requirements, resource assessments and projected completion dates.

Good Practice: a specific activity or application of a skill, tool or technique that has been proven to contribute positively to the execution of a process.

Grade: the category or level of the characteristics of a product or service.

Hammock: summary activities used in a high-level project network diagram.

Heuristics: rules of thumb for accomplishing tasks. Heuristics are easy and intuitive ways to deal with uncertain situations; however, they tend to result in probability assessments that are biased.

Indirect Costs: costs that are part of doing business and are shared among all ongoing projects.

Issue: a risk event that has occurred.

Knowledge Area: a collection of processes, inputs, tools, techniques and outputs associated with a topical area. Knowledge areas are a subset of the overall project management body of knowledge that recognizes "good practices."

Lag: the amount of time a successor's start or finish is delayed from the predecessor's start or finish. In a finish-to-start example, activity A (the predecessor) must finish before activity B (the successor) can start. If a lag of three days is also defined, it means that B will be scheduled to start three days after A is scheduled to finish.

Lead (negative lag): the amount of time a successor's start or finish can occur before the predecessor's start or finish. In a finish-to-start example, activity A (the predecessor) must finish before activity B (the successor) can start. A lead of three days means that B can be scheduled to start three days before A is scheduled to finish

Leadership: the ability to get an individual or group to work towards achieving an organization's objectives while accomplishing personal and group objectives at the same time.

Lean Six Sigma: a business improvement methodology that strives to achieve the fastest rate of improvement on quality, process speed and customer satisfaction while lowering costs and invested capital.

Letter Contract: a written preliminary contract authorizing the seller to begin work immediately; it is often used for small value contracts.

Letter of Intent: this is NOT a contract but simply a letter, without legal binding, that says the buyer intends to hire the seller.

Logical Relationships: there are four logical relationships between a predecessor and a successor: finish-to-start, finish-to-finish, start-to-start and start-to-finish.

Malcolm Baldrige: the national quality award given by the United States' National Institute of Standards and Technology. Established in 1987, the program recognizes quality in the business and other sectors. It was inspired by Total Quality Management (TQM).

Management Reserve: a dollar value, not included in the project budget, that is set aside for unplanned changes to project scope or time that are not currently anticipated.

Mean (μ): the sum of the means of individual tasks.

Milestone Charts: bar charts that only show the start or finish of major events or key external interfaces (e.g., a phase kickoff meeting or a deliverable); it consumes NO resources and has NO duration; these charts are effective for presentations and can be incorporated into a summary Gantt chart.

Network Diagram: a schematic display of project activities showing task relationships and dependencies; the precedence diagramming method (PDM) is useful for forcing the total integration of the project schedule, for simulations and "what if" exercises, for highlighting critical activities and the critical path and for determining the projected completion date.

Noise: anything that compromises the original meaning of the message.

Nonverbal Communication: about 55% of all communication, based on what is commonly called body language.

Operation: ongoing work performed by people, constrained by resources, planned, executed, monitored and controlled. Unlike a project, operations are repetitive; e.g., the work performed to carry out the day-to-day business of an organization is operational work.

Opportunities: risk events or conditions that are favorable to the project.

Opportunity Costs: costs of choosing one alternative over another and giving up the potential benefits of the other alternative.

Organizational Breakdown Structure (OBS): different from a responsibility assignment matrix (RAM). The OBS is a type of organizational chart in which work package responsibility is related to the organizational unit responsible for performing that work. It may be viewed as a very detailed use of the RAM with work packages of the work breakdown structure (WBS) and organizational units as the two dimensions.

Organizational Process Assets: any formal or informal processes, plans, policies, procedures, guidelines and on-going or historical project information such as lessons learned, measurement data, project files and estimates versus actuals.

Organizational Project Management Maturity Model (OPM3®): focuses on the organization's knowledge, assessment and improvement elements.

15

Output: a deliverable, result or service generated by the application of various tools or techniques within a process.

Paralingual Communication: optional vocal effects, the tone of voice that may help communicate meaning.

Percent Complete: the amount of work completed on an activity or WBS component.

Performance Domains: a broad category of duties and responsibilities that define a role. A performance domain expresses the actual actions of the project manager in a particular domain.

Phase: one of a collection of logically related project activities usually resulting in the completion of one or more major deliverables. A project phase is a component of a project life cycle.

Planning Package: a component of the work breakdown structure that is below the control account to support known uncertainty in project deliverables. Planning packages will include information on a deliverable but without any details associated with schedule activities.

Point of Total Assumption: in a fixed price contract, the point above which the seller will assume responsibility for all costs; it generally occurs when the contract ceiling price has been exceeded.

Portfolio: a collection of programs, projects and additional work managed together to facilitate the attainment of strategic business goals.

Power: the ability to influence people in order to achieve needed results.

Predecessor: the activity that must happen first when defining dependencies between activities in a network.

Privity: the contractual relationship between the two parties of a contract. If party A contracts with party B and party B subcontracts to party C. There is no privity between party A and party C.

Process: a collection of related actions performed to achieve a predefined desired outcome. The *PMBOK® Guide* defines a set of 42 project management processes, each with various inputs, tools, techniques and outputs. Processes can have predecessor or successor processes, so outputs from one process can be inputs to other processes. Each process belongs to one and only one of the five process groups and one and only one of the nine knowledge areas.

Process Groups: a set of project management processes that are required for any project; they are typically performed in sequence but have interdependencies within and across process groups.

Process Quality: specific to the type of product or service being produced and the customer expectations, the level of process quality will vary. Organizations strive to have efficient and effective processes in support of the product quality expected. For example, the processes associated with building a low-quality, low-cost automobile can be just as efficient, if not more so, than the processes associated with building a high-quality, high-cost automobile.

Product Life Cycle: the collection of stages that make up the life of a product. These stages are typically introduction, growth, maturity and retirement.

Product Quality: specific to the type of product produced and the customer requirements, product quality measures the extent to which the end product(s) of the project meets the specified requirements. Product quality can be expressed in terms that include, but are not limited to, performance, grade, durability, support of existing processes, defects and errors.

Program: a group of related projects managed in a coordinated way; e.g., the design and creation of the prototype for a new airplane is a project, while manufacturing 99 more airplanes of the same model is a program.

Progressive Elaboration: the iterative process of continuously improving the detailed plan as more information becomes available and estimates for remaining work can be forecasted more accurately as the project progresses.

Project: work performed by people, constrained by resources, planned, executed, monitored and controlled. It has definite beginning and end points and creates a unique outcome that may be a product, service or result.

Project Life Cycle: the name given to the collection of various phases that make up a project. These phases make the project easier to control and integrate. The result of each phase is one or more deliverables that are needed and utilized in the next few phases. The work of each phase is accomplished through the iterative application of the initiating, planning, executing, monitoring and controlling and closing process groups.

Project Management: the ability to meet project requirements by using various knowledge, skills, tools and techniques to accomplish project work. Project work is completed through the iterative application of initiating, planning, executing, monitoring and controlling and closing process groups. Project management is challenged by competing and changing demands for scope (customer needs, expectations and requirements), resources (people, time and cost), risks (known and unknown) and quality (of the project and product).

Project Management Information System: the collection of tools, methodologies, techniques, standards and resources used to manage a project. These may be formal systems and strategies determined by the organization or informal methods utilized by project managers.

Project Management Methodology: any structured approach used to guide the project team through the project life cycle. This methodology may utilize forms, templates and procedures standard to the organization.

Project Network Schedule Calculations: there are three types of project network schedule calculations: a forward pass, a backward pass and float. A forward pass yields early start and early finish dates, a backward pass yields late start and late finish dates, and these values are used to calculate total float.

Project Quality: typically defined within the project charter, project quality is usually expressed in terms of meeting stated schedule, cost and scope objectives. Project quality can also

15

be addressed in terms of meeting business objectives that have been specified in the charter. Solving the business problems for which the project was initiated is a measure of quality for the project.

Quality: the degree to which a set of inherent characteristics satisfies the stated or implied needs of the customer. To measure quality successfully, it is necessary to turn implied needs into stated needs via project scope management.

Quality Objective: a statement of desired results to be achieved within a specified time frame.

Quality Policy: a statement of principles for what the organization defines as quality.

Requirements Traceability Matrix: a matrix for recording each requirement and tracking its attributes and changes throughout the project life cycle to provide a structure for changes to product scope. Projects are undertaken to produce a product, service or result that meets the requirements of the sponsor, customer and other stakeholders. These requirements are collected and refined through interviews, focus groups, surveys and other techniques. Requirements may also be changed through the projects' configuration management activities.

Residual Risk: in implementing a risk response plan, the risk that cannot be eliminated.

Resource Calendar: a calendar that documents the time periods in which project team members can work on the project.

Responsibility Assignment Matrix (RAM): a structure that relates project roles and responsibilities to the project scope definition.

Risk: an uncertain event or condition that could have a positive or negative impact on the project objectives.

Rolling Wave Planning: a progressive elaboration technique that addresses uncertainty in detailing all future work for a project. Near-term work is planned to an appropriate level of detail; however, longer term deliverables are identified at a high level and decomposed as the project progresses.

Schedule Activity: an element of work performed during the course of a project. It is a smaller unit of work than a work package and the result of decomposition in the Define Activities process of project time management. Activities can be further subdivided into tasks.

Scheduling Charts: there are four types of scheduling charts: the Gantt chart, the milestone chart, the network diagram and the time-scaled network diagram.

Scope Baseline: the approved detailed project scope statement along with the WBS and WBS dictionary.

Secondary Risk: in implementing a risk response, a new risk that is introduced as a result of the response.

Seller: the bidder, contractor, source, subcontractor, vendor or supplier who will provide the goods and services to the buyer. The seller generally manages the work as a project, utilizing all processes and knowledge areas of project management.

Single Source: selecting a seller without competition. This may be appropriate if there is an emergency or prior business relationship.

Six Sigma: is an organized process that utilizes quality management for problem resolution and process improvement. It seeks to identify and remove the causes of defects.

Slack: see float.

Sole Source: selecting a seller because it is the only provider of the needed product or service.

Stakeholder Risk Tolerance: the stakeholders' attitude toward risk is an enterprise environmental factor that must be considered in the risk management plan. Risk responses should balance stakeholders' risk attitudes.

Stakeholders: individuals and organizations who are involved in or may be affected by project activities. Examples of stakeholders include the project manager, team members, the performing organization, the project sponsor and the customer. PMI advocates that any discrepancies between stakeholder requirements should be resolved in favor of the customer. Therefore, the customer is one of the most important stakeholders in any project.

Standard: a document that describes rules, guidelines, methods, processes and practices that can be used repeatedly to enhance the chances of success.

Standard Deviation (σ): the square root of the project variance, it is the measurement of the variability of the quantity measured, such as time or costs, from the average.

Start-to-Finish: a logical relationship in which the predecessor must start before the successor can finish. (This is the least used and some software packages do not even allow it.)

Start-to-Start: a logical relationship in which the successor can start as soon as the predecessor starts.

Statistical Terms: the primary statistical terms are the project mean, variance and standard deviation.

Subproject: a component of a project. Subprojects can be contracted out to an external enterprise or to another functional unit.

Successor: the activity that happens second or subsequently to a previous activity when defining dependencies between activities in a network.

Sunk Costs: money already spent; there is no more control over these costs. Since these are expended costs they should not be included when determining alternative courses of action.

Tailoring: the adaptation of the standard processes and their constituent inputs and outputs to fit appropriately with the needs of the project. The degree of rigor applied to each process considered must also be determined. The project manager, together with the project team, is responsible for determining the amount of tailoring to be carried out and documenting the decisions made by the project team in a work reference model or other project document.

Team Building: the process of getting a diverse group of individuals to work together effectively. Its purpose is to keep team members focused on the project goals and objectives and to understand their roles in the big picture.

Technique: a defined systematic series of steps applied by one or more individuals using one or more tools to achieve a product or result or to deliver a service.

Threat: risk events or conditions that are unfavorable to the project.

Time-Scaled Network Diagrams: a combination of a network diagram and a bar chart; it shows project logic, activity durations and schedule information.

Tool: a tangible item such as a checklist or template used in performing an activity to produce a product or result.

Total Float: see float.

Triangular Distribution or **Three-Point Estimating:** takes the average of three estimated durations — the optimistic value, the most likely value and the pessimistic value. By using the average of three values rather than a single estimate, a more accurate duration estimate for the activity is obtained.

Variable Costs: costs that increase directly with the size or number of units.

Variance: the sum of the variances of individual tasks.

Virtual Teams: groups of people with shared objectives who fulfill their roles with little or no time spent meeting face to face.

Warranties: assurance that the products are fit for use or the customer receives compensation. It could cover downtime and maintenance costs.

15

WBS Dictionary: houses the details associated with the work packages and control accounts. The level of detail needed will be defined by the project team.

Weighted Three-Point Estimates, or **Beta/PERT:** program evaluation and review technique (PERT) uses the three estimated durations of three-point estimating but weighs the most likely estimate by a factor of four. This weighted average places more emphasis on the most likely outcome in calculating the duration of an activity. Therefore, it produces a curve that is skewed to one side when possible durations are plotted against their probability of occurrence.

What-If Scenario Analysis: a technique used to assess the feasibility of the project schedule should unexpected events occur. This analysis is useful for preparing contingency and response plans to mitigate the impact of identified risk events and could involve simulations of various project durations using different sets of project assumptions. The most common simulation method is the **Monte Carlo Analysis** technique.

Work Breakdown Structure (WBS): a framework for defining project work into smaller, more manageable pieces, it defines the total scope of the project using descending levels of detail.

Work Package: the lowest level of a WBS; cost estimates are made at this level.

Workarounds: unplanned responses to risks that were previously unidentified or accepted.

APPENDIX D

BIBLIOGRAPHY

This study guide and the *PMBOK® Guide* provide enough material needed for most experienced project managers to pass the exam. However, if you feel that you need additional materials, here are some books that we have found useful and that we reference in the study guide.

Brake, Terence, Danielle Walker, and Thomas Walker. *Doing Business Internationally: The* Guide to Cross-cultural Success. New York: McGraw-Hill, 1995.

Cleland, David, Karen M. Bursic, Richard Puerzer, and A. Yaroslav Vlasak, eds. *Project Management Casebook.* Newtown Square, PA: Project Management Institute, 1998.

Clemen, Robert T. Making Hard Decisions: *An Introduction to Decision Analysis, Second Edition.* Pacific Grove, CA: Duxbury Press, 1996.

Ferraro, Gary P. *The Cultural Dimension of International Business, Fourth Edition.* Upper Saddle River, NJ: Prentice-Hall, 2002.

Fleming, Quentin W. and Joel M. Koppelman. *Earned Value Project Management, Second Edition.* Newtown Square, PA: Project Management Institute, 1996.

Garner, Bryan A., editor, *Black's Law Dictionary, Eighth Edition.* New York: Thomson West, 2004.

Ireland, Lewis R. *Quality Management for Projects and Programs.* Newtown Square, PA: Project Management Institute, 1991.

Kerzner, Harold. *Project Management: A Systems Approach to Planning, Scheduling, and Controlling, Eighth Edition.* New York: John Wiley & Sons, 2003.

15

Lewis, James P. *Fundamentals of Project Management.* New York: American Management Association, 1997.

----------. *Project Planning, Scheduling & Control.* Chicago: Probus Publishing, 1991.

Meredith, Jack R. and Samuel J. Mantel, Jr. *Project Management: A Managerial Approach, Fourth Edition.* New York: John Wiley & Sons, 2000.

Project Management Institute. *A Guide to the Project Management Body of Knowledge, Fourth Edition (PMBOK® Guide).* Newtown Square, PA: Project Management Institute, 2008.

----------. *Principles of Project Management.* Newtown Square, PA: Project Management Institute, 1997.

----------. *Project Management Experience and Knowledge Self-Assessment Manual.* Newtown Square, PA: Project Management Institute, 2000.

----------. *Project Management Professional (PMP) Examination Specification.* Newtown Square, PA: Project Management Institute, 2005.

Rosen, Robert, Patricia Digh, Marshall Singer, and Carl Phillips. *Global Literacies: Lessons on Business Leadership and National Cultures.* New York: Simon & Schuster, 2000.

Rosenau, Milton D., Jr. *Successful Project Management, A Step-by-Step Approach with Practical Examples, Third Edition.* New York: John Wiley & Sons, 1998.

Trompenaars, Fons, and Charles Hampden-Turner. *Riding the Waves of Culture: Understanding Diversity in Global Business, Second Edition.* New York: McGraw-Hill, 1998.

15

Verma, Vijay K. *Human Resource Skills for the Project Manager.* Newtown Square, PA: Project Management Institute, 1996.

----------. *Managing the Project Team.* Newtown Square, PA: Project Management Institute, 1995.

----------. *Organizing Projects for Success.* Newtown Square, PA: Project Management Institute, 1995.

Wideman, R. Max, ed. *A Framework for Project and Program Management Integration.* Newtown Square, PA: Project Management Institute, 1991.

----------. *Project and Program Risk Management: A Guide to Managing Project Risks & Opportunities.* Newtown Square, PA: Project Management Institute, 1992.

Wysocki, Robert K., Robert Beck Jr., and David B. Crane. *Effective Project Management: How to Plan, Manage, and Deliver a Project on Time and Within Budget.* New York: John Wiley & Sons, 2000.

15

INDEX

16